81/09

Edexcel

foundation

GCSE Modular Mathematics

unit 2

Keith Pledger

Gareth Cole

Peter Jolly

Graham Newman

Joe Petran

www.heinemann.co.uk
✓ Free online support
✓ Useful weblinks
✓ 24 hour online ordering

01865 888058

Heinemann
Inspiring generations

Heinemann is an imprint of Pearson Education Limited, a company incorporated in England and Wales, having its registered office at Edinburgh Gate, Harlow, Essex, CM20 2JE. Registered company number: 872828

Heinemann is a registered trademark of Pearson Education Limited

First published 2006

10 09
10 9 8 7 6 5 4 3 2

British Library Cataloguing in Publication Data is available from the British Library on request.

ISBN: 978 0 435585 28 0

Typeset by Tech-Set Ltd, Gateshead, Tyne and Wear
Original illustrations © Harcourt Education Limited, 2006
Cover design by mccdesign
Printed in China (CTPS/02)
Cover photo: Photolibrary

Acknowledgements

This high quality material is endorsed by Edexcel and has been through a rigorous quality assurance programme to ensure that it is a suitable companion to the specification for both learners and teachers. This does not mean that its contents will be used verbatim when setting examinations nor is it to be read as being the official specification – a copy of which is available at www.edexcel.org.uk.

The publisher's and authors' thanks are due to Edexcel Limited for permission to reproduce questions from past examination papers. These are marked with an [E]. The answers have been provided by the authors and are not the responsibility of Edexcel Limited.

The authors and publisher would like to thank the following individuals and organization for permission to reproduce photographs: Pearson Education Ltd/Debbie Rowe p**3**; Getty Images/ PhotoDisc pp**5, 6, 9, 13, 14, 29, 35, 53, 58, 132, 133**; MorgueFile/Kevin Conners p**15**; Corbis pp**24, 39, 107, 145**; iStockPhoto/Sandra O'Clare p**25**; Digital Vision pp**34, 142**; MorgueFile p**42**; Photos.com pp**65, 80, 97, 130**; Deere & Company p**66**; Devon Olugbena Shaw p**99**; Dreamstime.com/Michael Osterrieder p**106**; Dreamstime.com/Rick Parsons p**127**; iStockPhoto/ Andy Platt p**148**; Dreamstime.com/Kendy Kaveney p**152**; Dreamstime.com/Feng Yu p**165**

Every effort has been made to contact copyright holders of material reproduced in this book. Any omissions will be rectified in subsequent printings if notice is given to the publishers.

Publishing team

Editorial	Katherine Pate, James Orr, Evan Curnow, Laurice Suess, Elizabeth Bowden, Lindsey Besley
Design	Christopher Howson
Production	Helen McCreath
Picture Research	Chrissie Martin

Tel: 01865 888058   www.heinemann.co.uk

Quick reference to chapters

Contents

■ = New stage 1
■ = New stage 2

3 Powers, indices and calculations

9 Measures

10 Perimeter, area and volume

About this book

This book has been carefully matched to the new two-tier modular specification for Edexcel GCSE Maths. It covers everything you need to know to achieve success in Unit 2. The author team is made up of the Chief Examiner, the Chair of Examiners, Principal Examiners and Senior Moderators, all experienced teachers with an excellent understanding of the Edexcel specification.

Key features

Chapters are divided into **sections**. In each section you will find:
- **key points**, highlighted throughout like this

> • In a decimal number the decimal point separates the whole number from the part smaller than 1.

- **examples** that show you how to tackle questions
- an **exercise** to help develop your understanding.

Each chapter ends with a **mixed exercise** and a **summary of key points**. Mixed exercises, which include past exam questions marked with an [E], are designed to test your understanding across the chapter.

Hint boxes are used to make explanations clearer. They may also remind you of previously learned facts or tell you where in the book to find more information.

> Addition is the **inverse** of subtraction.

An examination practice paper is included to help you prepare for the exam at the end of the unit.

Answers are provided at the back of the book to use as your teacher directs.

Quick reference and detailed Contents pages

Use the thumb spots on the **Quick reference page** to turn to the right chapter quickly.

Use the detailed **Contents** to help you find a section on a particular topic. The summary and reference codes on the right show your teacher the part(s) of the specification covered by each section of the book. (For example, NA2a refers to Number and algebra, section 2 Numbers and the Number system, subsection a.)

Teaching and learning software

References to the Heinemann Edexcel GCSE Mathematics **Teaching and Learning Software** are included for you and your teacher.
(The number refers to the relevant chapter from the linear course on which the software is based.)

> ⊙ **2** Using factor trees

Use of a calculator

 These symbols show where you must, or must not, use a calculator.

1. Integers – four rules, rounding and ordering

1.1 Face value and place value

- Each digit in a number has a face value and a **place value**.
- An **integer** is any positive or negative whole number. Zero is also an integer.

Example 1

Draw a place value diagram and write in
(a) a three-digit number with a 2 in the Tens column
(b) a five-digit number with a 6 in the Thousands column.

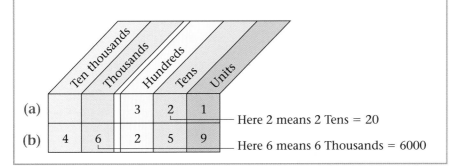

(a) | | | 3 | 2 | 1 | —— Here 2 means 2 Tens = 20

(b) | 4 | 6 | 2 | 5 | 9 | —— Here 6 means 6 Thousands = 6000

Exercise 1A

1 Draw a place value diagram and write in
   (a) a two-digit number with a 3 in the Tens column
   (b) a four-digit number with a 2 in the Hundreds column
   (c) a five-digit number with a 1 in the Units column and a 3 in the Hundreds column
   (d) a three-digit number with a 4 in the Hundreds column and a 2 in the Tens column
   (e) a five-digit number with a 3 in the Thousands column and a 2 in the Tens column.

2 Write down the value of the 5 in
   (a) 2502   (b) 351   (c) 54 321
   (d) 15   (e) 5489   (f) 10 050

1.2 Reading, writing and ordering numbers

Example 2

(a) Write 37 802 in words.
(b) Write the number five thousand three hundred and five in figures.

(a)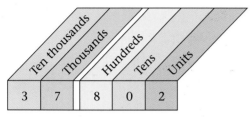

Thirty-seven thousand eight hundred and two.

(b) Five thousand three hundred and five.

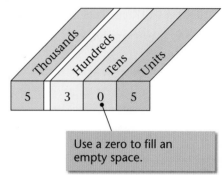

Use a zero to fill an empty space.

Example 3

Write these numbers in order of size, starting with the largest.

4532   4621   5831   425

The order is

5831   4621   4532   425

4621 ⎱ Both have
4532 ⎰ 4 Thousands.
4621 has 6 Hundreds.
4532 has 5 Hundreds.

Exercise 1B

1 Write these numbers in words.
(a) 237   (b) 6502   (c) 10 302   (d) 321   (e) 15

2 Write these numbers in figures.
(a) Three hundred and twenty-three
(b) Six thousand two hundred and four
(c) Forty-two
(d) Sixteen thousand seven hundred and thirty-two
(e) Nine hundred and ninety-nine

3 Write each set of numbers in order of size, starting with the largest.
(a) 18, 324, 3450, 67   (b) 234, 2681, 256, 963
(c) 10 002, 6554, 9999, 9460   (d) 56 762, 59 342, 56 745, 56 321

4 The table gives the prices of some second-hand cars.
   (a) Write down the price of each car in words.
   (b) Rewrite the list in price order, starting with the most expensive.

Car	Price
Peugeot 505	£7995
Focus	£11 495
Ka	£4835
Mini	£6549
Sharan	£13 205

5 The attendances at a football club's last five home matches were:

   37 992   43 845   43 621   39 042   39 681

   Rewrite these numbers in order of size, starting with the lowest attendance.

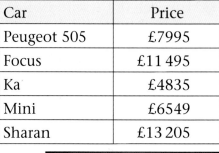

1.3 Number lines

- You can show the position of a number on a **number line**.
- You can use a number line to work out increases and decreases.

Example 4

Use a number line to
(a) increase 6 by 4
(b) decrease 23 by 8.

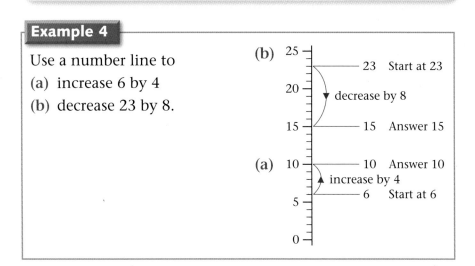

Exercise 1C

1 Draw a number line from 0 to 30.
   Mark these numbers on the number line.
   (a) 6   (b) 23   (c) 15   (d) 0   (e) 29

2 Use a number line from 0 to 25 to
   (a) increase 6 by 3   (b) decrease 15 by 7
   (c) increase 11 by 7   (d) increase 17 by 8
   (e) decrease 19 by 13   (f) decrease 16 by 8.

3 For each of these moves, write down whether it is an increase or decrease, and by how much.

(a) 10 to 6   (b) 15 to 21   (c) 10 to 3

(d) 24 to 29   (e) 13 to 5   (f) 19 to 25

1.4 Adding and subtracting

- Some words that show you have to add numbers are **add, plus, total** and **sum**.
- Some words that show you have to subtract numbers are **subtract, minus, take away** and **difference**.
- If the numbers are too big to add or subtract in your head you can set the calculation out in columns.
- You can use addition to check your subtraction.

For example

$$\begin{array}{r} \overset{3\ 1}{447} \\ -352 \\ \hline 95 \end{array} \qquad \begin{array}{r} \text{check:}\quad 352 \\ +95 \\ \hline 447 \\ {\scriptstyle 1} \end{array}$$

> Addition is the **inverse** of subtraction.

- You can use subtraction to check your addition.

For example

$$\begin{array}{r} 126 \\ +392 \\ \hline 518 \\ {\scriptstyle 1} \end{array} \qquad \begin{array}{r} \text{check:}\quad \overset{4\ 1}{518} \\ -392 \\ \hline 126 \end{array}$$

> Subtraction is the **inverse** of addition.

Example 5

(a) Add 3, 6 and 9.   (b) Take 6 away from 15.   (c) 27 + 73

(d) Find the sum of 58 and 84.

(e) Find the difference between 382 and 157.

(a) $3 + 6 + 9 = 18$ (b) $15 - 6 = 9$ (c) $27 + 73 = 100$

(d) $\begin{array}{r} 58 \\ +84 \\ \hline 142 \\ {\scriptstyle 1\ 1} \end{array}$ (e) $\begin{array}{r} \overset{7\ 1}{382} \\ -157 \\ \hline 225 \end{array}$

> You should be able to do these calculations in your head.

Exercise 1D

1 Add 6, 4 and 2.

2 Add these in your head.

(a) 51 + 49   (b) 37 + 63   (c) 39 + 61

(d) 84 + 16   (e) 46 + 54   (f) 9 + 91

3 Subtract these in your head.
  (a) $68 - 52$ (b) $57 - 18$ (c) $45 - 9$
  (d) $97 - 79$ (e) $62 - 59$ (f) $77 - 18$

4 Subtract 7 from 18.

5 Find the total of 3, 4, 9 and 10.

6 16 minus 5.

7 54 plus 97.

8 134 take away 67.

9 Karen buys three different cakes. They cost 27p, 34p and 52p. Find the total cost of the cakes.

10 Graham organises events. The attendances at four events were 89, 63, 42 and 24.
How many people attended altogether?

11 Julie has a collection of 325 DVDs. She sells 178 in a second-hand shop.
How many DVDs does she have left?

12 A school has 867 students. 498 students are girls.
How many students in the school are boys?

13 Find the sum of 623, 125 and 689.

14 Find the difference between 823 and 697.

15 Eryl has 87 CDs and Luisa has 139 CDs.
How many CDs do they have in total?

16 A book has 1142 pages. Veronica has read 738.
How many pages does she have left to read?

1.5 Multiplying and dividing

- Some words that show you have to multiply numbers are **times, product** and **multiply**.
- Some words that show you have to divide numbers are **share** and **divide**.
- You need to remember all the multiplication facts to 10×10.
- You can use multiplication to check your division.
  For example $48 \div 6 = 8$ check: $6 \times 8 = 48$

  > Multiplication is the inverse of division.

- You can use division to check your multiplication.
  For example $4 \times 32 = 128$ check: $128 \div 4 = 32$

  $$\text{or} \qquad 4\overline{)\underset{}{128}}^{\,32}$$

  > Division is the inverse of multiplication.

Example 6

(a) Find the product of 3 and 6. (b) Share 36 between 4.
(c) Multiply 23 and 4. (d) Divide 84 by 3.

(a) $3 \times 6 = 18$ (b) $36 \div 4 = 9$

(c)   23   (d)   2 8
     $\underline{\quad 4 \times}$ $3\overline{)8^24}$
       92
        1

Exercise 1E

1 (a) Find the product of 8 and 6.
  (b) Divide 72 by 9.

2 Multiply 19 and 5.   3 Divide 27 by 3.

4 $45 \div 9$ 5 82×6

6 15×10 7 234×100

8 Lesley buys 16 packs of Christmas cards. Each pack
  contains five cards.
  How many cards does she buy?

9 Three friends share a bunch of grapes. There are 81 grapes
  in the bunch.
  How many grapes does each person receive?

10 A school hires eight coaches for a trip to Alton Towers.
   Each coach holds 53 passengers.
   How many people can go to Alton Towers?

11 To complete a 200 m swimming race Jo has to swim eight
   lengths of the swimming pool.
   How long is the swimming pool?

12 A soap opera is broadcast four times a week.
   How many programmes will be broadcast in a year?

13 A lottery syndicate of four people share a win of £7832.
   How much does each person receive?

14 Each volume of an encyclopaedia has 1524 pages. There
   are eight volumes in the encyclopaedia.
   How many pages are there in the encyclopaedia
   altogether?

There are 52 weeks in a year.

1.6 Brackets and the order of operations

- Always work out brackets first. Then divide, multiply, add and subtract.
- When operations are the same you do them in the order they appear.

Example 7

Find the value of
(a) $6 + 3 \times 2$ (b) $(6 + 8) \div 2$ (c) $(12 - 3) \times (4 + 3)$

(a) $6 + \underbrace{3 \times 2}$

   $= 6 + \quad 6$

   $= 12$

Multiply first

(b) $\underbrace{(6 + 8)} \div 2$

   $= \quad 14 \quad \div 2$

   $= \quad 7$

Brackets first

(c) $\underbrace{(12 - 3)} \times \underbrace{(4 + 3)}$

   $= \quad 9 \quad \times \quad 7$

   $= 63$

Brackets first

Exercise 1F

1 Find the value of
   (a) $6 + (3 \times 2)$ (b) $7 - 3 - 2$
   (c) $18 \div (2 + 4)$ (d) $(3 \times 2) \div (5 - 2)$
   (e) $36 \div 4 - 2$ (f) $5 + 2 \times 4$
   (g) $3 + 2 \times 4 - 2$ (h) $(2 \times 7) - (18 \div 3)$
   (i) $18 - 6 \times 2$ (j) $9 \times 3 + (8 \div 2)$

2 Replace each * with +, −, × or ÷ to make these calculations correct. Use brackets if you need to.
   (a) $7 * 3 = 21$
   (b) $2 * 3 * 4 = 14$
   (c) $3 * 5 * 2 = 21$
   (d) $10 * 4 * 2 = 3$

1.7 Rounding numbers

- To round to the nearest 10 look at the digit in the Units column:
  - if it is less than 5 round down.
  - if it is 5 or more round up.
- To round to the nearest 100 look at the digit in the Tens column:
  - if it is less than 5 round down.
  - if it is 5 or more round up.
- To round to the nearest 1000 look at the digit in the Hundreds column:
  - if it is less than 5 round down.
  - if it is 5 or more round up.

Example 8

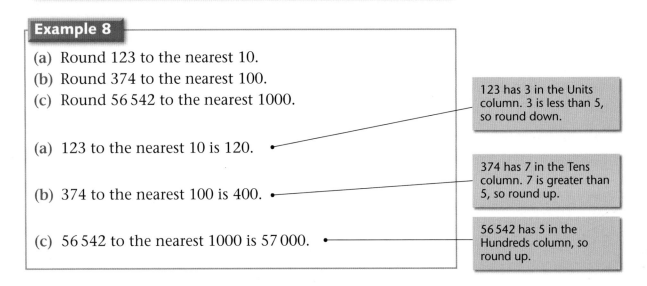

(a) Round 123 to the nearest 10.
(b) Round 374 to the nearest 100.
(c) Round 56 542 to the nearest 1000.

(a) 123 to the nearest 10 is 120.

123 has 3 in the Units column. 3 is less than 5, so round down.

(b) 374 to the nearest 100 is 400.

374 has 7 in the Tens column. 7 is greater than 5, so round up.

(c) 56 542 to the nearest 1000 is 57 000.

56 542 has 5 in the Hundreds column, so round up.

Exercise 1G

1   Round these numbers to the nearest 10.
   (a) 12   (b) 18   (c) 6   (d) 67   (e) 75
   (f) 114   (g) 299   (h) 1055   (i) 2007   (j) 3145

2   Round these numbers to the nearest 100.
   (a) 237   (b) 568   (c) 58   (d) 850   (e) 708
   (f) 3745   (g) 5955   (h) 9041   (i) 10 078   (j) 50 350

3   Round these numbers to the nearest 1000.
   (a) 7892   (b) 6432   (c) 2500   (d) 4005   (e) 13 982
   (f) 16 432   (g) 156 540   (h) 784   (i) 500   (j) 372 450

4 Round these numbers to the nearest multiple of 10 given in the brackets.

(a) 13 (10) (b) 25 (10) (c) 76 (10)
(d) 378 (100) (e) 4759 (1000) (f) 194 268 (10 000)
(g) 364 582 (100) (h) 2500 (1000)

5 Acme Furnishings has 1468 employees.
Write the number of employees to the nearest hundred.

6 47 891 people attended a rugby match.
Write the attendance to the nearest 1000.

7 In 2006, 54 239 candidates took Edexcel GCSE Mathematics.
Write the number of candidates to the nearest 10 000.

1.8 Factors, multiples and common factors

- A **factor** of a number is a whole number that divides into the number without a remainder. The factors of a number include 1 and the number itself.
- **Multiples** of a number are made by multiplying the number by the positive whole numbers, 1, 2, 3, 4 … etc.
- A **common factor** of two numbers is a whole number that is a factor of both numbers.

Example 9

Write down all the factors of 12.

The factors of 12 are 1, 2, 3, 4, 6 and 12.

> 1, 2, 3, 4, 6 and 12 all divide into 12 without a remainder.

Example 10

Write down the first four multiples of 4.

The first four multiples of 4 are 4, 8, 12 and 16.

> $1 \times 4 = 4$
> $2 \times 4 = 8$
> $3 \times 4 = 12$
> $4 \times 4 = 16$

Example 11

Write down the common factors of 9 and 6.

The factors of 9 are ①, ③, 9
The factors of 6 are ①, 2, ③, 6

1 and 3 are factors of both 9 and 6.
They are the common factors of 9 and 6.

Exercise 1H

1 Write down all the factors of

(a) 6   (b) 10   (c) 15   (d) 17

(e) 27   (f) 36   (g) 90   (h) 120

2 Find the common factors of

(a) 4 and 6   (b) 10 and 15   (c) 24 and 36

(d) 3 and 18   (e) 10, 15 and 30

3 List the first five multiples of

(a) 3   (b) 7   (c) 4

(d) 10   (e) 13

4 From the numbers in the cloud write down the numbers that are

(a) factors of 24

(b) multiples of 5

(c) factors of 16

(d) multiples of 3

(e) common factors of 16 and 24

(f) common factors of 10 and 25.

5   6   8   1
4   12   20
16   9   13   15

1.9 LCM, HCF and prime factor decomposition

2 Using factor trees

- A **prime number** is a whole number greater than 1 that has only two factors: itself and 1.
- A number written as a product of prime numbers is written in **prime factor form**.
- The **highest common factor** (HCF) of two numbers is the highest factor common to both of them.
- The **lowest common multiple** (LCM) of two numbers is the lowest multiple common to both of them.

Example 12

(a) Write 36 in prime factor form.
(b) Find the highest common factor (HCF) of 36 and 12.
(c) Find the lowest common multiple (LCM) of 3 and 4.

(a) **Method 1**

$36 = 2 \times 18$
$\quad = 2 \times 2 \times 9$
$\quad = 2 \times 2 \times 3 \times 3$

which can be simplified to $2^2 \times 3^2$.

> 2^2 (two squared) $= 2 \times 2$. For more on powers see Chapter 3.

Method 2

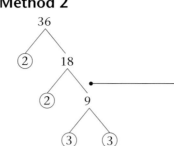

$= 2 \times 2 \times 3 \times 3$

> This is called a factor tree.

(b) $36 = ② \times ② \times 3 \times ③$
$24 = ② \times ② \times 2 \times ③$

The HCF of 24 and 36 is $2 \times 2 \times 3 = 12$.

> Write each number in prime factor form. Pick out the factors common to both numbers.

(c) 3: 3, 6, 9, ⑫, 15

4: 4, 8, ⑫, 16

The LCM of 3 and 4 is 12.

> Write a list of multiples for each number. The LCM is the lowest number that appears in both lists.

Exercise 1I

1 Write down all the factors of

(a) 48   (b) 360   (c) 29   (d) 100

(e) 71   (f) 645

2 Write down the numbers in question **1** that are prime numbers.

3 Write down the first five multiples of

(a) 5   (b) 8   (c) 11   (d) 20

4 Write these numbers in prime factor form.

(a) 50   (b) 72   (c) 450   (d) 840

> Write your answers using powers. For example $5 \times 5 \times 5 \times 5 = 5^4$.

5 Find the HCF of

(a) 9 and 15   (b) 4 and 14   (c) 12 and 20

(d) 6, 15 and 21   (e) 8, 24 and 36

6 Find the LCM of

(a) 6 and 8   (b) 5 and 7   (c) 4 and 6

(d) 2, 3 and 4   (e) 5, 6 and 10

1.10 Negative numbers

- The **negative numbers** are less than zero on the number line.

Example 13

Write the largest and the smallest numbers in this list.

3, −2, 0, −6, 8

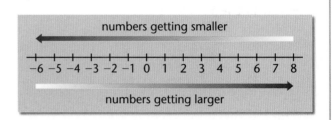

−6 is the smallest number.
8 is the largest number.

Exercise 1J

1 Write the largest and the smallest number in each list.
   (a) −4, 0, 5, −8, 1   (b) −6, −3, 0, 10, 2
   (c) 8, −4, 1, 2, −9   (d) −3, −6, −18, −11, −1
   (e) −3, −11, 0, −2, −9

2 Use the number line to find the number that is
   (a) 3 more than −1   (b) 3 less than −1
   (c) 6 less than 5   (d) 7 more than −2
   (e) 8 more than −9   (f) 4 less than −4
   (g) 4 more than 0   (h) 3 less than 0
   (i) 7 less than −3   (j) 5 more than −8

3 What number is
   (a) 10 more than −20   (b) 30 less than −10
   (c) 100 more than −300   (d) 200 less than 100
   (e) 70 less than −150   (f) 300 less than 50
   (g) 150 more than −500   (h) 80 more than −250
   (i) 400 less than 70   (j) 180 more than −700?

4 The table gives the highest and lowest temperatures for five days in one week.

	Mon	Tues	Wed	Thurs	Fri
Highest	11°C	9°C	3°C	−2°C	0°C
Lowest	−1°C	−4°C	−6°C	−8°C	−7°C

10 ⊣
9 ⊣
8 ⊣
7 ⊣
6 ⊣
5 ⊣
4 ⊣
3 ⊣
2 ⊣
1 ⊣
0 ⊣
−1 ⊣
−2 ⊣
−3 ⊣
−4 ⊣
−5 ⊣
−6 ⊣
−7 ⊣
−8 ⊣
−9 ⊣
−10 ⊣

(a) On which day was the lowest temperature recorded?

(b) On which day was the highest temperature recorded?

(c) On which day was the difference between the highest temperature and lowest temperature the greatest?

5 The temperature at the bottom of a mountain is 3 °C. The temperature at the top of the mountain is 8 degrees less. What is the temperature at the top of the mountain?

1.11 Calculations with negative numbers

- You can calculate with negative numbers.
- Adding a negative number is the same as subtracting the positive number.
- Subtracting a positive number is the same as adding the negative number.
- Subtracting a negative number is the same as adding the positive number.
- This table shows the signs you get when you multiply or divide two numbers.

+	×/÷	+	=	+
+	×/÷	−	=	−
−	×/÷	+	=	−
−	×/÷	−	=	+

Negative number × positive number → negative answer

Example 14

Work out

(a) $2 - +3$

(b) $-3 - -2$

(c) $4 + -2$

(d) $-3 + +1$

(a) $2 - +3 = -1$

(b) $-3 - -2 = -1$

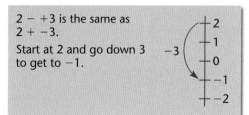

$2 - +3$ is the same as $2 + -3$.

Start at 2 and go down 3 to get to −1.

$-3 - -2$ is the same as $-3 + +2$.

Start at −3 and go up 2 to get to −1.

(c) $4 + -2 = 2$

4 + −2 is the same as
4 − 2.

Start at 4 and go down 2
to get to +2.

$$\begin{array}{c} +4 \\ -2 \left(\begin{array}{c} +3 \\ \searrow +2 \\ +1 \\ +0 \end{array} \right. \end{array}$$

(d) $-3 + +1 = -2$

Start at −3 and go up 1
to get to −2.

$$\begin{array}{c} +0 \\ +-1 \\ +1 \left(\begin{array}{c} -2 \\ -3 \end{array} \right. \end{array}$$

Example 15

Work out
(a) 15×-3
(c) -16×-3

(b) $-8 \div -2$
(d) $-10 \div 5$

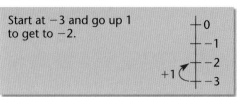

(a) $15 \times -3 = -45$
(c) $-16 \times -3 = +48$

(b) $-8 \div -2 = +4$
(d) $-10 \div 5 = -2$

Exercise 1K

1 Work out
  (a) $-4 + -3$ **(b)** $9 - +5$ **(c)** $8 - -2$
  (d) $5 + +4$ **(e)** $-7 - -6$ **(f)** $-2 + +4$
  (g) $6 + -8$ **(h)** $-3 - +7$

2 Work out
  (a) -3×-8 **(b)** -5×3 **(c)** $24 \div -3$
  (d) $-36 \div -12$ **(e)** -8×5 **(f)** $-48 \div 8$
  (g) 6×-5 **(h)** $-50 \div -5$

3 A diver dives to a depth of -27 metres. A second diver
dives to a depth of -16 metres.
What is the difference in the depths of the dives?

4 The temperature at the Arctic Circle is recorded as $-18\,°C$
one night. The following day it rises by $6\,°C$.
What is the temperature during the day?

5 Copy and complete these tables.

(a)

		1st number		
	$\times$	-2	6	-7
2nd	5		30	
number	-3			
	8	-16		

(b)

		1st number		
	$-$	2	-3	8
2nd	-4			
number	5		-8	
	-1			

(c)

	1st number		
+	−3	−4	2
2nd 5	2		
number 1			
−6			

(d)

	1st number		
÷	16	−24	−36
2nd −2			12
number 4			
−8			

Mixed exercise 1

1 Write down the value of the underlined digit in each number.

(a) 2<u>7</u>   (b) 9<u>3</u>   (c) 2<u>7</u>4   (d) 6<u>7</u>82   (e) <u>9</u>536

2 The distances in kilometres from Calais to some other European cities are given in the table.

City	Distance (km)
Brussels	204
Athens	3175
Bordeaux	845
Hanover	1096
Lisbon	2052

The Parthenon in Athens is an enduring symbol of Ancient Greece.

(a) Write the numbers in the list in words.

(b) Rewrite the list in order, starting with the city furthest away from Calais.

3 Draw a number line from 0 to 20. Show these on your number line.

(a) 6 increased by 3   (b) 12 decreased by 5

(c) 8 increased by 6   (d) 20 decreased by 12

(e) 13 decreased by 4   (f) 2 increased by 13

4 Work out

(a) 7 plus 3   (b) 20 minus 6

(c) 13 times 4   (d) 27 shared between 3

5 (a) Find the total of 6, 10 and 23.

(b) Sum 28, 57 and 39.

(c) Find the difference between 237 and 93.

(d) Multiply 132 by 8.

(e) Divide 480 by 3.

6 A snooker player plays three games. He scores 97, 104 and 86. Find his total score.

 7 226 g of flour is taken from a 1 kg bag of flour. How much flour is left in the bag?

> 1 kg = 1000 g

 8 1862 people pay £8 each to see a film. How much money is this altogether?

 9 A builder can carry eight bricks at a time. How many trips will the builder need to make to move a pile of 952 bricks?

10 Find the value of
(a) $3 + 2 \times 5$ (b) $6 + (3 + 8)$ (c) $(6 \times 7) \div 3$
(d) $8 - 18 \div 3$ (e) $(5 + 3) \times (8 - 4)$

11 Write these numbers to the nearest multiple of 10 given in the brackets.
(a) 236 (10)   (b) 6892 (100)   (c) 9823 (100)
(d) 5545 (1000)   (e) 2378 (1000)   (f) 6351 (100)

12 Here is a list of numbers:

   6, 7, 8, 9, 10, 11, 12, 13, 14, 15

From the list write down all the numbers that are
(a) factors of 18   (b) factors of 14
(c) multiples of 3   (d) multiples of 6
(e) common factors of 24 and 36
(f) common factors of 14 and 21.

13 Write in prime factor form
(a) 180   (b) 196   (c) 600

14 Find the highest common factor (HCF) of
(a) 12 and 18   (b) 42 and 24   (c) 6, 12 and 15

15 Find the lowest common multiple (LCM) of
(a) 4 and 5   (b) 6 and 8   (c) 2, 6 and 8

16 What number is
(a) 4 more than -2 (b) 6 less than 1
(c) 11 more than 0   (d) 14 more than -7
(e) 6 less than 0   (f) 30 more than -70
(g) 25 less than -100 (h) 140 less than -50?

17 Work out

(a) $-6 + -3$ (b) $7 - -3$ (c) $8 - +4$ (d) $-3 + +5$

18 Work out

(a) -8×2 (b) $-10 \div -5$ (c) $6 \div -3$ (d) -7×-5

Summary of key points

1 Each digit in a number has a face value and a **place value**.

2 An **integer** is any positive or negative whole number. Zero is also an integer.

3 You can show the position of a number on a **number line**.

4 You can use a number line to work out increases and decreases.

5 Some words that show you have to add numbers are **add, plus, total** and **sum**.

6 Some words that show you have to subtract numbers are **subtract, minus, take away** and **difference**.

7 If the numbers are too big to add or subtract in your head you can set the calculation out in columns.

8 You can use addition to check your subtraction.

For example

$$\begin{array}{r} \overset{3\,1}{4}47 \\ -352 \\ \hline 95 \end{array} \qquad \begin{array}{r} \text{check:}\ \ 352 \\ +95 \\ \hline 447 \\ \hline {\scriptstyle 1} \end{array}$$

9 You can use subtraction to check your addition.

For example

$$\begin{array}{r} 126 \\ +392 \\ \hline 518 \\ {\scriptstyle 1} \end{array} \qquad \begin{array}{r} \text{check:}\ \ \overset{4\,1}{5}18 \\ -392 \\ \hline 126 \end{array}$$

10 Some words that show you have to multiply numbers are **times, product** and **multiply**.

11 Some words that show you have to divide numbers are **share** and **divide**.

12 You need to remember all the multiplication facts to 10×10.

13 You can use multiplication to check your division.

For example $48 \div 6 = 8$ check: $6 \times 8 = 48$

14 You can use division to check your multiplication.

For example $4 \times 32 = 128$ check: $128 \div 4 = 32$

$$\text{or} \qquad \begin{array}{r} 32 \\ 4\overline{)128} \end{array}$$

15 Always work out brackets first. Then divide, multiply, add and subtract.

16 When operations are the same you do them in the order they appear.

17 To round to the nearest 10 look at the digit in the Units column:
- if it is less than 5 round down.
- if it is 5 or more round up.

18 To round to the nearest 100 look at the digit in the Tens column:
- if it is less than 5 round down.
- if it is 5 or more round up.

19 To round to the nearest 1000 look at the digit in the Hundreds column:
- if it is less than 5 round down.
- if it is 5 or more round up.

20 A **factor** of a number is a whole number that divides into the number without a remainder. The factors of a number include 1 and the number itself.

21 **Multiples** of a number are made by multiplying the number by the positive whole numbers, 1, 2, 3, 4 ... etc.

22 A **common factor** of two numbers is a whole number that is a factor of both numbers.

23 A **prime number** is a whole number greater than 1 that has only two factors: itself and 1.

24 A number written as a product of prime numbers is written in **prime factor form**.

25 The **highest common factor** (HCF) of two numbers is the highest factor common to both of them.

26 The **lowest common multiple** (LCM) of two numbers is the lowest multiple common to both of them.

27 The **negative numbers** are less than zero on the number line.

28 You can calculate with negative numbers.

29 Adding a negative number is the same as subtracting the positive number.

30 Subtracting a positive number is the same as adding the negative number.

31 Subtracting a negative number is the same as adding the positive number.

32 This table shows the signs you get when you multiply or divide two numbers.

+	×/÷	+	=	+
+	×/÷	−	=	−
−	×/÷	+	=	−
−	×/÷	−	=	+

2 Fractions, decimals and percentages

2.1 Improper fractions and mixed numbers

- In a fraction:

  The top number shows how many parts you have.

  The top number is called the **numerator**.

  $$\frac{3}{4}$$

  The bottom number shows how many parts there are.

  The bottom number is called the **denominator**.

- A fraction whose numerator is larger than its denominator is called an **improper fraction**.

  For example, $\frac{5}{2}$ is an improper fraction.

- An improper fraction can be written as a **mixed number**, with a whole number part and a fraction part.

  For example, $2\frac{1}{2}$ is a mixed number.

Example 1

Change these improper fractions to mixed numbers.

(a) $\frac{17}{12}$ (b) $\frac{23}{8}$ (c) $\frac{7}{2}$

(a) $\frac{17}{12} = \frac{12}{12} + \frac{5}{12} = 1\frac{5}{12}$

(b) $\frac{23}{8} = \frac{8}{8} + \frac{8}{8} + \frac{7}{8} = 2\frac{7}{8}$

(c) $\frac{7}{2} = \frac{2}{2} + \frac{2}{2} + \frac{2}{2} + \frac{1}{2} = 3\frac{1}{2}$

Example 2

Change these mixed numbers to improper fractions.

(a) $1\frac{3}{4}$ (b) $2\frac{1}{5}$

(a) $1\frac{3}{4} = \frac{4}{4} + \frac{3}{4} = \frac{7}{4}$

(b) $2\frac{1}{5} = \frac{5}{5} + \frac{5}{5} + \frac{1}{5} = \frac{11}{5}$

Exercise 2A

1 Change these improper fractions to mixed numbers.

(a) $\frac{5}{4}$ (b) $\frac{3}{2}$ (c) $\frac{7}{5}$ (d) $\frac{9}{7}$ (e) $\frac{13}{11}$

(f) $\frac{5}{2}$ (g) $\frac{11}{5}$ (h) $\frac{13}{5}$ (i) $\frac{17}{7}$ (j) $\frac{20}{8}$

(k) $\frac{9}{2}$ (l) $\frac{13}{4}$ (m) $\frac{17}{6}$ (n) $\frac{19}{4}$ (o) $\frac{23}{3}$

2 Change these mixed numbers to improper fractions.

(a) $1\frac{1}{5}$ (b) $1\frac{3}{7}$ (c) $1\frac{3}{4}$ (d) $1\frac{1}{2}$ (e) $1\frac{3}{10}$

(f) $2\frac{4}{5}$ (g) $2\frac{2}{3}$ (h) $2\frac{1}{4}$ (i) $2\frac{5}{9}$ (j) $2\frac{6}{7}$

(k) $3\frac{1}{3}$ (l) $3\frac{3}{4}$ (m) $4\frac{2}{10}$ (n) $5\frac{1}{3}$ (o) $5\frac{7}{10}$

2.2 Equivalent fractions

- You can simplify a fraction if the numerator and denominator have a common factor. When you have divided by all the common factors, the fraction is in its **simplest form**.

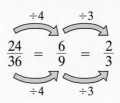

- **Equivalent fractions** are fractions that have the same value. For example, $\frac{3}{4} = \frac{6}{8} = \frac{12}{16}$

Example 3

Write the fraction $\frac{18}{24}$ in its simplest form.

$\frac{18}{24} = \frac{3}{4}$

Divide the numerator and denominator by the *same* number.

$\frac{3}{4}$ is equivalent to $\frac{18}{24}$

Example 4

Change $\frac{3}{7}$ to an equivalent fraction with a denominator of 21.

$\frac{3}{7} = \frac{9}{21}$

Multiply the numerator and denominator by the *same* number.

Exercise 2B

1 Write these fractions in their simplest form.

(a) $\frac{6}{8}$ (b) $\frac{12}{15}$ (c) $\frac{16}{24}$ (d) $\frac{25}{35}$ (e) $\frac{18}{27}$

> Divide the numerator and denominator by a common factor.

2 Copy the table.
Draw lines to join the equivalent fractions.

$\frac{1}{5}$	$\frac{5}{8}$
$\frac{3}{4}$	$\frac{12}{16}$
$\frac{15}{24}$	$\frac{3}{7}$
$\frac{5}{10}$	$\frac{3}{15}$
$\frac{6}{14}$	$\frac{1}{2}$
$\frac{2}{5}$	$\frac{8}{20}$

3 Copy these sets of fractions. Write in the missing numbers to make the fractions equivalent.

(a) $\frac{2}{5} = \frac{}{10} = \frac{}{20} = \frac{}{30} = \frac{}{100}$ (b) $\frac{1}{6} = \frac{}{12} = \frac{4}{} = \frac{}{30} = \frac{8}{}$ (c) $\frac{3}{8} = \frac{}{48} = \frac{12}{} = \frac{}{24}$

4 Write down two fractions equivalent to each of these.

(a) $\frac{4}{5}$ (b) $\frac{27}{36}$ (c) $\frac{8}{12}$ (d) $\frac{1}{9}$

2.3 Ordering fractions

- To write a list of fractions in order of size
  - ○ write them all as equivalent fractions with the same denominator
  - ○ order them using the numerators.

Example 5

Write these fractions in order, starting with the largest.

$$\frac{1}{3}, \quad \frac{2}{5}, \quad \frac{3}{10}, \quad \frac{1}{6}$$

$$\frac{1}{3} = \frac{10}{30} \qquad \frac{2}{5} = \frac{12}{30} \qquad \frac{3}{10} = \frac{9}{30} \qquad \frac{1}{6} = \frac{5}{30}$$

In order

$$\frac{12}{30}, \quad \frac{10}{30}, \quad \frac{9}{30}, \quad \frac{5}{30}$$

So the order is $\frac{2}{5}, \frac{1}{3}, \frac{3}{10}, \frac{1}{6}$

> Largest to smallest is **descending order**.

> Rewrite the fractions with a common denominator of 30.

> Remember to write the *original* fractions in order for the answer.

Exercise 2C

1 Which is larger

   (a) $\frac{1}{4}$ or $\frac{1}{5}$ (b) $\frac{2}{3}$ or $\frac{3}{5}$ (c) $\frac{7}{10}$ or $\frac{11}{15}$ (d) $\frac{6}{7}$ or $\frac{2}{3}$?

> **Ascending order** means from smallest up to largest.

2 Write these fractions in ascending order.

   $$\frac{1}{2}, \ \frac{2}{5}, \ \frac{3}{10}, \ \frac{1}{4}$$

> Hint: use a common denominator of 20.

3 Keith eats $\frac{1}{3}$ of a cake. Mary eats $\frac{1}{4}$ of the same cake. Who eats the larger piece?

4 A book is divided into four sections. The table below shows what fraction of the book each section is.

Section 1	$\frac{1}{8}$
Section 2	$\frac{2}{3}$
Section 3	$\frac{1}{6}$
Section 4	$\frac{1}{24}$

   (a) Which section is the largest?

   (b) Which section is the smallest?

5 Write the fractions $\frac{7}{8}, \frac{13}{16}, \frac{1}{4}, \frac{2}{3}$ in descending order.

2.4 Decimal place value

- In a decimal number the decimal point separates the whole number from the part smaller than 1.

Example 6

Write down the value of the underlined digit in each number.

(a) 41.<u>3</u>   (b) 0.28<u>5</u>   (c) 16.8<u>9</u>

	Tens	Units	.	tenths	hundredths	thousandths	
(a)	4	1	.	3			3 tenths
(b)		0	.	2	8	5	5 thousandths
(c)	1	6	.	8	9		9 hundredths

Exercise 2D

1 Draw a place value diagram like the one in Example 6 and write in these numbers.

(a) 5.82   (b) 7.801   (c) 19.1   (d) 20.02

(e) 13.381   (f) 0.76   (g) 0.5   (h) 0.001

2 Write down the value of the underlined digit in each of these numbers.

(a) 10.3<u>2</u>   (b) 11.19<u>2</u>   (c) 0.<u>7</u>6   (d) 0.80<u>1</u>

(e) <u>1</u>.308   (f) 7.<u>9</u>2   (g) 0.00<u>1</u>   (h) 1.00<u>2</u>

(i) <u>1</u>2.3   (j) 15.<u>8</u>9

3 Write down the value of the 6 in each of these numbers.

(a) 0.062   (b) 2.631   (c) 6.21   (d) 60.82   (e) 0.006

2.5 Ordering decimals

- You can sort decimals in order of size by first comparing the whole numbers, then the digits in the tenths place, then the digits in the hundredths place, and so on.

Example 7

Write these decimal numbers in order of size, starting with the largest.

    0.36   2.5   0.58   0.621   0.003

Largest value digits:

0.36	2.5	0.58	0.621	0.003
↑	↑	↑	↑	↑
3 tenths	2 units	5 tenths	6 tenths	3 thousandths

In order:
2.5, 0.621, 0.58, 0.36, 0.003

Exercise 2E

1 Write these decimal numbers in order of size, starting with the largest.

(a) 2.1, 3.68, 0.20, 0.03   (b) 0.76, 0.75, 0.07, 0.001

(c) 9.08, 0.98, 0.09, 9.009   (d) 6.01, 1.06, 0.016, 0.61

(e) 0.9, 0.09, 0.009, 9.0   (f) 0.03, 30.0, 0.30, 0.303

2 The times of five runners in a 100 m race are given below.

Alex	10.96 s
Jack	11.02 s
Ameet	10.93 s
Tom	11.13 s
Ben	10.87 s

Rewrite the list in order, starting with the fastest time.

3 A sports drink can lists these amount of vitamins per 100 ml of the drink.

B2	0.08 mg
Niacin	0.89 mg
B6	0.10 mg
Pantothenic acid	0.30 mg

Rewrite the list of vitamins in order, starting with the largest amount.

4 The table gives the heights in metres of five basketball players.

Karim	Peter	Leroy	Curtis	Greg
2.10	1.92	2.15	1.96	2.06

Write the heights in descending order (starting with the tallest).

2.6 Adding and subtracting decimals

- When adding and subtracting decimals make sure you write the digits in their correct place value columns.

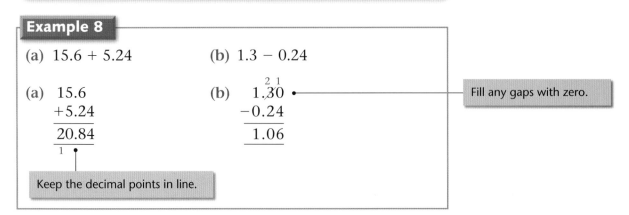

Example 8

(a) 15.6 + 5.24   (b) 1.3 − 0.24

(a)   15.6
     +5.24
     ─────
      20.84
        1

Keep the decimal points in line.

(b)   ² ¹
        1.30 ●────── Fill any gaps with zero.
       −0.24
       ─────
        1.06

Exercise 2F

1 Work out
   (a) 5.3 + 2.6   (b) 4.5 + 0.7   (c) 2.13 + 3.14
   (d) 0.32 + 0.49   (e) 1.2 + 1.58   (f) 6.94 + 0.7
   (g) 30.8 + 2.79   (h) 23.1 + 0.23   (i) 5.78 + 0.031
   (j) 21.3 + 0.02

2 Work out
   (a) 7.8 − 3.6   (b) 6.1 − 2.9   (c) 18.2 − 0.7
   (d) 9.23 − 1.8   (e) 6.2 − 2.34   (f) 2.9 − 0.36
   (g) 15.1 − 1.51   (h) 20.01 − 6.2   (i) 9 − 3.62
   (j) 0.36 − 0.036

3 Alix is making some cakes. She uses 1.5 kg of flour, 0.75 kg of margarine and 0.325 kg of sugar.
What is the total weight of these ingredients?

4 A set of triplets weigh 2.3 kg, 2 kg and 2.05 kg at birth.
What is their total birth weight?

5 A relay team runs a race. The times for the four runners are 10.02 seconds, 10.3 seconds, 9.98 seconds and 10 seconds. How long does the whole team take to run the race?

6 Harry wants to put his wardrobe, chest of drawers and desk along one wall in his bedroom. The wall is 4.1 metres long. The wardrobe is 0.98 metres, the desk 1.4 metres and the chest of drawers 1.75 metres. Will they all fit?

7 Dina is packing to go on holiday. The baggage allowance is 20 kg. Her suitcase weighs 2.6 kg, her clothes weigh 11.3 kg, her shoes weigh 3.7 kg and her toiletries weigh 2.3 kg. Is her packed suitcase within the 20 kg limit?

2.7 Multiplying and dividing decimals by 10, 100 or 1000

- To **multiply by 10** move the digits **one place** to the **left**.
- To **multiply by 100** move the digits **two places** to the **left**.
- To **multiply by 1000** move the digits **three places** to the **left**.
- To **divide by 10** move the digits **one place** to the **right**.
- To **divide by 100** move the digits **two places** to the **right**.
- To **divide by 1000** move the digits **three places** to the **right**.

Example 9

Work out

(a) 3.14×10 (b) $6.89 \div 10$

(c) 0.361×100 (d) $2.36 \div 100$

(e) $78.19 \div 1000$ (f) 2.3×1000

(a) $3.14 \times 10 = 31.4$ (b) $6.89 \div 10 = 0.689$

(c) $0.361 \times 100 = 36.1$ (d) $2.36 \div 100 = 0.0236$

(e) $78.19 \div 1000 = 0.078\ 19$ (f) $2.3 \times 1000 = 2300$

- To multiply or divide by a decimal, write the decimal as a whole number divided by 10 or 100 or 1000.

Example 10

Work out

(a) 13.4×3 (b) $8.19 \div 9$

$\boxed{13.4 = 134 \div 10}$ $\boxed{8.19 = 819 \div 100}$

(a) 13.4×3
$= 134 \div 10 \times 3$
$= 134 \times 3 \div 10$
$= 402 \div 10$
$= 40.2$

(b) $8.19 \div 9$
$= 819 \div 100 \div 9$
$= 819 \div 9 \div 100$
$= 91 \div 100$
$= 0.91$

Exercise 2G

1 Work out

   (a) 2.1×10 (b) 0.1×100 (c) 2.3×10 (d) 0.017×100

   (e) 0.28×1000 (f) 3.1×10 (g) 4.6×100 (h) 0.36×1000

   (i) 3.14×100 (j) 3.14×1000

2 Work out

   (a) $28.1 \div 10$ (b) $36.9 \div 100$ (c) $6.89 \div 10$ (d) $123.1 \div 1000$

   (e) $23.1 \div 100$ (f) $0.23 \div 10$ (g) $1.3 \div 100$ (h) $3.14 \div 10$

   (i) $3.14 \div 100$ (j) $0.02 \div 1000$

3 Work out

   (a) 2.1×10 (b) $6.2 \div 10$ (c) 0.162×1000 (d) $3.89 \div 100$

   (e) 0.3×100 (f) $2.38 \div 1000$ (g) 0.35×100 (h) $0.2 \div 1000$

4 Work out

(a) 8.3×4 (b) 2.5×6 (c) 11.1×5 (d) 3.11×4

(e) 2.31×8 (f) $18.2 \div 2$ (g) $28.4 \div 4$ (h) $65.5 \div 5$

(i) $6.48 \div 8$ (j) $7.07 \div 7$

2.8 Multiplying and dividing decimal numbers

- When you multiply decimals the answer must have the same number of decimal places as the total number of decimal places in the numbers you multiply.

- When you divide by a decimal: multiply the number you are dividing *by* by 10, 100 or 1000 to change it into a whole number. Then multiply the number you are dividing *into* by the same number (10, 100 or 1000).

Example 11

Work out the cost of 16 CDs at £8.45 each.
Do not use a calculator.

```
    8 4 5
  ×   1 6
  5 0²7³0          845 × 6
  8 4 5 0          845 × 10
  1 3 5 2 0
      1
```

These are the carries.

Multiply the numbers together, ignoring the decimals.

Add them together.

This is sometimes called long multiplication.

Count the number of decimal places:

16   no places   } total 2 places
8.45   2 places

So $16 \times £8.54 = £135.20$

The answer has two decimal places.

Example 12

Work out 6.3×5.4 using equivalent fractions.

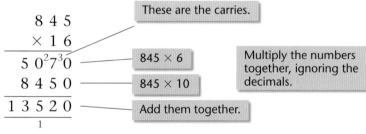

$$6.3 = \frac{63}{10} \quad \text{and} \quad 5.4 = \frac{54}{10}$$

So $\quad 6.3 \times 5.4 = \frac{63}{10} \times \frac{54}{10}$

$$= \frac{63 \times 54}{10 \times 10}$$

$$= \frac{3402}{100}$$

$$= 34.02$$

Work out 63×54 by long multiplication:

```
      6 3
    × 5 4
    2 5¹2        63 × 4
  3 1¹5 0        63 × 50
  3 4 0 2
      1
```

Example 13

Work out 0.08×0.14

$$
\begin{array}{r}
1\ 4 \\
\times\ 8 \\
\hline
1\ 1^3 2
\end{array}
$$

The answer is 0.0112   The answer must have 4 d.p.

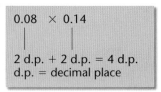

0.08 $\times$ 0.14

2 d.p. + 2 d.p. = 4 d.p.
d.p. = decimal place

Example 14

Work out $3.25 \div 0.05$

Method 1

$0.05\overline{)3.25}$

$\times$ by 100

$$
\begin{array}{r}
6\ 5 \\
5\overline{)3\ 2^2 5}
\end{array}
$$

$3.25 \div 0.05 = 65$

Method 2

$3.25 \div 0.05$

$325 \div 5$

$$
\begin{array}{r}
65 \\
5\overline{)325} \\
30 \\
\hline
25
\end{array}
$$

Multiply both numbers by 100 to remove the decimal point.

 **Exercise 2H**

Work these out, showing all your working.

1 Work out the cost of
  (a) 8 paperbacks at £5.45 each
  (b) 5 boxes of crackers at £8.19 each
  (c) 26 bottles of oil at £2.36 each
  (d) 3.5 kg of potatoes at £0.46 per kilogram
  (e) 14 pairs of socks at £3.89 a pair.

2 Use the method of equivalent fractions to work out
  (a) 0.4×0.7 (b) 0.8×0.6 (c) 3.2×1.4
  (d) 8.5×6.7 (e) 9.1×4.5 (f) 4.1×0.6

3 Work out
  (a) 0.3×5 (b) 0.6×0.7 (c) 2.34×0.2 (d) 3.67×0.09
  (e) 12.7×0.6 (f) 3.93×1.2 (g) 16.2×3.7 (h) 7.12×0.032

4 Work out
  (a) $15.6 \div 6$ (b) $209.2 \div 4$ (c) $28.5 \div 4$ (d) $10.56 \div 0.6$
  (e) $2.36 \div 0.8$ (f) $58.6 \div 2.5$ (g) $2.34 \div 0.32$ (h) $3.26 \div 0.16$

5 A piece of fabric 23.4 m long is cut into five equal lengths. How long is each length?

6 Work out the total weight of eight bags of dried fruit weighing 0.375 kg each.

7 A glass holds 0.3 *l*. How many glasses of lemonade can be poured from a 1.5 *l* bottle?

8 A car will travel 17.2 km on 1 litre of petrol. How far will the car travel on 8.5 litres of petrol?

9 How many stamps costing £0.32 can be bought with £5.76?

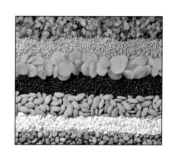

2.9 Converting between fractions and decimals

- You can convert a fraction to a decimal by dividing the numerator by the denominator.
- You can convert a decimal to a fraction by writing it as a number of tenths/hundredths/thousandths.
- Not all fractions have an exact decimal equivalent.
- **Recurring decimal** notation:
  - $0.\dot{3}$ means 0.333 333 recurring
  - $0.1\dot{7}$ means 0.171 717 recurring
  - $0.\dot{1}2\dot{3}$ means 0.123 123 recurring.
- A **terminating decimal** can be written as an **exact fraction** using a place value table.
- You need to remember these fraction to decimal conversions:

  $\frac{1}{2} = 0.5$ $\frac{1}{5} = 0.2$ $\frac{1}{3} = 0.\dot{3}$

  $\frac{1}{4} = 0.25$ $\frac{1}{10} = 0.1$ $\frac{2}{3} = 0.\dot{6}$

Example 15

Convert these fractions into decimals.

(a) $\frac{2}{5}$ (b) $\frac{5}{12}$ (c) $\frac{2}{11}$

(a) $2 \div 5 = 0.4$

(b) $5 \div 12 = 0.416\,666 = 0.41\dot{6}$ The 6 repeats

(c) $2 \div 11 = 0.181\,818 = 0.\dot{1}\dot{8}$ Both 1 and 8 repeat

> 0.416 666 7
>
> If you work out 5 ÷ 12 on a calculator, the result on the display could be 0.416 666 7. The result has been rounded to 7 significant figures by the calculator.

> For more on significant figures see Section 2.10.

Example 16

Convert these decimals into fractions.

(a) 0.6   (b) 0.148   (c) 0.36

(a) $0.6 = \frac{6}{10} = \frac{3}{5}$ $\frac{6}{10}$ simplifies to $\frac{3}{5}$ (dividing top and bottom by 2).

(b) $0.148 = \frac{148}{1000} = \frac{37}{250}$ Simplify by dividing top and bottom by 4.

(c) $0.36 = \frac{36}{100} = \frac{9}{25}$ Simplify by dividing top and bottom by 4.

Exercise 2I

1 Convert these fractions into decimals.

(a) $\frac{1}{5}$ (b) $\frac{3}{5}$ (c) $\frac{5}{8}$ (d) $\frac{9}{20}$ (e) $\frac{3}{4}$

(f) $\frac{1}{3}$ (g) $\frac{4}{9}$ (h) $\frac{7}{12}$ (i) $\frac{7}{22}$ (j) $\frac{7}{27}$

2 Convert these decimals into fractions. Give your answers in their simplest form.

(a) 0.7   (b) 0.5   (c) 0.12   (d) 0.65

(e) $0.8\dot{3}$ (f) 0.362   (g) 0.137   (h) 0.685

3 Which of these fractions have exact decimal equivalents?

(a) $\frac{4}{5}$ (b) $\frac{5}{9}$ (c) $\frac{7}{25}$ (d) $\frac{4}{13}$ (e) $\frac{8}{17}$

2.10 Rounding to one significant figure

- The first significant figure is the first non-zero digit in a number, counting from the left.
- To write a number to one significant figure (1 s.f.), look at the place value of the first significant figure and round the number to this place value.

Example 17

Round these numbers to one significant figure.

(a) 325   (b) 5720

(c) 8.3   (d) 0.028

> 325
> ↑
> 3 is the 1st significant figure. It is in the Hundreds column, so round this number to the nearest hundred.

(a) 325 to 1 s.f. is 300.

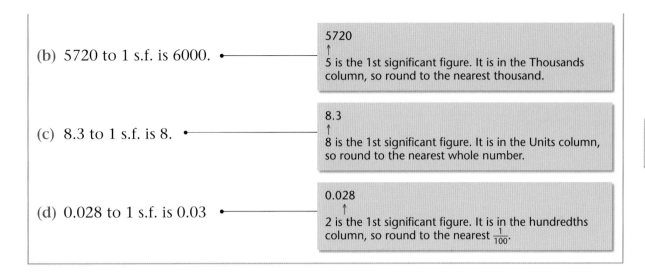

(b) 5720 to 1 s.f. is 6000.

> 5720
> ↑
> 5 is the 1st significant figure. It is in the Thousands column, so round to the nearest thousand.

(c) 8.3 to 1 s.f. is 8.

> 8.3
> ↑
> 8 is the 1st significant figure. It is in the Units column, so round to the nearest whole number.

(d) 0.028 to 1 s.f. is 0.03

> 0.028
> ↑
> 2 is the 1st significant figure. It is in the hundredths column, so round to the nearest $\frac{1}{100}$.

Exercise 2J

1 Round each number to the nearest multiple of 10 given in the brackets.

(a) 27 (10)   (b) 328 (10)   (c) 482 (100)

(d) 2771 (100)   (e) 3256 (1000)   (f) 4789 (1000)

(g) 5821 (10)   (h) 476 (100)

In questions **2–4** round the numbers to 1 s.f.

2 (a) 326   (b) 4821   (c) 301   (d) 42

(e) 5231   (f) 69 231   (g) 28   (h) 30 021

3 (a) 4.9   (b) 2.1   (c) 8.38   (d) 6.701

(e) 9.31   (f) 9.87   (g) 2.01   (h) 3.07

4 (a) 0.34   (b) 0.69   (c) 0.081   (d) 0.0632

(e) 0.003 21   (f) 0.0025   (g) 0.0802   (h) 0.961

5 The number of students in Shefford High School is 1487.
Write this number to 1 s.f.

6 The number of spectators at a rugby match is 34 682.
Write this number to 1 s.f.

7 Ted's salary is £19 800.
Write down Ted's salary to 1 s.f.

2.11 Using significant figures to estimate answers

• To estimate the answer to a calculation round all the numbers to one significant figure and do the simpler calculation.

You can use estimated answers to check that an answer to a question is about the right size.

Example 18

For each of these calculations write down a calculation that can be used to estimate an answer, and work out the value of your estimate.

(a) $\dfrac{27 \times 321}{9.2}$

(b) 9.2×0.73

(a) $\dfrac{27 \times 321}{9.2}$

Estimate:

$\dfrac{30 \times 300}{9}$

$= \dfrac{9000}{9} = 1000$

(b) 9.2×0.73

Estimate:

$9 \times 0.7 = 6.3$

Write all the numbers in the question to 1 s.f.

Example 19

For each calculation

(i) work out the exact value by calculator

(ii) check that your answer is about the right size by estimating.

(a) 482×0.92

(b) $\dfrac{285 \times 79}{586}$

(a) (i) $482 \times 0.92 = 443.44$

(ii) Estimate: $500 \times 0.9 = 450$

(b) (i) $\dfrac{285 \times 79}{586} = 38.421\,501\,71$

(ii) Estimate: $\dfrac{300 \times 80}{600} = 40$

Using a calculator.

450 is about the same size as 443.44

Exercise 2K

1 For each of these calculations

(i) write down a calculation that can be used to work out an estimated answer

(ii) work out the estimated answer.

(a) 382×43

(b) $962 \div 39$

(c) $\dfrac{823 \times 4872}{3261}$

(d) 634×2.7

(e) $382 \div 4.9$

(f) 6.9×2.1

(g) $8.7 \div 1.9$

(h) $\dfrac{3.6 \times 4.5}{9.8}$

(i) $\dfrac{2.4 \times 7.9}{3.9 \times 2.3}$

2 For each of these calculations
   (i) use your calculator to work out the exact value
   (ii) check your answer by estimating.
   (a) 683×23 (b) 47×2.7 (c) 3.1×9.4
   (d) $385 \div 35$ (e) $335.4 \div 8.6$ (f) $9.6 \div 3.2$
   (g) $\dfrac{912 \div 24}{4.9}$ (h) $\dfrac{2.8 \times 3.1}{24}$

2.12 Giving a sensible answer

- You may need to round an answer up or down, depending on the context of the question.

Example 20

Electricity is charged at 8.66p per unit. Sue uses 136 units.
Work out the cost of the electricity she uses.

Sue uses 136 units that cost 8.66p each.
   So the total cost $= 136 \times 8.66$p
   $= 1177.76$p
   Total cost $= 1178$p or £11.78

> You cannot pay 0.76p. Round to the nearest penny.

Example 21

221 people are going on a coach trip. One coach can carry
52 passengers. Work out the number of coaches needed for
the trip.

Number of coaches needed is $221 \div 52 = 4.25$
Five coaches are needed.

> You can't hire 0.25 of a coach.
> If you hire four coaches, there won't be enough room for all the passengers. This time you need to round up.

Example 22

Malcolm is asked to draw a square that has an area of 50 cm.
He calculates that each side should be 7.071 cm.
Explain why his figure is not sensible, and give a more
sensible figure.

7.071 cm is 7 cm and 0.71 mm.
You could not measure 0.71 mm.
A side of 7.1 cm would be more sensible, as you could
actually measure this distance.

Exercise 2L

Remember to check that your answers are sensible.

1 An electricity company charges 7.44p per unit of electricity. Work out the cost of 176 units of electricity.

2 Meia is buying books of stamps. Stamps come in books of 12. She has 135 letters to post. How many books of stamps does she need to buy?

3 A farmer collects 50 eggs from his chickens. How many egg boxes will he need if each box holds 6 eggs?

4 Mr Lowry gives his six grandchildren £40 to share between them. How much will each grandchild receive?

5 Gas costs £0.025 per kWh. Sasha uses 312 kWh. Calculate the cost of Sasha's gas bill.

6 A kilogram of bread dough is divided into two dozen bread rolls. Work out the weight of each bread roll.

> Remember: 1 kg = 1000 g
> 1 dozen = 12

7 Dominic is asked to draw a circle with a circumference of 30 cm. He calculates that the diameter should be 9.549 cm. Explain why his answer is not sensible. Give a more sensible answer.

8 Mary carries out a survey of shoe sizes in her class. She says the average size is 4.3. Explain why this is not a sensible answer.

9 The car deck of a ferry is 30 m long. Each car is given 1.8 m. How many cars can be carried in one lane on the ferry?

10 Mr Jewitt earns £7.30 an hour. He is paid overtime at time and a third. Mr Jewitt works 4 hours' overtime and makes a request for £38.933 333 overtime payment. Explain why Mr Jewitt's request is not sensible.

> For each hour of overtime he is paid $1\frac{1}{3}$ × his hourly rate.

2.13 Using trial and improvement to solve problems

- If there is no simple method to solve a problem, you can use **trial and improvement**.
- To solve a problem using trial and improvement:
  - ○ **try** an estimated value in the calculation
  - ○ use the answer to your calculation to **improve** your estimate.

Example 23

A group of people go to the cinema. The group pay a total of £25 for their tickets. Adult tickets cost £8 and children's tickets cost £3. How many adults and children are in the group?

1    $\dfrac{£25}{£3} = 8$ remainder 1

Total cost

Cost of 1 child

The group is not made up only of children.

$\dfrac{£25}{£8} = 3$ remainder 1

Total cost

Cost of 1 adult

The group is not made up only of adults.

2   Try 1 adult in the group: 1 adult pays £8.
$£25 - £8 = £17$

$\dfrac{£17}{£3} = 5$ remainder 2 •——— The other people are not all children.

3   Try 2 adults: 2 adults pay £16.
$£25 - £16 = £9$

$\dfrac{£9}{£3} = 3$ •——— £9 is 3 children's tickets

The group is made up of 2 adults and 3 children.

> First check that the group is not just all adults or all children.

> Check whether £17 could be just children's tickets.

> Check whether £9 could be just children's tickets.

Exercise 2M

1   A group of friends visit a sports centre. Some of the group go swimming and the rest play squash. Tickets for swimming cost £3 and tickets for squash cost £5. The total cost of their tickets is £22. Work out how many of the group went swimming and how many played squash.

2   Ballpoint pens cost 22p and gel pens cost 60p. Kwame bought a mixture of ballpoint pens and gel pens for £2.30. How many of each did he buy?

3   A football team plays four matches over Christmas. They score a total of 7 points. If they score 3 points for a win, 1 point for a draw and no points for a defeat, how many games did they win, draw and lose?

4 Two moons, Zeus and Hermes, orbit the same planet. Zeus takes 24 days to orbit the planet and Hermes takes 32 days. If the two moons start in line with each other, how long will it be before they line up again?

5 A café charges £1.20 for coffee and £1.10 for tea. Faisal buys coffee and tea for his friends. He pays £9.20 for the drinks. How many cups of tea and coffee does he buy?

2.14 Understanding percentages

- Percentage
  %   mean 'number of parts per hundred'.
  pc
- A percentage can be written as a fraction with denominator (bottom) 100.

Example 24

This rectangle is divided into 100 squares.

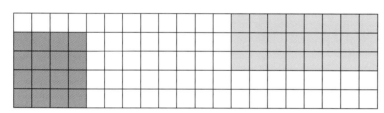

(a) What percentage of the rectangle is coloured red?
(b) What percentage of the rectangle is coloured blue?
(c) What percentage of the rectangle is not coloured?
(d) Write your answers to parts (a), (b) and (c) as fractions.

The rectangle is divided into 100 equal parts.
(a) 16 parts out of 100 are coloured red.
    16% of the rectangle is red.
(b) 24 parts are coloured blue
    24% of the rectangle is blue.
(c) 60 parts are not coloured.
    60% of the rectangle is not coloured.
(d) $16\% = \frac{16}{100}$ $\qquad 24\% = \frac{24}{100}$ $\qquad 60\% = \frac{60}{100}$

$\qquad\quad = \frac{4}{25}$ $\qquad\qquad = \frac{6}{25}$ $\qquad\qquad = \frac{3}{5}$

Exercise 2N

1 This rectangle is divided into 100 squares.

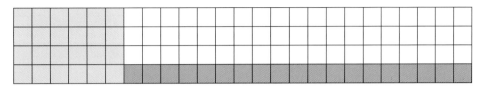

   (a) What percentage of the rectangle is coloured blue?

   (b) What percentage of the rectangle is coloured red?

   (c) What percentage of the rectangle is not coloured?

   (d) Write your answers to parts (a), (b) and (c) as fractions.

2 100 Year 11 students were asked which person they wanted to win a reality TV show.
The table below shows their replies.

Person	No. of students
Brian	63
Dan	16
Makosi	18
Fariah	3

   (a) What percentage of the students chose Brian?

   (b) What percentage chose Fariah?

   (c) Write down the percentage and fraction who chose Dan.

> Work out the total number of students first.

3 A cereal manufacturer lists the following nutritional information on a packet of cornflakes.

Nutrient	Typical value per 100 g
Carbohydrates	82 g
Fat	1 g
Protein	8 g

   (a) What percentage of a serving of cornflakes is carbohydrates?

   (b) What percentage of a serving of cornflakes is protein?

   (c) What percentage of a serving is something other than carbohydrates, fat or protein?

   (d) Write your answers to parts (a), (b) and (c) as fractions.

4 Draw a rectangle 20 cm long and 5 cm wide.

(a) Shade 25% of the rectangle blue.

(b) Shade 13% of the rectangle red.

(c) What percentage of your rectangle is left unshaded?

2.15 Comparing different proportions using percentages

Example 25

In four class tests Liberty scored
9 out of 10 in History
13 out of 20 in French
68 out of 100 in Mathematics
35 out of 50 in English.
Which test did she do best in?

Liberty's scores are

History $\frac{9}{10}$ French $\frac{13}{20}$ Maths $\frac{68}{100}$ English $\frac{35}{50}$

History	$\frac{9}{10} = \frac{90}{100} = 90\%$
French	$\frac{13}{20} = \frac{65}{100} = 65\%$
Maths	$\frac{68}{100} = 68\%$
English	$\frac{35}{50} = \frac{70}{100} = 70\%$

Liberty did best in History.

> To compare these fractions, change them to percentages.

> First write each fraction with a denominator of 100.

Exercise 20

1 The number of games won by three football teams is shown below together with the total number of matches played.

Team	Played	Won
Greenfield FC	10	4
Millbrook Utd	5	3
Carrbrook Town	20	9

(a) Write down the number of matches won by each team as a percentage of the games they played.

(b) Which team was the most successful?

2 Jessica bought three packets of sweets. The packets were different sizes. She counted the numbers of the different flavoured sweets in each packet. Her results were:

Flavour	Packet 1 (20 sweets)	Packet 2 (50 sweets)	Packet 3 (100 sweets)
Strawberry	6	13	29
Blackcurrant	3	6	6
Lime	7	24	45
Orange	4	7	20

(a) What percentage of each packet was strawberry sweets?

(b) Which packet had the highest proportion of lime sweets?

(c) Which packet had the lowest proportion of orange sweets?

2.16 Working out a percentage of an amount

- To work out a percentage of an amount write the percentage as a fraction with a denominator of 100. Then multiply the fraction by the amount.

Example 26

Work out 15% of 40.

$$\frac{15}{100} \times 40 = 6$$

Write 15% as a fraction with a denominator of 100. Multiply by 40.

Exercise 2P

1 Work out

(a) 5% of 60 (b) 10% of 30 (c) 15% of 70 (d) 25% of 36

(e) 45% of 80 (f) 10% of £2 (g) 15% of £9 (h) 24% of £10

(i) 36% of £50 (j) 90% of £145

2 Peter scored 75% in an English test. The test was marked out of 60. How many marks did Peter score?

3 10% of the passengers booked on to a flight did not turn up. The plane carries 130 passengers. How many passengers did not turn up?

4 A tennis player won 86% of the 50 games he played in a season. How many games did he win?

5 An MP3 player normally costs £80. In a sale it is reduced by 20%.
   (a) How much is the MP3 player reduced by?
   (b) How much does the MP3 player cost in the sale?

6 The normal price of a dress is £36. Its price is reduced by 15% in a sale. How much does the dress cost in the sale?

Mixed exercise 2

1 Change these improper fractions to mixed numbers.
   (a) $\frac{9}{8}$ (b) $\frac{15}{9}$ (c) $\frac{20}{6}$ (d) $\frac{25}{8}$

2 Change these mixed numbers to improper fractions.
   (a) $1\frac{1}{4}$ (b) $1\frac{2}{3}$ (c) $2\frac{2}{5}$ (d) $3\frac{5}{7}$

3 Write these fractions in their simplest form.
   (a) $\frac{6}{8}$ (b) $\frac{9}{15}$ (c) $\frac{16}{18}$ (d) $\frac{24}{30}$

4 Fill in the missing numbers to make these fractions equivalent.
   (a) $\frac{3}{4} = \frac{}{12}$ (b) $\frac{5}{8} = \frac{}{16}$ (c) $\frac{}{4} = \frac{24}{32}$
   (d) $\frac{}{7} = \frac{6}{21}$ (e) $\frac{3}{} = \frac{12}{20}$ (f) $\frac{3}{8} = \frac{}{40}$

5 In an office, $\frac{1}{5}$ of the employees go out for lunch, $\frac{3}{4}$ eat lunch at their desk and $\frac{1}{20}$ do not eat lunch.
   (a) What do the largest number of employees do at lunchtime?
   (b) What do the smallest number of employees do at lunchtime?

6 Write the fractions $\frac{1}{3}$, $\frac{3}{5}$, $\frac{3}{10}$ and $\frac{5}{6}$ in ascending order.

7 Write down the value of the underlined digit.
   (a) 11.3<u>8</u>   (b) 0.02<u>1</u>   (c) 1.0<u>3</u>2   (d) 0.<u>6</u>8

8 Write these numbers in ascending order.
      8.078, 0.878, 0.087, 0.87, 0.8

9 Work out
   (a) 8.9 + 0.36   (b) 6.89 − 1.36   (c) 5 + 2.13
   (d) 1.3 − 0.24   (e) 31.3 + 2.95   (f) 7.8 − 0.78
   (g) 16.1 + 0.38   (h) 10 − 2.93

10 Work out
   (a) 6.3 × 10   (b) 0.9 ÷ 10   (c) 3.2 × 1000
   (d) 17.91 × 100   (e) 11 ÷ 100   (f) 2.36 ÷ 1000

11 Work out
    (a) 2.4×6 (b) 13.1×3 (c) 2.42×5
    (d) $10.6 \div 2$ (e) $33.6 \div 3$ (f) $4.88 \div 8$

 12 Write down the answers to
    (a) $31.3 \div 10$ (b) 4.38×10 (c) $2.56 \div 100$
    (d) 0.2×100 (e) $5.6 \div 1000$ (f) 2.13×1000

 13 (a) A packet of biscuits weighs 0.375 kg. How much do
        100 packets of biscuits weigh?
    (b) 1000 sheets of paper weigh 6.8 kg. How much does
        1 sheet of paper weigh?

 14 Work out
    (a) 3.28×1.3 (b) $4.84 \div 1.1$
    (c) 2.6×32.1 (d) $0.576 \div 0.16$

 15 A packet of cornflakes contains 0.45 kg of cornflakes.
A serving of cornflakes is 0.03 kg. Calculate the number of
servings in the packet.

16 Tiles costs £17.50 per square metre. Calculate the cost of
5.5 square metres of tiles.

17 Change these fractions into decimals.
    (a) $\frac{4}{5}$ (b) $\frac{7}{8}$ (c) $\frac{5}{9}$

18 Change these decimals into fractions in their simplest
form.
    (a) 0.16   (b) 0.6   (c) 0.485

19 Greeting cards are sold in packs of four. Darius wants to
send a card to each of his 17 friends. How many packs
should he buy?

20 Terry is asked to draw an equilateral triangle with a
perimeter of 20 cm. He works out that the length of each
side of the triangle should be 6.6666 cm. Explain why his
answer is not sensible. Give a more sensible answer.

21 Round these numbers to 1 s.f.
    (a) 32   (b) 45   (c) 237
    (d) 5800   (e) 3.7   (f) 0.02

22 23 970 people attended a pop concert. Write this number
to 1 significant figure.

23 For each of these calculations
   (i) write down a calculation that can be used to work out an estimate of the answer
   (ii) work out the estimated answer.

   (a) 372×54 (b) $\dfrac{234 \div 39}{4.9}$ (c) $\dfrac{3.7 \times 8.2}{7.9 \div 2.1}$

24 For each of these calculations
   (i) use your calculator to work out an exact answer
   (ii) check your answer by estimating.

   (a) 587×28 (b) 3.2×7.8 (c) $8.2 \div 1.7$ (d) $\dfrac{56 \times 38}{27}$

25 Mr Heath uses 174 kWh of gas. Gas costs 2.62p per kWh. Work out the cost of the gas used by Mr Heath. Give your answer to a sensible degree of accuracy.

26 In a café, biscuits cost 55p and cakes cost 90p. Robert bought a mixture of biscuits and cakes for £3.10. How many biscuits and how many cakes did Robert buy?

27 A gardener plants 100 tulips. 35 tulips are red, 42 are yellow and the rest are purple.
   (a) What percentage of the tulips are red?
   (b) What percentage of the tulips are purple?

28 Draw a square with sides 10 cm.
   (a) Shade 15% of the square blue.
   (b) Shade 43% of the square red.
   (c) What percentage of the square is left?

29 Kate takes three modular tests in Science. Her scores are:
   Biology   13 out of 20
   Chemistry   31 out of 50
   Physics   64 out of 100
   (a) Write down Kate's scores as percentages.
   (b) Which test did Kate do best in?

30 Work out
   (a) 10% of 30   (b) 15% of 60   (c) 18% of 50
   (d) 25% of £6   (e) 30% of £10   (f) 12% of £15

31 8% of a yogurt is fat. How many grams of fat are there in a yogurt weighing 150 g?

32 The attendance at a concert is 4800. Of the spectators, 26% are women. How many spectators are women?

33 How much will Flash trainers cost in the sale?

FLASH TRAINERS
Normal Price £85
SALE: 20% OFF
NORMAL PRICE

Summary of key points

1 In a fraction:

The top number shows how many parts you have.

The top number is called the **numerator**.

$$\frac{3}{4}$$

The bottom number shows how many parts there are.

The bottom number is called the **denominator**.

2 A fraction whose numerator is larger than its denominator is called an **improper fraction**.

3 An improper fraction can be written as a **mixed number**, with a whole number part and a fraction part.

4 You can simplify a fraction if the numerator and denominator have a common factor. When you have divided by all the common factors, the fraction is in its **simplest form**.

5 **Equivalent fractions** are fractions that have the same value.

6 To write a list of fractions in order of size
  ○ write them all as equivalent fractions with the same denominator
  ○ order them using the numerators.

7 In a decimal number the decimal point separates the whole number from the part smaller than 1.

8 You can sort decimals in order of size by first comparing the whole numbers, then the digits in the tenths place, then the digits in the hundredths place, and so on.

9 When adding and subtracting decimals make sure you write the digits in their correct place value columns.

10 To **multiply by 10** move the digits **one place** to the **left**.

11 To **multiply by 100** move the digits **two places** to the **left**.

12 To **multiply by 1000** move the digits **three places** to the **left**.

13 To **divide by 10** move the digits **one place** to the **right**.

14 To **divide by 100** move the digits **two places** to the **right**.

15 To **divide by 1000** move the digits **three places** to the **right**.

16 To multiply or divide by a decimal, write the decimal as a whole number divided by 10 or 100 or 1000.

17 When you multiply decimals the answer must have the same number of decimal places as the total number of decimal places in the numbers you multiply.

18 When you divide by a decimal: multiply the number you are dividing *by* by 10, 100 or 1000 to change it into a whole number. Then multiply the number you are dividing *into* by the same number (10, 100 or 1000).

19 You can convert a fraction to a decimal by dividing the numerator by the denominator.

20 You can convert a decimal to a fraction by writing it as a number of tenths/hundredths/thousandths.

21 Not all fractions have an exact decimal equivalent.

22 **Recurring decimal** notation:
   ○ $0.\dot{3}$ means 0.333 333 recurring
   ○ $0.\dot{1}\dot{7}$ means 0.171 717 recurring
   ○ $0.\dot{1}2\dot{3}$ means 0.123 123 recurring.

23 A **terminating decimal** can be written as an **exact fraction** using a place value table.

24 You need to remember these fraction to decimal conversions:

$\frac{1}{2} = 0.5$ $\frac{1}{10} = 0.1$ $\frac{1}{3} = 0.\dot{3}$ $\frac{1}{5} = 0.2,$

$\frac{1}{4} = 0.25$ $\frac{1}{100} = 0.01$ $\frac{2}{3} = 0.\dot{6}$ $\frac{1}{8} = 0.125$

25 The first significant figure is the first non-zero digit in a number, counting from the left.

26 To write a number to one significant figure (1 s.f.), look at the place value of the first significant figure and round the number to this place value.

27 To estimate the answer to a calculation round all the numbers to one significant figure and do the simpler calculation.

28 You may need to round an answer up or down, depending on the context of the question.

29 If there is no simple method to solve a problem, you can use **trial and improvement**.

30 To solve a problem using trial and improvement:
   ○ **try** an estimated value in the calculation
   ○ use the answer to your calculation to **improve** your estimate.

31 Percentage
    %   mean 'number of parts per hundred'.
    pc

32 A percentage can be written as a fraction with denominator 100.

33 To work out a percentage of an amount write the percentage as a fraction with a denominator of 100. Then multiply the fraction by the amount.

3 Powers, indices and calculations

3.1 Squares, cubes, square and cube roots

- **Square numbers** are the result of multiplying a whole number by itself.

  3×3 can be written as

  3 squared   the square of 3 3^2

- To square a number multiply the number by itself.

- A **square root** is a number that has been multiplied by itself to make another number.

- If $x \times x = A$ then x is the square root of A, written $\sqrt{A}$.

- Every positive number has a positive and a negative square root.

- **Cube numbers** are the result of multiplying a whole number by itself then multiplying again.

  $3 \times 3 \times 3$ can be written as

  3 cubed   the cube of 3 3^3

- To cube a number multiply the number by itself, then multiply by the number again.

- A **cube root** is a number that has been multiplied by itself and by itself again to make another number.

- If $y \times y \times y = A$ then y is the cube root of A, written $\sqrt[3]{A}$.

- A positive number has a positive cube root. A negative number has a negative cube root.

$7 \times 7 = 49$

7×7 can be written as 7^2 (7 squared).

$\sqrt{49}$ means the square root of 49.

7 is the positive square root of 49 because 7 is a positive number and $7 \times 7 = 49$.

-7 is the negative square root of 49 because $-7 \times -7 = 49$.

$7 \times 7 \times 7$ can be written as 7^3 (7 cubed).

$\sqrt[3]{27}$ means the cube root of 27.

3 is the cube root of 27 because $3 \times 3 \times 3 = 27$.

Example 1

From the numbers in the cloud, write down

(a) the square numbers

(b) the cube numbers.

> 16   5
> 10   1   27
> 8   4

(a) 1, 4 and 16 are square numbers because
$$1 = 1 \times 1$$
$$4 = 2 \times 2$$
$$16 = 4 \times 4$$

(b) 1, 8 and 27 are cube numbers because
$$1 = 1 \times 1 \times 1$$
$$8 = 2 \times 2 \times 2$$
$$27 = 3 \times 3 \times 3$$

Example 2

Work out
(a) 6^2 (b) 2^3 (c) $\sqrt{25}$
(d) the positive square root of 100.

(a) $6^2 = 6 \times 6 = 36$
(b) $2^3 = 2 \times 2 \times 2 = 8$
(c) $\sqrt{25} = 5$ or -5, because $5 \times 5 = 25$ and $-5 \times -5 = 25$
(d) The positive square root of 100 is 10 because
    $10 \times 10 = 100$

- You can use the function keys on a calculator to work out squares, cubes, square roots and cube roots.

> Make sure you know how to work these out with your calculator.

Example 3

Work out
(a) 3.2^2 (b) 5.1^3 (c) $\sqrt{64}$
(d) $\sqrt[3]{8}$ (e) $\sqrt[3]{-1.331}$

(a) $3.2^2 = 10.24$ (b) $5.1^3 = 132.651$ (c) $\sqrt{64} = 8$
(d) $\sqrt[3]{8} = 2$
(e) $\sqrt[3]{-1.331} = -1.1$

> Use the square, cube, square root and cube root functions on your calculator.

> The calculator only gives 8, but $-8 \times -8 = 64$.

Exercise 3A

1 Write down the first five square numbers.

2 Write down the first five cube numbers.

3 Write down the value of
  (a) 2.1^2 (b) 3.3^3
  (c) $\sqrt{5.76}$ (d) $\sqrt[3]{42.875}$
  (e) 14 squared   (f) 10 cubed
  (g) the positive square root of 961 (h) the cube of 17
  (i) the cube root of 64   (j) 152^2
  (k) $\sqrt{625}$ (l) $\sqrt[3]{-216}$
  (m) the square of -15 (n) 21.3 squared
  (o) $\sqrt{0.36}$ (p) the negative square root of 0.81
  (q) 1^2 (r) 1^3
  (s) $\sqrt[3]{-1}$ (t) the negative square root of 1.

3.2 Power facts you need to know

- You need to memorise all the square numbers from 2^2 to 15^2 and the corresponding square roots.
- You need to memorise the cubes of 2, 3, 4, 5 and 10.

Example 4

Estimate, to the nearest whole number, the value of $\sqrt{98}$.

$9^2 = 81$ and $10^2 = 100$
98 is closer to 100 than to 81.
$\sqrt{98}$ is between 9 and 10.
An estimate for $\sqrt{98}$ is 10, to the nearest whole number.

Exercise 3B

1 Write down from memory
   (a) 3^2 (b) 4^3 (c) 7^2 (d) 8^2 (e) 10^2 (f) 2^2 (g) 6^2
   (h) 3^3 (i) 10^3 (j) 4^2 (k) 5^3 (l) 12^2 (m) 13^2 (n) 2^3
   (o) 5^2 (p) 9^2 (q) 11^2 (r) 14^2 (s) 15^2

2 Write down from memory
   (a) $\sqrt{64}$ (b) $\sqrt{9}$ (c) $\sqrt{25}$ (d) $\sqrt{144}$ (e) $\sqrt{169}$
   (f) $\sqrt{225}$ (g) $\sqrt{4}$ (h) $\sqrt{100}$ (i) $\sqrt{36}$ (j) $\sqrt{121}$
   (k) $\sqrt{49}$ (l) $\sqrt{81}$ (m) $\sqrt{16}$ (n) $\sqrt{196}$

3 Estimate, to the nearest whole number, the value of
   (a) $\sqrt{50}$ (b) $\sqrt{38}$ (c) $\sqrt{128}$ (d) $\sqrt{69}$ (e) $\sqrt{24}$

3.3 Indices and powers

- The ^{2} in 7^2 is called an **index** or a **power**. It tells you how many times the given number must be multiplied by itself.

The mathematical plural of 'index' is 'indices'.

Example 5

Find the value of
(a) 2^4 (b) 3 to the power 5   (c) $2^2 \times 3^3$

(a) $2^4 = 2 \times 2 \times 2 \times 2 = 16$
(b) 3 to the power 5 $= 3^5 = 3 \times 3 \times 3 \times 3 \times 3 = 243$
(c) $2^2 = 2 \times 2 = 4$ and $3^3 = 3 \times 3 \times 3 = 27$
    $2^2 \times 3^3 = 4 \times 27 = 108$

$3 \times 3 \times 3 \times 3 \times 3$ written in index form is 3^5 because 3 has been multiplied by itself 5 times.

Example 6

Rewrite these expressions using index notation.

(a) $3 \times 3 \times 3$ (b) $4 \times 4 \times 3 \times 3 \times 3$

(c) $2 \times 2 \times 2 \times 2 \times 2$ (d) 3

(a) 3^3 (b) $4^2 \times 3^3$ (c) 2^5 (d) 3^1

Example 7

Find the value of x when

(a) $6^x = 36$ (b) $2^x = 32$ (c) $4^x = 256$

(a) $6 \times 6 = 36$ so $6^2 = 36$ and $x = 2$.
(b) $2 \times 2 \times 2 \times 2 \times 2 = 32$ so $2^5 = 32$ and $x = 5$.
(c) $4 \times 4 \times 4 \times 4 = 256$ so $4^4 = 256$ and $x = 4$.

Exercise 3C

1 Find the value of
   (a) 2^5 (b) 4 to the power 4
   (c) 1^6 (d) 10 to the power 4
   (e) 5^4 (f) 6 to the power 5.

2 Write these using index notation.
   (a) $2 \times 2 \times 2 \times 2$ (b) $4 \times 4 \times 4 \times 4 \times 4$
   (c) $1 \times 1 \times 1 \times 1 \times 1 \times 1$ (d) $8 \times 8 \times 8$
   (e) 6×6 (f) $7 \times 7 \times 7 \times 7$
   (g) $3 \times 3 \times 8 \times 8 \times 8 \times 8$ (h) $4 \times 4 \times 4 \times 4 \times 2 \times 2 \times 2$

3 Work out the value of
   (a) 2^4 (b) 3^5 (c) 6^3 (d) 5^2
   (e) 8^3 (f) $2^4 \times 9^3$ (g) $2^6 \times 4^5$ (h) $5^3 \times 3^4$
   (i) $2^7 \times 3^5$ (j) $4^3 \times 4^1$

4 Copy and complete the table for powers of 10.

Power of 10	Index	Value	Value in words
	3		One thousand
10^2		100	
		1 000 000	One million
	1	10	
10^5	5		

5 Work out the value of

(a) $4^3 \times 10^2$ (b) 4×10^2 (c) 6×10^3

(d) $10^2 \div 5^2$ (e) $10^3 \div 2^3$ (f) $4^3 \div 2^2$

6 Find x when

(a) $5^x = 125$ (b) $3^x = 81$ (c) $2^x = 64$

(d) $10^x = 10\,000$ (e) $9^x = 81$ (f) $3^x = 27$

(g) $2^x = 16$ (h) $7^x = 49$

3.4 BIDMAS

- **BIDMAS** is a made-up word to help you remember the order of operations:

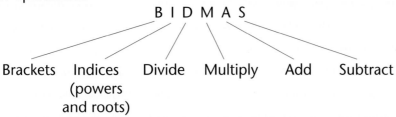

B I D M A S

Brackets   Indices   Divide   Multiply   Add   Subtract
          (powers
          and roots)

- When operations are the same you do them in the order they appear.

Example 8

Work out

(a) $6 + 3 \times 4$ (b) $\dfrac{48 - 16}{4^2}$

(c) $(2^2 + 3^2) \div 2$ (d) $32 \div 4 \div 2$

(a) $6 + \underbrace{3 \times 4}$

     $= 6 + \quad 12$

     $= 18$

(b) $\dfrac{48 - 16}{4^2}$ *(This line acts as a bracket.)*

     $= \underbrace{(48 - 16)} \div 4^2$

     $= 32 \div \underbrace{4^2}$

     $= 32 \div 16$

     $= 2$

(c) $\underbrace{(2^2 + 3^2)} \div 2$

   $= (\underbrace{(2 \times 2)} + \underbrace{(3 \times 3)}) \div 2$

   $= \quad \underbrace{(4 \quad + \quad 9)} \div 2$

   $= \qquad\qquad 13 \div 2$

   $= 6.5$

(d) $32 \div 4 \div 2$

   $= \underbrace{(32 \div 4)} \div 2$

   $= 8 \div 2$

   $= 4$

Exercise 3D

1 Work out

(a) $5 + 4 \times 7$ (b) $8 - 8 \div 2$

(c) $(6 + 2) \times 3$ (d) $(5 + 3) \times (6 - 4)$

(e) $\dfrac{9 \times 3}{5 \times 2}$ (f) $(2 + 7)^2$

(g) $\sqrt{(5 + 4)}$ (h) $3^2 + 7$

(i) $\dfrac{\sqrt{(5 + 20)}}{3 + 2}$ (j) $\dfrac{6^2}{\sqrt{9} \times 2}$

(k) $(5 + 4)^2 - (3 - 5)^2$ (l) $8 + 2^2 \times 3 \div (10 - 6)$

2 Make these equations correct by replacing each * with +, −, × or ÷. Use brackets if you need to.

(a) $3 * 4 * 5 = 27$ (b) $2 * 3 * 2 * 3 = 25$

(c) $6 * 7 * 8 * 9 = 1$ (d) $10 * 9 * 8 * 7 = 34$

(e) $3 * 3 * 3 = 0$ (f) $3 * 3 * 3 = 2$

3.5 Calculations using a calculator

- Make sure you know how to enter calculations involving brackets, powers and roots into your calculator.
- Estimate the solution to a calculation first, so you can check that your answer is sensible.

> For more on estimating see Section 2.11.

Example 9

Work out

(a) $\dfrac{57 \times 3.4}{25 + 41}$ (b) $3.2^2 \times \sqrt{5 - 3.79}$ (c) $\dfrac{\sqrt{1.96}}{2.5^3 \times 4}$

> Remember to use BIDMAS to work out the order of operations (see Section 3.4).

(a) $\dfrac{57 \times 3.4}{25 + 41} = \dfrac{(57 \times 3.4)}{(25 + 41)}$

    $= 2.936\,363\,636$

> Estimate: $\dfrac{60 \times 3}{30 + 40} = \dfrac{180}{70} = 2.6$

(b) $3.2^2 \times \sqrt{5 - 3.79} = 3.2^2 \times \sqrt{(5 - 3.79)}$

    $= 11.264$

> Estimate: $3^2 \times \sqrt{5 - 4} = 9 \times 1 = 9$

(c) $\dfrac{\sqrt{1.96}}{2.5^3 \times 4} = \dfrac{(\sqrt{1.96})}{(2.5^3 \times 4)}$

    $= 0.0224$

> Estimate: $\dfrac{\sqrt{2}}{27 \times 4} = 0.013$

⊞ **Exercise 3E**

1 Work out

(a) $\dfrac{64}{3 + 5}$ (b) $\dfrac{4.7 - 1.1}{2 \times 3}$ (c) $\dfrac{16.4 \div 0.2}{41 \times 0.4}$

2 Work out

(a) 4.7^2 (b) 2.1^3 (c) 5.7^4 (d) 1.2^6 (e) $\sqrt{6.25}$ (f) $\sqrt{5.29}$

3 Work out

(a) $\sqrt{15.2 - 2.24}$ (b) $\sqrt{3.2 + 3.05}$
(c) $(2.3)^2 \times \sqrt{11.56}$ (d) $4.1^2 \times \sqrt{4.5 - 2.1}$
(e) $\sqrt{2.7 \times 1.5} \times 2.1^2$

4 Work out

(a) $\dfrac{2.1^2 \times 3.2^2}{5.2 - 1.1}$ (b) $\dfrac{6.8 - 2.4}{\sqrt{6.1 - 2.1}}$ (c) $\dfrac{5.3 \times 2.7^3}{3.4^2 \times \sqrt{2.5}}$ (d) $\sqrt{\dfrac{5.3 - 2.1}{1.1 + 2.3}}$

5 Work out

(a) $\dfrac{1}{4(3 + 2)}$ (b) $\dfrac{1}{\sqrt{25}}$ (c) $\dfrac{1}{0.2 \times 0.4}$ (d) $\dfrac{1}{\sqrt{0.09}}$

3.6 Index laws

- To multiply powers of the same number, add the indices.
  In general: $x^n \times x^m = x^{n+m}$

- To divide powers of the same number, subtract the indices.
  In general: $x^n \div x^m = x^{n-m}$

Example 10

Simplify
(a) $3^2 \times 3^4$ (b) $4^3 \times 4^5$ (c) $2^5 \div 2^1$

(d) $10^4 \div 10^2$ (e) $\dfrac{2^6 \times 2^3}{2^4}$ (f) $x^3 \times x^2$

(a) $3^2 \times 3^4 = 3^{2+4} = 3^6$ •——— The powers are of the **same** number.
(b) $4^3 \times 4^5 = 4^{3+5} = 4^8$
(c) $2^5 \div 2^1 = 2^{5-1} = 2^4$ •——— You can write 2 as 2^1.
(d) $10^4 \div 10^2 = 10^{4-2} = 10^2$
(e) $\dfrac{2^6 \times 2^3}{2^4} = \dfrac{2^{6+3}}{2^4} = \dfrac{2^9}{2^4} = 2^{9-4} = 2^5$
(f) $x^3 \times x^2 = x^{3+2} = x^5$

Exercise 3F

Simplify these.

1 $8^2 \times 8^4$ **2** $3^4 \times 3^2$ **3** $2^6 \times 2^3$

4 5×5^2 **5** $3^4 \div 3^2$ **6** $7^4 \div 7^2$

7 $8^5 \div 8^3$ **8** $10^4 \div 10$ **9** $8^2 \times 8^3 \times 8^4$

10 $2^3 \times 2^5 \times 2$ **11** $4^3 \times 4 \times 4^0$ **12** $\dfrac{6^3 \times 6^2}{6^3}$

13 $\dfrac{2^5 \div 2^2}{2^4}$ **14** $\dfrac{4^8 \times 4^4}{4^2}$ **15** $\dfrac{9^4 \div 9^2}{9}$

16 $\dfrac{10^6 \div 10^2}{10^4}$ **17** $x^4 \times x^3$ **18** $y^4 \div y^2$

19 $\dfrac{a^2 \times a^4}{a^3}$ **20** $\dfrac{z^4 \div z}{z^2}$

3.7 Writing numbers in standard form

- A number is in **standard form** when it is written like this:

$$7.2 \times 10^6$$

This part is a number from 1 up to (but not including) 10.

This part is written as a power of 10, and the power is an integer.

> Standard form is an alternative way of writing very large or very small numbers.

Example 11

Write in standard form
(a) 35 600   (b) 2 876 000

	10^6	10^5	10^4	10^3	10^2	10^1	10^0	$\cdot$	Standard form
(a) 35 600			3	5	6	0	0	$\cdot$	3.56×10^4
(b) 2 876 000	2	8	7	6	0	0	0	$\cdot$	2.876×10^6

> The power of 10 is the place value of the first significant figure.

Example 12

Write as ordinary numbers
(a) 2.3×10^3 (b) 3.78×10^5

> To multiply by a positive power of 10, move the digits to the left by the number of places of the power of 10.

Standard form	10^5	10^4	10^3	10^2	10^1	10^0	$\cdot$	
2.3×10^3			2	3	0	0	$\cdot$	(a) $2.3 \times 10^3 = 2300$
3.78×10^5	3	7	8	0	0	0	$\cdot$	(b) $3.78 \times 10^5 = 378\,000$

Example 13

Write in standard form
(a) 0.48   (b) 0.0025

	10^0	.	10^{-1}	10^{-2}	10^{-3}	10^{-4}	Standard form
(a) 0.48	0	.	4	8			4.8×10^{-1}
(b) 0.0025	0	.	0	0	2	5	2.5×10^{-3}

Example 14

Write as ordinary numbers
(a) 2.4×10^{-2} (b) 5.63×10^{-4}

> To multiply by a negative power of 10 move the digits to the right by the number of places of the power of 10.

Standard form	10^0	.	10^{-1}	10^{-2}	10^{-3}	10^{-4}	10^{-5}	10^{-6}	
2.4×10^{-2}	0	.	0	2	4				(a) $2.4 \times 10^{-2} = 0.024$
5.63×10^{-4}	0	.	0	0	0	5	6	3	(b) $5.63 \times 10^{-4} = 0.000\,563$

Standard form on a calculator

When the answer to a calculation is very large or very small, the calculator may display the answer in standard form.

Different calculators display the answer in different ways. Here are two ways of displaying 2.3×10^3.

Some bacteria measure only 5×10^{-7} m in size.

Display 1

This is the power of 10.

Display 2

2.3 E03

The power of 10 is 3.

This shows the answer is in standard form.

> Make sure you know how to enter a number in standard form into your calculator.

• You can enter numbers in standard form into a calculator.

Exercise 3G

1 Write these numbers in standard form.
   (a) 800   (b) 7000   (c) 90 000
   (d) 872   (e) 9200   (f) 8700
   (g) 98 400   (h) 834 000   (i) 1 200 000

2 Write as ordinary numbers
   (a) 3×10^2 (b) 5×10^4 (c) 8×10^6
   (d) 2.5×10^4 (e) 3.8×10^6 (f) 2.36×10^4
   (g) 4.78×10^6 (h) 2.94×10^5 (i) 3.84×10^7

3 Write in standard form
   (a) 0.8   (b) 0.72   (c) 0.04
   (d) 0.02   (e) 0.0053   (f) 0.0089
   (g) 0.0032   (h) 0.0485   (i) 0.000 041

4 Write as ordinary numbers
   (a) 2×10^{-1} (b) 3×10^{-2} (c) 5×10^{-4}
   (d) 2.1×10^{-2} (e) 3.4×10^{-5} (f) 5.8×10^{-4}
   (g) 2.38×10^{-6} (h) 4.39×10^{-8} (i) 2.61×10^{-8}

5 Write, in standard form, the number shown on these
   calculator displays.

(a) 7.0^{05} / 1.0   (b) $3.6 \ E{-}02$

(c) $9.8 \ E \ 10$ (d) 5.7^{-06}

6 Use your calculator to work out
   (a) $2.3 \times 10^4 \times 5$ (b) $4.7 \times 10^{-3} \times 2$
   (c) $5.1 \times 10^6 \times 3$ (d) $8.2 \times 10^{-4} \times 4$

Mixed exercise 3

1 Write down these using index notation.
   (a) $6 \times 6 \times 6$ (b) 11×11 (c) $2 \times 2 \times 2 \times 2 \times 2 \times 2$

2 Write down the value of
   (a) 5^4 (b) 2^7 (c) 10^3 (d) 10^5

3 Work out the value of
   (a) $3^2 \times 4^2$ (b) $2^4 \times 7^2$ (c) 4×10^2 (d) 3×10^4

4 Use your calculator to work out
   (a) $\dfrac{5.1 \times 2.3}{5.6 - 2.1}$ (b) $2.1^2 \times \sqrt{3.1 + 2.2}$

   (c) $\sqrt{\dfrac{2.4^3 \times 3.1}{2.1 \times 1.4}}$ (d) $\dfrac{1}{\sqrt{0.49}}$

5 Write down from memory
  (a) 4^2 (b) 12^2 (c) 8^2 (d) 13^2
  (e) $\sqrt{49}$ (f) $\sqrt{196}$ (g) $\sqrt{225}$ (h) 4^3
  (i) 5^3 (j) 10^3

6 Rewrite these expressions using index notation.
  (a) $2 \times 2 \times 3 \times 3 \times 3$ (b) $5 \times 5 \times 7 \times 7$
  (c) $4 \times 4 \times 8 \times 8 \times 8 \times 8$ (d) $6 \times 6 \times 6 \times 2 \times 2 \times 2$

7 Work out
  (a) 8^3 (b) 10^4 (c) 5^3
  (d) $2^4 \times 3^2$ (e) $5^2 \times 2^5$

8 Find x when
  (a) $3^x = 81$ (b) $2^x = 32$ (c) $10^x = 1000$

9 Write down the value of
  (a) 5^2 (b) the square of 10
  (c) 4 cubed   (d) $\sqrt[3]{64}$
  (e) $\sqrt{36}$ (f) 2^3
  (g) 6.3 squared   (h) the cube of 2.4
  (i) the positive square root of 5.76 (j) $\sqrt[3]{-8}$

10 Use BIDMAS to work out the value of
  (a) $(7 - 3) \times (5 + 3)$ (b) $\dfrac{100}{4 \times 5}$

  (c) $(2 + 5)^2 \div (9 - 2)$ (d) $5 + 3^2 \times 2 \div (3 - 9)$

11 Find the HCF and LCM of 8, 16 and 36.
  Write your answers using powers.

12 Simplify
  (a) $2^3 \times 2^4$ (b) $5^3 \times 5^2$ (c) 3×3^4 (d) $7^5 \div 7^2$
  (e) $9^8 \div 9^4$ (f) $8^3 \div 8$ (g) $\dfrac{7^2 \times 7^4}{7^3}$ (h) $\dfrac{6^4 \div 6}{6^2}$

13 Write in standard form
  (a) 3000   (b) 5800   (c) 789 000
  (d) 86 300   (e) 0.5   (f) 0.061
  (g) 0.000 21   (h) 0.000 381

14 Write as ordinary numbers

    (a) 2×10^4 (b) 2.3×10^3 (c) 3.84×10^5

    (d) 8.97×10^7 (e) 3×10^{-4} (f) 2.1×10^{-6}

    (g) 7.92×10^{-3} (h) 8.26×10^{-2}

15 Write, in standard form, the number shown on these calculator displays.

    (a)   (b)

16 Use your calculator to work out

    (a) $2.68 \times 10^4 \times 3$ (b) $3.82 \times 10^{-5} \times 4$

Summary of key points

1 **Square numbers** are the result of multiplying a whole number by itself.

2 To square a number multiply the number by itself.

3 A **square root** is a number that has been multiplied by itself to make another number.

4 If $x \times x = A$ then x is the square root of A, written $\sqrt{A}$.

5 Every positive number has a positive and a negative square root.

6 **Cube numbers** are the result of multiplying a whole number by itself then multiplying again.

7 To cube a number multiply the number by itself, then multiply by the number again.

8 A **cube root** is a number that has been multiplied by itself and by itself again to make another number.

9 If $y \times y \times y = A$ then y is the cube root of A, written $\sqrt[3]{A}$.

10 A positive number has a positive cube root. A negative number has a negative cube root.

11 You can use the function keys on a calculator to work out squares, cubes, square roots and cube roots.

12 You need to memorise all the square numbers from 2^2 to 15^2 and the corresponding square roots.

13 You need to memorise the cubes of 2, 3, 4, 5 and 10.

14 The ^{2} in 7^2 is called an **index** or a **power**. It tells you how many times the given number must be multiplied by itself.

15 **BIDMAS** is a made-up word to help you remember the order of operations:

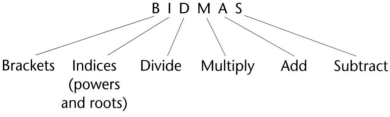

Brackets   Indices   Divide   Multiply   Add   Subtract
(powers
and roots)

16 When operations are the same you do them in the order they appear.

17 Make sure you know how to enter calculations involving brackets, powers and roots into your calculator.

18 Estimate the solution to a calculation first, so you can check that your answer is sensible.

19 To multiply powers of the same number, add the indices. In general: $x^n \times x^m = x^{n+m}$

20 To divide powers of the same number, subtract the indices. In general: $x^n \div x^m = x^{n-m}$

21 A number is in **standard form** when it is written like this:

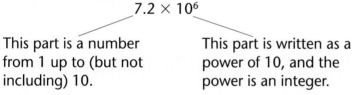

$$7.2 \times 10^6$$

This part is a number from 1 up to (but not including) 10.   This part is written as a power of 10, and the power is an integer.

22 You can enter numbers in standard form into a calculator.

4 Coordinates and essential algebra

4.1 Coordinates in the first quadrant

- **Coordinates** are 'across the floor' and 'up the wall'.
  (3, 2) means 3 across (in the x-direction) and 2 up (in the y-direction).

You can also remember 'x comes before y'.

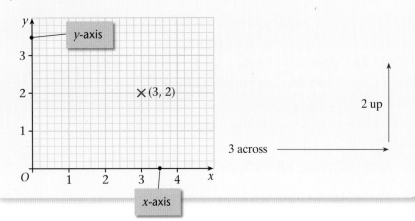

Exercise 4A

1 Write down the coordinates of the points marked on the grid.

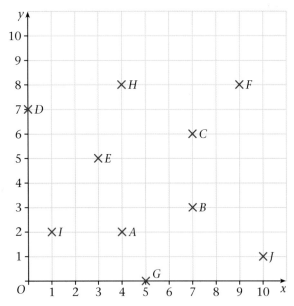

2 Plot these points on a coordinate grid. The grid needs to go up to 10 in each direction.

$A(4, 3)$	$B(2, 6)$	$C(0, 4)$	$D(7, 0)$
$E(8, 1)$	$F(3, 9)$	$G(8, 7)$	$H(5, 2)$

You can copy the coordinate grid from question **1**.

4.2 Coordinates in all four quadrants

- The x- and y-axes can both be extended to include negative numbers.
- Coordinates can include positive and negative numbers.

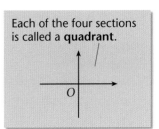

Each of the four sections is called a **quadrant**.

Example 1

What are the coordinates of the points A, B and C on the grid?

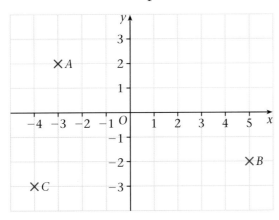

A is $(-3, 2)$ B is $(5, -2)$ C is $(-4, -3)$

Exercise 4B

1 Write down the coordinates of the points marked on the grid.

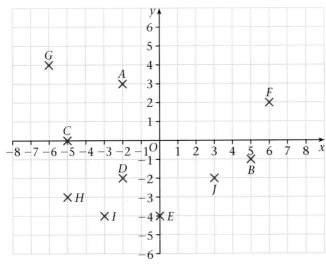

2 Plot these points on a coordinate grid. The grid needs to go from -6 to $+6$ in each direction.

$A(-3, 0)$ $B(-4, 5)$ $C(5, -4)$ $D(-4, -5)$
$E(3, -3)$ $F(-2, 6)$ $G(-3, -1)$ $H(0, -5)$

You could copy the coordinate grid from question **1**.

4.3 Coordinates to complete shapes

Example 2

Give the coordinates of the points that could complete the parallelogram in the diagram.

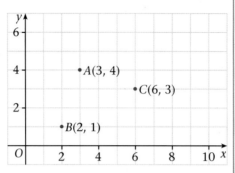

There are three possibilities:

1 Suppose *BA* is a side of the parallelogram. This is 1 unit right (*x*-direction) and 3 up (*y*-direction).
   C to *D* must also be 1 right and 3 up.
   D is (7, 6).

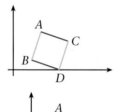

> For a parallelogram, *CD* is parallel to *AB*.

2 If *AB* is the side then *A* to *B* is 1 unit left and 3 down.
   C to *D* must also be 1 left and 3 down.
   D is (5, 0).

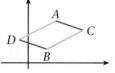

3 There is another possibility: *CB* is a side of the parallelogram.
   C to *B* is 4 units left and 2 down.
   This means *D* would be (−1, 2).

Exercise 4C

1 Copy each diagram and find a point to complete an isosceles triangle. Find one where the given line is one of the equal sides and one where it is the unequal side. Are there any others?

> An isosceles triangle has two equal sides. For more on isosceles triangles see Sections 7.3 and 7.5.

(a)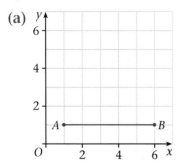

(b)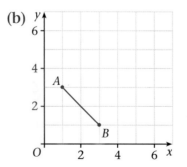

(c)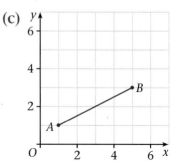

2 Draw axes which run 0 to 8 for x and 0 to 6 for y.
Plot $A(2, 3)$, $B(4, 3)$ and $C(5, 1)$.
Find three points which could complete a parallelogram.

3 Draw axes running from 0 to 6.
Plot points $P(2, 4)$ and $Q(4, 3)$.
These are two vertices of a square.
Find three pairs of points which could complete the square.

4 Draw the x-axis to run from 0 to 8 and the y-axis from 0 to 5.
Plot points $A(7, 1)$, $B(2, 1)$ and $C(1, 3)$.
Find the coordinates of D to complete trapezium $ABCD$.

> A trapezium has one pair of parallel sides. For more on trapezia see Section 7.4.

5 Draw the x-axis from -10 to $+10$ and the y-axis from -8 to $+6$. Plot points $A(-3, 5)$, $B(-8, 0)$ and $C(-7, -7)$.
  (a) Find the coordinates of D to complete a rhombus.
  (b) Find four pairs of integer coordinates that would complete a kite.

> An integer is a whole number. For more on rhombuses and kites see Section 7.4.

4.4 Mid-points of line segments

* The **mid-point** of the line segment joining (a, b) and (c, d) is
$$\left(\frac{a + c}{2}, \frac{b + d}{2}\right)$$

> A line can continue for ever. The part of the line between points A and B is called the **line segment AB**.

Worked examination question (modified)

(a) Write down the coordinates of
  (i) point A
  (ii) point B.

(b) (i) On the grid, plot the point $(-2, 5)$.
    Label it point P.
  (ii) On the grid, plot the point $(5, 0)$.
    Label it point Q.

(c) Find the coordinates of the mid-point of PQ.

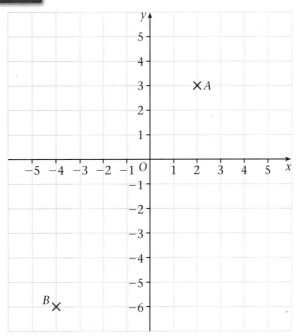

(a) (i) A is $(2, 3)$
(ii) B is $(-4, -6)$

(b)

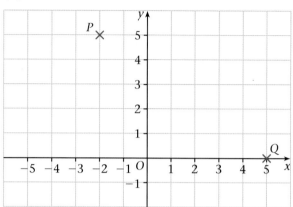

(c) $P = (-2, 5)$, $Q = (5, 0)$
Mid-point of PQ:

x-coordinate $= \dfrac{-2 + 5}{2} = 1\frac{1}{2}$

y-coordinate $= \dfrac{5 + 0}{2} = 2\frac{1}{2}$

So mid-point $= (1\frac{1}{2}, 2\frac{1}{2})$

Example 3

The points A, B and C have coordinates $A(1, 1)$, $B(4, 3)$ and $C(2, 6)$.
$ABCD$ is a square.

(a) Find the coordinates of D.

(b) Find the coordinates of the mid-points of AC and BD.

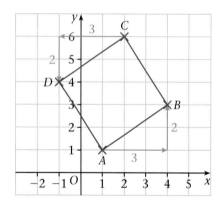

> The shift from A to B is 3 right, 2 up.
>
> So the shift from C to D must be 3 left, 2 down.

(a) D is $(-1, 4)$

(b) A is $(1, 1)$, C is $(2, 6)$
The mid-point of AC is

$$\left(\frac{1 + 2}{2}, \frac{1 + 6}{2} \right) = \left(\frac{3}{2}, \frac{7}{2} \right) \text{ or } (1\frac{1}{2}, 3\frac{1}{2})$$

The mid-point of DB is

$$\left(\frac{-1 + 4}{2}, \frac{4 + 3}{2} \right) = (1\frac{1}{2}, 3\frac{1}{2})$$

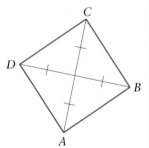

Exercise 4D

1 The diagram shows a triangle *ABC*.

(a) Write down the coordinates of
  (i) point *A*
  (ii) point *B*
  (iii) point *C*.

(b) *ABCD* is a parallelogram.
 Find the coordinates of *D*.

(c) Find the coordinates of the mid-point of
  (i) *AC*
  (ii) *CD*.

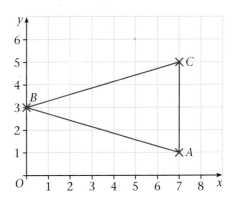

2 Draw a coordinate grid for *x* and *y* from −8 to +8.
Plot the points

A(4, 6)	*B*(1, 3)	*C*(6, 6)	*D*(8, 6)
E(4, −2)	*F*(−2, 4)	*G*(−4, −6)	*H*(−5, 3)

Find the coordinates of the mid-points of the line segments
 AC, *AE*, *EF*, *FH*, *EG*, *EH* and *BH*.

3 Find the mid-point of the line segment joining
(a) (3, −2) to (−4, 3)
(b) (−2, −6) to (3, 5).

4 The point (5, 6) is the mid-point of a line segment starting from (2, 1).
Find the coordinates of the other end of this line segment.

4.5 1-D, 2-D or 3-D?

> 🔎 **16** 3-D coordinates on shapes

- The number line goes in one direction.
  It is **one-dimensional** (**1-D** for short).
- Coordinates on a grid go in two directions. They cover a flat shape which is **two-dimensional** (**2-D** for short).
- Solid shapes, space and volumes are **three-dimensional** (**3-D** for short).
  To describe positions in space a third axis is used. This is the z-axis.
  3-D coordinates look like this: (4, 5, 7).

> (4, 5, 7) means
> 4 units in the *x*-direction
> 5 units in the *y*-direction
> 7 units in the *z*-direction

Example 4

Write down the coordinates of points *A*, *B*, *C*, *D* of this cuboid.

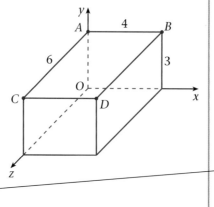

A(0, 3, 0)

B(4, 3, 0)

C(0, 3, 6)

D(4, 3, 6)

> zero in the *x*-direction
> 3 in the *y*-direction
> zero in the *z*-direction.

> From *O* you go
> 4 in the *x*-direction
> 3 in the *y*-direction
> 6 in the *z*-direction.

Exercise 4E

1 List these shapes in a table with headings '2-D' and '3-D'.

   pentagon, pyramid, hexagon, triangle, cylinder, cone, trapezium, cuboid, rectangle, sphere, square, circle

> 2-D shapes are flat.
> 3-D shapes are solids.

2 Make a list of the three-dimensional coordinates from the following:

   (1, 4, 2)   (3, 3)   (6.2, 1.4)   (0, 3)   (2, 3, 4)
   (4, 5, 0)   (6, 0, 7)   (6, 3)   (3)   (−3, 0, 0)

3 Write down the coordinates of each vertex of this cuboid.

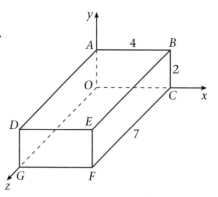

4.6 Writing expressions

> ⊙ **3** Introduction to algebra

- In algebra, you use letters to represent numbers.
- When you multiply letters and numbers, leave out the × sign.

Example 5

y is a number. Write down an expression for a number which is

(a) 3 less than y (b) 5 times y.

(a) $y - 3$

> 3 less than y is $y - 3$.

(b) $5y$

> $5y$ is short for $5 \times y$.

Example 6

There are c people in an office and g of them are women. Write down an expression for the number of men in the office.

Number of men is $c - g$.

> Subtract the number of women from the number of people.

Example 7

x sweets are shared equally between 6 children. Write down an expression for the number of sweets each child receives.

$$x \div 6 = \frac{x}{6}$$

Exercise 4F

1 Use algebra to write down an expression for each of these numbers:

   (a) 6 less than x (b) 4 more than y (c) 3 times a
   (d) c with 7 added   (e) p multiplied by 8   (f) q with 2 subtracted
   (g) t more than 9   (h) n less than 5   (i) p times 2
   (j) c more than d (k) m less than n (l) p multiplied by q
   (m) a is divided by 3   (n) one quarter of b (o) x divided by y

2 There are m men and w women in an office. Write down an expression for the total number of people in the office.

3 The sum of two numbers is 20. One of the numbers is n. Write down an expression for the other number.

4 A cinema ticket costs £8. Write down an expression for the cost, in pounds, of c cinema tickets.

5 x and y are two numbers. Write down an expression for the product of x and y.

The **product** of x and y is x multiplied by y.

6 John's age is y years. Kate is three years younger than John. Write down an expression for Kate's age.

7 Write down an expression for the number of days in w weeks.

8 Himal has 10 strawberries. She eats s of them. Write down an expression for the number of strawberries she has left.

9 A box of apples is shared amongst c children. Each child receives n apples and there are none left over. Write down an expression for the number of apples that were in the box.

Strawberry picking is a popular part-time summer job.

4.7 Collecting like terms

- **Like terms** have the same power(s) of the same letter(s).
- You can simplify algebraic expressions by **collecting like terms**.

Example 8

Simplify

(a) $c + c + c + c$ (b) $8p - 3p$ (c) $5t - 2t + t$

(a) $c + c + c + c = 4c$ (b) $8p - 3p = 5p$ (c) $5t - 2t + t = 4t$

Remember: t means $1t$.

Example 9

Simplify

(a) $4a + 5b + 2a + 3b$ (b) $7x + 5 - 4x + 2$
(c) $8p + 2q - 7p - 2q$ (d) $3c + 4d + 5c - 7d$

(a) $4a + 5b + 2a + 3b = 4a + 2a + 5b + 3b = 6a + 8b$
(b) $7x + 5 - 4x + 2 = 7x - 4x + 5 + 2 = 3x + 7$
(c) $8p + 2q - 7p - 2q = 8p - 7p + 2q - 2q = p$
(d) $3c + 4d + 5c - 7d = 8c - 3d$

Keep each term with its sign.

$3c + 5c + 4d - 7d$

Example 10

The length of each side of an equilateral triangle is l centimetres.
Write down, as simply as possible, an expression for its perimeter.

Perimeter is $l + l + l = 3l$ cm

Perimeter is the distance all the way round a shape.

Exercise 4G

Simplify these expressions by collecting like terms.

1 $d + d + d$

2 $q + q + q + q + q$

3 $n + n + n + n - n$

4 $7a + 3a$

5 $8c - 2c$

6 $5d + d$

7 $9e - 5c$

8 $5c + 3c + 4c$

9 $8t - 5t + 2t$

10 $3x + 5x - 7x$

11 $10h - 2h - 5h$

12 $5a + 3b + 2a + 6b$

13 $4p + 5q + 2p + 3q$

14 $3x + 4y + 2x$

15 $7t + 5 - 3t + 4$

16 $8m + 5n - 2m + 4n$

17 $5c + 6d - 2c - 3d$

18 $4p + 3q + 5p - 2q$

19 $5x + 2y + 3x - 2y$

20 $2a + 7b - 4b + 5c$

21 $6d + 4e + 2d - 7e$

22 $4y + 3 - 2y - 6$

23 $9a - 5b + 3b$

24 $7c + 5d + c - 6d$

25 $6p - 4q - 3p - 2q$

26 $6 + 5x + 2 - 6x$

27 $m + 4n - 2m$

28 $3x + 2y + 4x - 3y - y$

29 $6d + 4e - 5d - 3e - e$

30 $7 - 3t - 1 - 2t + t$

In questions **31–35**, give your answers as simply as possible.

31 The length of each side of a square is d centimetres. Write down an expression for its perimeter.

32 The length of a rectangle is a centimetres and its width is b centimetres. Write down an expression for its perimeter.

33 The lengths, in centimetres, of the sides of a triangle are $2d + 1$, $4d + 5$ and $3d - 4$. Find an expression for its perimeter.

Draw a diagram.

34 Emma's age is t years. David is three times as old as Emma. Write down an expression for the sum of their ages.

35 Mel's height is $7h$ and Nadia's height is $5h$. Write down an expression for the difference in their heights.

4.8 Simplifying products

- When there is a number in an expression, write the number before the letter(s).
- Write the letters in alphabetical order.

Example 11

Write these expressions in a simpler form.

(a) $p \times 2$ (b) $m \times n$ (c) $5 \times b \times a$ (d) $c \times d \times e$

(a) $p \times 2 = 2p$ (b) $m \times n = mn$

(c) $5 \times b \times a = 5ab$ (d) $c \times d \times e = cde$

Example 12

Multiply these expressions and give your answer as simply as possible.

(a) $2p \times 6q$ (b) $3d \times 2e \times 5f$

| $2 \times 6 = 12$ | | $3 \times 2 \times 5 = 30$ |

(a) $2p \times 6q = 12pq$ (b) $3d \times 2e \times 5f = 30def$

| $p \times q = pq$ | | $d \times e \times f = def$ |

Exercise 4H

Write these expressions in a simpler form.

1 $c \times 2$ **2** $t \times a$ **3** $8 \times d$

4 $7 \times f \times g$ **5** $5 \times x \times y$ **6** $a \times b \times c$

7 $p \times q \times r$ **8** $3 \times c \times d \times e$

Multiply these expressions and give your answer as simply as possible.

9 $4x \times 5y$ **10** $7f \times 3g$ **11** $6p \times q$

12 $8d \times 3$ **13** $4 \times 5y$ **14** $m \times 2n$

15 $7 \times pq$ **16** $3s \times 4t \times 2u$ **17** $5a \times 4b \times 3c$

18 $8d \times 3e \times f$ **19** $6x \times y \times 2z$ **20** $8bc \times 5d$

4.9 Using brackets

- Always work out brackets first in a calculation.
- **BIDMAS** helps you remember the order of operations.

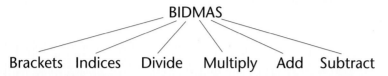

BIDMAS

Brackets Indices Divide Multiply Add Subtract

> For more on BIDMAS see Section 3.4.

Example 13

Find the value of each of these expressions.

(a) $5 \times (6 - 2)$ (b) $(5 \times 6) - 2$

(c) $30 \div 5 + 3$ (d) $48 \div 6 \div 2$

(a) $5 \times (6 - 2) = 5 \times 4$
$\qquad\qquad\quad = 20$

(b) $(5 \times 6) - 2 = 30 - 2$
$\qquad\qquad\quad = 28$

(c) $30 \div 5 + 3 = 6 + 3$
$\qquad\qquad\quad = 9$

(d) $48 \div 6 \div 2 = 8 \div 2$
$\qquad\qquad\quad = 4$

Exercise 4I

Find the value of each of these expressions.

1 $6 \times (4 + 3)$ **2** $6 \times 4 + 3$ **3** $6 + 4 \times 3$

4 $8 - 4 \div 2$ **5** $(8 - 4) \div 2$ **6** $8 - (4 \div 2)$

7 $9 + 5 - 4$ **8** $9 + (5 - 4)$ **9** $10 - 7 - 3$

10 $10 - (7 - 3)$ **11** $10 - 7 + 3$ **12** $(8 - 3) \times 2$

13 $8 - 3 \times 2$ **14** $30 \div 6 \div 5$ **15** $10 - (3 \times 3)$

16 $(10 - 3) \times 3$ **17** $9 + 6 \div 3$ **18** $(9 + 6) \div 3$

19 $(4 + 2) \times (5 - 1)$ **20** $4 + 2 \times 5 - 1$ **21** $28 \div 4 - 3 \times 2$

Copy these calculations and insert brackets to make them correct.

22 $8 - 5 \times 6 = 18$ **23** $7 - 5 - 1 = 3$ **24** $3 \times 5 + 3 \times 2 = 48$

Make these calculations correct by replacing each * with +, −, × or ÷ and using brackets if you need to.

25 $5 * 2 = 3$ **26** $6 * 3 = 18$ **27** $3 * 2 * 4 = 1$

28 $5 * 2 * 7 = 21$ **29** $5 * 2 * 7 = 17$ **30** $5 * 2 * 7 = 19$

4.10 Expanding brackets

- When you **expand** brackets, you multiply every term inside the brackets by the term outside.

Example 14

Expand the brackets in these expressions.

With practice, you should be able to write the answer straight down, without the working.

(a) $4(a + b)$ (b) $5(3c - 2)$ (c) $p(q + 6)$ (d) $3f(4g - 5h)$

(a) $4(a + b) = 4 \times a + 4 \times b$
$= 4a + 4b$

(b) $5(3c - 2) = 5 \times 3c - 5 \times 2$
$= 15c - 10$

(c) $p(q + 6) = p \times q + p \times 6$
$= pq + 6p$

(d) $3f(4g - 5h) = 3f \times 4g - 3f \times 5h$
$= 12fg - 15fh$

Exercise 4J

Expand the brackets in these expressions.

1 $6(c + d)$	**2** $5(p - q)$	**3** $2(x + 3)$	**4** $4(y - 2)$
5 $7(3a + 2)$	**6** $6(4p - 5)$	**7** $5(2c + 3d)$	**8** $8(3p - 4q)$
9 $a(b + 2)$	**10** $c(d - 2)$	**11** $x(y + z)$	**12** $p(q - r)$
13 $m(n - 1)$	**14** $2(5 - x)$	**15** $2f(5g + h)$	**16** $3p(q - 4r)$
17 $4x(5y + 3z)$	**18** $5b(6c - 5)$	**19** $7d(3e + 1)$	**20** $8a(3b - 2c)$

4.11 Simplifying expressions with brackets

- To simplify an expression with brackets, expand the brackets and collect like terms.

Example 15

Simplify $2(3x - y) + 5(y - 2x)$.

$$2(3x - y) + 5(y - 2x)$$

This is 5 lots of $(y - 2x)$.

This is 2 lots of $(3x - y)$.

$$2 \times (3x - y) = 6x - 2y \qquad 5 \times (y - 2x) = 5y - 10x$$

$$6x - 2y + 5y - 10x = 3y - 4x$$

Exercise 4K

Expand and simplify

1 $3(x + 2) + 2(x + 4)$ 2 $4(2x - 1) + 3(4x + 7)$

3 $5(3x + 2) + 4(2x + 1)$ 4 $7(3 - 2x) + 3(2x - 3)$

5 $6(4 - 2x) - 3(5 + 3x)$ 6 $4(3 - 2x) + 3(1 - 5x)$

7 $2(3x - 5y) + 3(2x - 4y)$ 8 $5(6y + 2x) - 4(3x + 2y)$

9 $3(2x - 3y) - 2(5x + 6y)$ 10 $3(2x + 3y) - 5(x + y)$

11 $4(3y - 2) - 5(y - 2)$ 12 $2(3x + 6) - 3(2x - 5)$

13 $4(3 - 2x) - 3(5 - 3x)$ 14 $2(3 - y - 2x) - 3(4x - 3y)$

15 $3(2x - 3y) + 5(3x - 2y)$ 16 $5(3y - 5x) - 2(x - 3y)$

17 $(4x - 3y) + 2(3x - 2y)$ 18 $7(3x - 5y) - (x - 3y)$

19 $x(2y + 1) + 2x(3y + 1)$ 20 $2x(3y + 1) + y(2x + 1)$

21 $2y(3x - 2) + 3x(2 - 3y)$ 22 $4x(2y - 5x) + 2y(x - 3y)$

4.12 Factorising

- **Factorising** is the reverse process to expanding brackets.
- To factorise an expression, find the common factor of the terms in the expression and write the common factor outside a bracket. Then complete the brackets with an expression which, when multiplied by the common factor, gives the original expression.

> The common factor may be a number or it may be a letter. For example, the common factor of $8x$ and $12y$ is 4 and the common factor of ab and ac is a.

Example 16

Factorise $5a + 15b$.

$$5a + 15b = 5(a + 3b)$$

> 5 is a common factor of $5a$ and $15b$. Write 5 outside the bracket. For more on common factors see Section 1.8.

Example 17

Factorise $8x - 12y$.

$$8x - 12y = 4(2x - 3y)$$

> 4 is a common factor of $8x$ and $12y$. Write 4 outside the bracket.

Example 18

Factorise $ab + ac$.

$$ab + ac = a(b + c)$$

> a is a common factor of ab and ac.

Example 19

Factorise $x^2 - 4x$.

$$x^2 - 4x = x(x - 4)$$

> x is a common factor of x^2 and $4x$.

Example 20

Factorise $2a^2 + 6ab$.

$$2a^2 + 6ab = 2a(a + 3b)$$

> This has two terms: $2a^2$ and $6ab$.
> 2 and a are factors of both terms so $2a$ is a common factor.

Exercise 4L

Factorise

1 $3x + 12$	**2** $7x - 21$	**3** $15x + 20$	**4** $9x - 12$
5 $4x + 6$	**6** $9x - 15$	**7** $12x + 18$	**8** $21 + 28x$
9 $14 + 21y$	**10** $35x - 15$	**11** $6x - 3y$	**12** $14x + 7y$
13 $10x - 5y$	**14** $25a + 15b$	**15** $3a - 9b$	**16** $17p + 51q$
17 $36c - 9d$	**18** $24s + 16t$	**19** $x^2 + 6xy$	**20** $2x^2 - 3xy$
21 $4xy + y^2$	**22** $5ab - a^2$	**23** $6bc + b^2$	**24** $4b^2 + 5bc$
25 $3ab - 5bc$	**26** $2x^2 + 6xy$	**27** $3x^2 - 9xy$	**28** $8p^2 + 4pq$
29 $14x^2 + 21xy$	**30** $10ab - 15bc$	**31** $4a^2 - 6abc$	**32** $2x^3 + 4x^2y$

4.13 Multiplying expressions with brackets

- To multiply two expressions with brackets, multiply every term in the second bracket by every term in the first bracket.

$$(e + f)(g + h) = e(g + h) + f(g + h)$$
$$= eg + eh + fg + fh$$

Example 21

Multiply and simplify $(x + 3)(x + 5)$.

$$(x + 3)(x + 5) = x(x + 5) + 3(x + 5)$$
$$= x \times x + x \times 5 + 3 \times x + 3 \times 5$$
$$= x^2 + 5x + 3x + 15$$
$$= x^2 + 8x + 15$$

> With practice, you should not need this line of working.

Example 22

Multiply and simplify $(2y - 3)(5y + 4)$.

$$
\begin{aligned}
(2y - 3)(5y + 4) &= 2y(5y + 4) - 3(5y + 4) \\
&= 2y \times 5y + 2y \times 4 - 3 \times 5y - 3 \times 4 \\
&= 10y^2 + 8y - 15y - 12 \\
&= 10y^2 - 7y - 12
\end{aligned}
$$

Example 23

Multiply $(3a + 4)(2b - 1)$.

$$
\begin{aligned}
(3a + 4)(2b - 1) &= 3a(2b - 1) + 4(2b - 1) \\
&= 6ab - 3a + 8b - 4
\end{aligned}
$$

> You cannot simplify this answer.

Example 24

Multiply and simplify $(c - 5)^2$.

$$
\begin{aligned}
(c - 5)^2 &= (c - 5)(c - 5) \\
&= c(c - 5) - 5(c - 5) \\
&= c^2 - 5c - 5c + 25 \\
&= c^2 - 10c + 25
\end{aligned}
$$

> The last term is $-5 \times -5 = +25$.

Exercise 4M

1 Multiply and simplify
   (a) $(a + 3)(a + 6)$ (b) $(b + 5)(b + 1)$ (c) $(c + 2)(c + 8)$
   (d) $(d + 4)(d + 3)$ (e) $(e + 9)(e + 4)$ (f) $(f + 7)(f + 5)$

2 Multiply
   (a) $(a + 4)(b + 5)$ (b) $(c + 6)(d - 2)$ (c) $(p - 1)(q - 4)$
   (d) $(x - 8)(y + 3)$ (e) $(a - 9)(t - 1)$ (f) $(b + 3)(c - 7)$

3 Multiply and simplify
   (a) $(a + 4)(a - 1)$ (b) $(b - 6)(b + 3)$ (c) $(c - 7)(c - 2)$
   (d) $(d - 4)(d + 4)$ (e) $(e - 3)(e - 9)$ (f) $(f + 6)(f - 4)$
   (g) $(g - 8)(g + 5)$ (h) $(x + 6)(x - 6)$ (i) $(y + 9)(y - 2)$

4 Multiply and simplify where possible.
   (a) $(3a + 1)(a - 2)$ (b) $(2b - 5)(3b + 4)$
   (c) $(4c - 3)(2c - 7)$ (d) $(2c - 3)(d + 2)$
   (e) $(5e - 3)(2e - 9)$ (f) $(5e + 4)(2f - 3)$
   (g) $(3g + 5)(3g - 5)$ (h) $(3x + 8)(4x + 1)$
   (i) $(4y - 9)(4y + 9)$ (j) $(2a + b)(3a - 2b)$
   (k) $(4a + 3b)(2c - 5d)$ (l) $(7x - 3y)(2x - 5y)$
   (m) $(7p + 2q)(7p - 2q)$

5 Multiply and simplify
  (a) $(a + 5)^2$ (b) $(b - 1)^2$ (c) $(c + 8)^2$
  (d) $(d - 7)^2$ (e) $(2e + 3)^2$ (f) $(3f - 4)^2$
  (g) $(5g + 1)^2$ (h) $(7h - 2)^2$ (i) $(a + b)^2$
  (j) $(3x - y)^2$ (k) $(3m + 5n)^2$ (l) $(4p - 7q)^2$

6 Multiply and simplify
  (a) $7 + (a - 1)(a + 5)$
  (b) $(4b + 3)(b - 1) + 7b - 2$
  (c) $(c + 4)(c - 3) + (c - 5)(c - 2)$
  (d) $(d + 4)^2 + (d - 3)^2$
  (e) $(3e + 5)^2 - 9e^2$
  (f) $(f + 2)^2 - (f - 2)^2$

4.14 Dividing algebraic expressions

- To simplify algebraic expressions involving division, divide the numerator and denominator by their common factors.

Example 25

Simplify (a) $\dfrac{15x}{5}$ (b) $\dfrac{6ab}{4a}$

(a) $\dfrac{15x}{5} = \dfrac{\cancel{5} \times 3x}{\cancel{5}} = 3x$ → Divide numerator and denominator by 5.

(b) $\dfrac{6ab}{4a} = \dfrac{\cancel{2} \times 3 \times \cancel{a} \times b}{\cancel{2} \times 2 \times \cancel{a}}$ → Divide numerator and denominator by 2a.

$= \dfrac{3 \times b}{2} = \dfrac{3b}{2}$

For more on simplifying fractions see Section 2.2.

Exercise 4N

Simplify these expressions.

1 $\dfrac{8pq}{2}$ **2** $\dfrac{24x^2}{3}$ **3** $\dfrac{14p}{7}$ **4** $\dfrac{25b}{15}$

5 $\dfrac{2ab}{a}$ **6** $\dfrac{6cd}{2d}$ **7** $\dfrac{21pqr}{14q}$ **8** $\dfrac{4xyz}{2xz}$

9 $\dfrac{4abc}{12a}$ **10** $\dfrac{9xy}{12y}$

Mixed exercise 4

1 Draw coordinate axes for x and y from -5 to $+5$.

   (a) Plot these points.

      $A(2, 3)$ $B(2, -4)$ $C(-1, 3)$ $D(-5, -3)$

      $E(0, -4)$ $F(3, 0)$ $G(-2, -3)$ $H(5, -2)$

   (b) Work out the coordinates of the mid-points of the line segments BE, AG, AC, DG, EH, CD, GH and CE.

2 $A(1, 4)$, $B(2, 6)$ and $C(6, 3)$ are three points. Find the coordinates of the three possible points, D, which could complete a parallelogram.

3 $A(-2, 5)$ and $C(4, 3)$ are opposite corners of a square. Find the coordinates of the other two corners.

4 The diagram shows a cube. Say whether the shape made by these (lettered) points is 1-D, 2-D or 3-D.

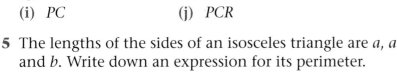

   (a) AB **(b)** ABC

   (c) $ABCD$ **(d)** PR

   (e) $PABC$ **(f)** PSB

   (g) $PQDA$ **(h)** $PQRSC$

   (i) PC **(j)** PCR

5 The lengths of the sides of an isosceles triangle are a, a and b. Write down an expression for its perimeter. Give your answer as simply as possible.

6 Write these expressions in a simpler form.

   (a) $3 \times d$ **(b)** $m \times n$ **(c)** $9 \times d \times e$ **(d)** $b \times c \times d$

   (e) $a \times 3b$ **(f)** $3p \times 4q$ **(g)** $2m \times 5n$ **(h)** $2a \times 4b \times 3c$

7 Simplify these expressions as fully as possible.

   (a) $2x + 3x - 4y$ **(b)** $6p - 3q + 2p - 2q$

   (c) $4t + 3s + 7s - 2t$ **(d)** $5c - 4d - 3d - 6c$

   (e) $2ab + 3ab$ **(f)** $5cd - 2dc$

   (g) $4pq + 3pq - 2pq$ **(h)** $a^2 + a + 3a$

   (i) $5b^2 - 2b + 3b$ **(j)** $2a + 3ab + 3a + 4b$

   (k) $2xy - y + 4x - 5x + 3yx + y$

8 Expand the brackets in these expressions.

   (a) $3(p + q)$ **(b)** $6(a - b)$ **(c)** $y(y + 4)$

   (d) $c(c - 1)$ **(e)** $a(2x + 3y)$ **(f)** $n(5a - 4b)$

   (g) $y(2y - 5)$ **(h)** $c(6c + 1)$ **(i)** $p(a - b)$

9 Expand and simplify
  (a) $3a(b - 2a) + 2b(3a - 2b)$ (b) $4p(2q + 3p) + 3p(2p + q)$
  (c) $5c(3c + 2d) - 2c(c - d)$ (d) $a(a + b) + b(a + b)$
  (e) $3a(b + c) + 2b(a + c) - c(2a + 3b)$
  (f) $2a(b - 2c) - 3b(2a + 3c)$

10 Multiply and simplify where possible.
  (a) $(a + 5)(a + 3)$ (b) $(b + 4)(b - 2)$
  (c) $(c - 5)(c - 6)$ (d) $(d + 5)(d - 5)$
  (e) $(f + 3)^2$ (f) $(8g + 1)(8g - 1)$
  (g) $(3h + 4)^2$ (h) $(8j - 3)(3j + 2)$
  (i) $(6k + 7)(2k + 5)$ (j) $(4m + n)(3m - 5n)$
  (k) $(3p - 4q)(3p - 4q)$ (l) $(5t - 4u)^2$

11 Factorise
  (a) $5x + 15y$ (b) $15p - 9q$ (c) $cd + ce$
  (d) $x^2 - 7x$ (e) $t^2 + at$ (f) $bx^2 - x$
  (g) $3p^2 + py$ (h) $aq^2 - at$

12 Simplify
  (a) $\dfrac{8q}{4}$ (b) $\dfrac{25at}{5a}$ (c) $\dfrac{14b^2c}{7c}$ (d) $\dfrac{32rs^2}{8s}$

13 (a) Simplify $3p + q - p + 2q$
  (b) Simplify $3y^2 - y^2$
  (c) Simplify $5c + 7d - 2c - 3d$
  (d) Simplify $4p \times 2q$ [E]

14 (a) Expand and simplify $(x + 7)(x - 4)$
  (b) Expand $y(y^3 + 2y)$
  (c) Factorise $p^2 + 6p$
  (d) Factorise completely $6x^2 - 9xy$ [E]

Summary of key points

> **1 Coordinates** are 'across the floor' and 'up the wall'. (3, 2)
>   means 3 across (in the x-direction) and 2 up (in the y-direction).
>
> **2** The x- and y-axes can both be extended to include negative
>   numbers.
>
> **3** Coordinates can include positive and negative numbers.

4 The **mid-point** of the line segment joining (a, b) and (c, d) is

$$\left(\frac{a + c}{2}, \frac{b + d}{2}\right)$$

5 The number line goes in one direction. It is **one-dimensional** (**1-D** for short).

6 Coordinates on a grid go in two directions. They cover a flat shape which is **two-dimensional** (**2-D** for short).

7 Solid shapes, space and volumes are **three-dimensional** (**3-D** for short). To describe positions in space a third axis is used. This is the z-axis.
3-D coordinates look like this: (4, 5, 7).

8 In algebra, you use letters to represent numbers.

9 When you multiply letters and numbers, leave out the $\times$ sign.

10 **Like terms** have the same power(s) of the same letter(s).

11 You can simplify algebraic expressions by **collecting like terms**.

12 When there is a number in an expression, write the number before the letter(s).

13 Write the letters in alphabetical order.

14 Always work out brackets first in a calculation.

15 **BIDMAS** helps you remember the order of operations.

BIDMAS

Brackets Indices Divide Multiply Add Subtract

16 When you **expand** brackets, you multiply every term inside the brackets by the term outside.

17 To simplify an expression with brackets, expand the brackets and collect like terms.

18 **Factorising** is the reverse process to expanding brackets.

19 To factorise an expression, find the common factor of the terms in the expression and write the common factor outside a bracket. Then complete the brackets with an expression which, when multiplied by the common factor, gives the original expression.

20 To multiply two expressions with brackets, multiply every term in the second bracket by every term in the first bracket.
$$(e + f)(g + h) = e(g + h) + f(g + h)$$
$$= eg + eh + fg + fh$$

21 To simplify algebraic expressions involving division, divide the numerator and denominator by their common factors.

5 Sequences

5.1 Term to term rules

- A **sequence** is a succession of numbers formed according to a rule.
- The numbers in a sequence are called the **terms** of the sequence.
- The **term to term rule** for a sequence tells you what to do to each term to obtain the next term in the sequence.

> For example, in the sequence 4, 7, 10, … 4 is the first term and 7 is the second term.

> The term to term rule for the sequence 4, 7, 10, 13, … is **add 3**.

Example 1

The first term in a sequence is 3. The term to term rule for the sequence is **add 5**.

(a) Find the next three terms in the sequence.

(b) Find the tenth term of the sequence.

(a) second term $= 3 + 5 = 8$
third term $= 8 + 5 = 13$
fourth term $= 13 + 5 = 18$
The next three terms are 8, 13, 18.

(b) To find the tenth term, you have to add **nine** 5s to 3.
So tenth term $= 3 + 5 \times 9 = 3 + 45 = 48$

> To get the next term add 5.

- To find the rule for a sequence, it often helps to find the **differences** between consecutive terms.

> **Consecutive** terms are next to each other.

Example 2

The first five terms of a sequence are 22, 18, 14, 10, 6.
Find the term to term rule for this sequence.

Sequence   22   18   14   10   6

Differences -4 -4 -4 -4

The term to term rule is **subtract 4**.

> The differences are all -4.

Exercise 5A

1 Find the next three terms for each of these sequences.
  (a) First term = 1; rule is **add 3**.
  (b) First term = 16; rule is **subtract 5**.
  (c) First term = 4; rule is **multiply by 3**.
  (d) First term = 24; rule is **divide by 2**.
  (e) First term = 5; rule is **multiply by 2 then subtract 1**.
  (f) First term = 24; rule is **add 8 then divide by 2**.

2 Find the term to term rule for each of these sequences.
  (a) 13, 11, 9, 7, ...   (b) 1, 7, 13, 19, ...
  (c) 3, 9, 27, 81, ...   (d) 1, 10, 100, 1000, ...
  (e) 1000, 100, 10, 1, ...   (f) 64, 32, 16, 8, ...

3 The first term of a sequence is 7 and the rule is **add 4**.
  Find the tenth term of the sequence.

4 The first term of a sequence is 35 and the rule is **subtract 2**.
  Find the 15th term of the sequence.

5 The first five terms of a sequence are 5, 7, 9, 11, 13.
  (a) Find the rule for the sequence.
  (b) Find the 20th term of the sequence.

5.2 Position to term rules

- The **position to term rule** for a sequence tells you what to do to the term number to obtain that term in the sequence.

Example 3

The position to term rule for a sequence is **multiply the term number by 5 and add 2**.
Find the first four terms of the sequence.

The first term is term number 1.
So   first term $= 1 \times 5 + 2 = 7$
Similarly, second term $= 2 \times 5 + 2 = 12$
            third term $= 3 \times 5 + 2 = 17$
            fourth term $= 4 \times 5 + 2 = 22$
The first four terms are 7, 12, 17, 22.

Notice that the differences between the terms are all 5.

Example 4

The rule for a sequence is **subtract 2 from the term number and multiply by 5**. Find the ninth term.

The ninth term is term number 9.
So ninth term $= (9 - 2) \times 5$
$$= 7 \times 5$$
$$= 35$$

Exercise 5B

1 For each of these rules, find
   (i) the first three terms of the sequence
   (ii) the tenth term of the sequence.
   (a) Add 9 to the term number.
   (b) Multiply the term number by 7.
   (c) Multiply the term number by 4 and subtract 1.
   (d) Add 3 to the term number and multiply by 2.
   (e) Multiply the term number by 6 and add 5.

2 The rule for a sequence is **subtract 4 from the term number and multiply by 10**. Find the twelfth term.

3 The rule for a sequence is **divide the term number by 2 and add 9**. Find the 22nd term.

5.3 Sequences of shapes

• Sequences of shapes can lead to number sequences.

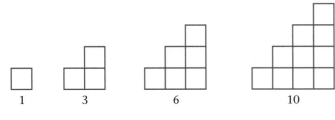

1   3   6   10

These are the **triangle numbers**.
Each time you add on 1 more than you did the time before.

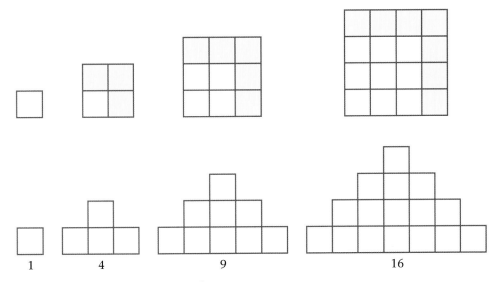

1   4   9   16

These are the **square numbers**.
Each time you add on the next odd number.

Example 5

Here are the first three shapes in a sequence of shapes made from matchsticks.

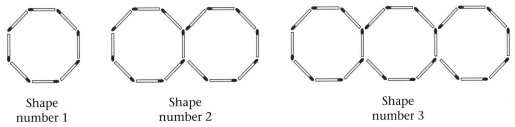

Shape   Shape   Shape
number 1   number 2   number 3

(a) (i) Draw shape number 4.
     (ii) Find the number of matchsticks in shape number 4.

(b) Work out the number of matchsticks in
     (i) shape number 5
     (ii) shape number 12.

(a) (i)

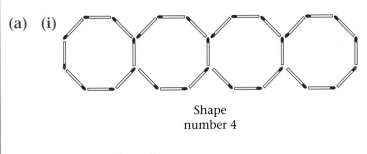

Shape
number 4

(ii) 29 matchsticks

(b) **(i)** The table shows the number of matchsticks in each of the first four shapes.

Shape number	1	2	3	4
Number of matchsticks	8	15	22	29

Differences   +7   +7   +7

> In shape number 5, there are $8 + 7 \times 4$ matchsticks.

In shape number 5, there are $29 + 7 = 36$ matchsticks.

(ii) In shape number 12, there are $8 + 7 \times 11 = 85$ matchsticks.

Exercise 5C

1 Here are the first four shapes in a sequence of shapes made from matchsticks.

Shape   Shape   Shape   Shape
number 1   number 2   number 3   number 4

(a) **(i)** Draw shape number 5.

(ii) Find the number of matchsticks in shape number 5.

(b) Work out the number of matchsticks in

(i) shape number 6

(ii) shape number 15.

> Draw a table, as in Example 5.

2 (a) The first odd number is 1.

(i) Find the 3rd odd number.

(ii) Find the 12th odd number.

(b) Write down a method you could use to find the 100th odd number.

Here are some patterns with dots.

Pattern number 1   Pattern number 2   Pattern number 3

(c) Draw pattern number 4.

The table shows the number of dots used to make each pattern.

(d) Copy and complete the table

Pattern number	1	2	3	4	5
Number of dots	5	8	11		

[E]

3 Here are the first four patterns in a sequence of patterns made with square tiles.

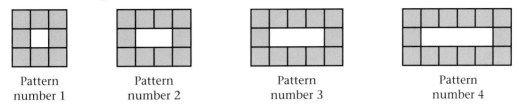

Pattern number 1   Pattern number 2   Pattern number 3   Pattern number 4

(a) (i) Draw pattern number 5.
    (ii) Find the number of tiles in pattern number 5.
(b) Work out the number of tiles in
    (i) pattern number 6   (ii) pattern number 17.

4 Here are the first three patterns in a sequence of patterns made from dots.

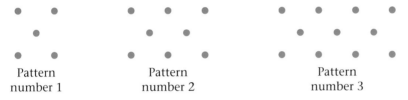

Pattern number 1   Pattern number 2   Pattern number 3

(a) Draw pattern number 4.
(b) Copy and complete the table.

Pattern number	1	2	3	4	5
Number of dots	5	8	11		

(c) Work out the number of dots in pattern number 25.

5 Here are the first four patterns in a sequence of patterns made with square tiles.

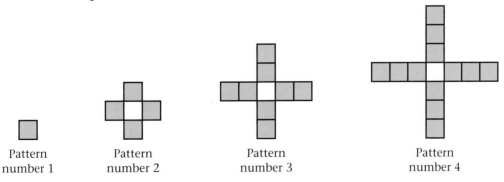

Pattern number 1   Pattern number 2   Pattern number 3   Pattern number 4

(a) (i) Draw pattern number 5.
    (ii) Find the number of tiles in pattern number 5.
(b) Work out the number of tiles in
    (i) pattern number 6   (ii) pattern number 12.

5.4 The nth term

- You can use the nth term to generate any term in a sequence. Substitute the number of the term you want for n.

- A sequence where the differences between the terms are all the same (the same number is added or subtracted each time to obtain the next term) is called an **arithmetic series**.

For example, for the fourth term substitute $n = 4$.

Example 6

The nth term of a sequence is $3n + 5$. Find the first four terms.

substituting $n = 1$,   first term $= 3 \times 1 + 5 = 3 + 5 = 8$
substituting $n = 2$,   second term $= 3 \times 2 + 5 = 6 + 5 = 11$
substituting $n = 3$,   third term $= 3 \times 3 + 5 = 9 + 5 = 14$
substituting $n = 4$,   fourth term $= 3 \times 4 + 5 = 12 + 5 = 17$

The first four terms are 8, 11, 14, 17.

The differences are all 3, the same as the coefficient of n in the nth term.

Example 7

The nth term of a sequence is $19 - 4n$. Find the first four terms.

substituting $n = 1$,   first term $= 19 - 4 \times 1 = 19 - 4 = 15$
substituting $n = 2$,   second term $= 19 - 4 \times 2 = 19 - 8 = 11$
substituting $n = 3$,   third term $= 19 - 4 \times 3 = 19 - 12 = 7$
substituting $n = 4$,   fourth term $= 19 - 4 \times 4 = 19 - 16 = 3$

The first four terms are 15, 11, 7, 3.

The differences are all -4. The coefficient of n in the nth term is -4.

Example 8

The nth term of a sequence is $7n - 23$. Find the tenth term.

substituting $n = 10$, tenth term $= 7 \times 10 - 23$
$= 70 - 23$
$= 47$

- When the differences between terms are all d, the nth term includes dn.

d is a positive or negative number.

Example 9

The first five terms of a sequence are 5, 11, 17, 23, 29.
Find an expression for the nth term of the sequence.

Sequence   5   11   17   23

Differences   +6   +6   +6   +6

$6n$ 6   12   18   24

*n*th term is $6n - 1$

> The differences are all +6.
> The *n*th term will include $6n$.

> Each term is 1 more than in the sequence.

Example 10

The first five terms of a sequence are 8, 5, 2, −1, −4.
Find an expression for the *n*th term of the sequence.

Sequence   8   5   2   −1   −4

Differences   −3   −3   −3   −3

$-3n$ −3   −6   −9   −12   −15

*n*th term is $-3n + 11$ or $11 - 3n$

> $-15 + 11 = -4$

Exercise 5D

1 For each of these position to term rules, find
   (i) the first five terms in the sequence
  (ii) the twelfth term of the sequence.
     (a) Multiply the term number by 5 and subtract 2.
     (b) Add 1 to the term number and multiply by 6.
     (c) Multiply the term number by 8 and add 3.
     (d) Multiply the term number by 3 and subtract from 16.

2 Write down an expression for the *n*th term of each of the sequences in question **1**.

3 For sequences with these *n*th terms, find
   (i) the first five terms in the sequence
  (ii) the twelfth term of the sequence.
     (a) $8n$ **(b)** $2n + 1$ **(c)** $5n - 4$
     (d) $40 - 3n$ **(e)** $19 - 6n$

4 Here are the first five terms of some sequences.
Find an expression for the *n*th term of each of the sequences.
     (a) 9, 18, 27, 36, 45, ...   **(b)** 9, 14, 19, 24, 29, ...
     (c) 12, 13, 14, 15, 16, ...   **(d)** 21, 17, 13, 9, 5, ...
     (e) 3, 13, 23, 33, 43, ...   **(f)** 8, 7, 6, 5, 4, ...
     (g) 23, 15, 7, −1, −9, ...   **(h)** −12, −3, 6, 15, 24, ...

5 Find an expression for the *n*th term of each of these sequences:

  (a) even numbers starting with 2

  (b) odd numbers starting with 1

  (c) multiples of 8 starting with 8

  (d) even numbers starting with 6

  (e) odd numbers starting with 9

  (f) multiples of 5 starting with 25.

5.5 *n*th term for shape sequences

> • You can find an expression for the *n*th term of a shape sequence.

> **4** Deriving simple formulae from sequences
> **4** Finding the rule and generating sequences.

Example 11

Here are the first four shapes in a sequence of shapes made from matchsticks.

| Shape number 1 | Shape number 2 | Shape number 3 | Shape number 4 |

The table shows the number of matchsticks in each of these shapes.

Shape number (*n*)	1	2	3	4
Number of matchsticks	3	5	7	9

(a) Work out the number of matchsticks in shape number 5 and in shape number 6.

(b) Find an expression for the number of matchsticks in shape number *n*.

(c) Find the number of matchsticks in shape number 20.

(d) Find the shape number of the shape with 57 matchsticks.

> In other words, find the *n*th term of the sequence 3, 5, 7, 9, ...

(a) Matchsticks   3   5   7   9

  Differences   +2   +2   +2

  shape number 5: 9 + 2 = 11 matchsticks
  shape number 6: 11 + 2 = 13 matchsticks

(b) The *n*th term will include 2*n*.

Matchsticks	3	5	7	9
2*n*		2	4	6	8

To get the matchstick sequence number you need to add 1 each time.

*n*th term = 2*n* + 1.

(c) Number of matchsticks in shape 20 = 2 × 20 + 1 = 40 + 1 = 41 | *n* = 20 |

(d) For the shape with 57 matchsticks

2*n* + 1 = 57

2*n* = 56 | Subtract 1 from both sides. |

n = 28 | Divide both sides by 2. |

Shape number 28 has 57 matchsticks.

Exercise 5E

Work out an expression for the number of matchsticks in shape number *n* for each of these sequences.

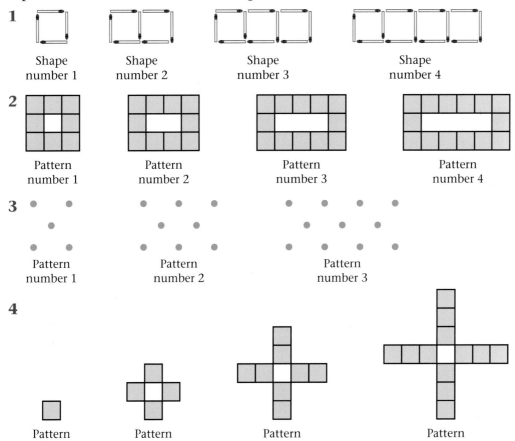

1

Shape number 1   Shape number 2   Shape number 3   Shape number 4

2

Pattern number 1   Pattern number 2   Pattern number 3   Pattern number 4

3

Pattern number 1   Pattern number 2   Pattern number 3

4

Pattern number 1   Pattern number 2   Pattern number 3   Pattern number 4

Mixed exercise 5

1 Find the next three terms in each of these sequences.
You are given the first term and the term to term rule.
 (a) First term = 13; rule is **add 7**.
 (b) First term = 3; rule is **multiply by 4**.
 (c) First term = 5; rule is **multiply by 6 then subtract 1**.
 (d) First term = 11; rule is **subtract 5 then multiply by 2**.

2 For each of these sequences
 (i) find the term to term rule for the sequence
 (ii) find the next two terms in the sequence.
   (a) 3, 11, 19, 27, 35, ...   (b) 8, 4, 2, 1, $\frac{1}{2}$, ...
   (c) 20, 16, 12, 8, 4, ...   (d) 3, 7, 15, 31, 63, ...

3 For each of these position to term rules, find
 (a) the first five terms in the sequence
 (b) the tenth term in the sequence
 (c) an expression for the nth term of the sequence.
   (i) Multiply the term number by 7 and add 5.
   (ii) Multiply the term number by 9 and subtract 8.
   (iii) Multiply the term number by 5 and subtract from 20.

4 For sequences with these nth terms, find
 (a) the first five terms in the sequence
 (b) the 20th term of the sequence.
   (i) $9n$ (ii) $3n + 7$ (iii) $5n - 11$
   (iv) $28 - 7n$ (v) $8 - 9n$

5 Here are the first five terms of some sequences.
Find an expression for the nth term of each of the sequences.
 (a) 7, 13, 19, 25, 31, ...   (b) 23, 20, 17, 14, 11, ...
 (c) 0, 7, 14, 21, 28, ...   (d) 5, −4, −13, −22, −31, ...

6 The nth term of a sequence is $8n - 3$. A term of the
sequence is 101. Find the term number of 101.

7 The nth term of a sequence is $3 - 8n$. A term of the
sequence is −141. Find the term number of −141.

8 47 is a term of the sequence 2, 11, 20, 29, 38, ...
Find the term number of 47.

9 −94 is a term of the sequence 8, 5, 2, −1, −4, ...
Find the term number of −94.

10 Here are the first four shapes in a sequence of shapes made from matchsticks.

  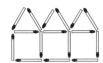 

Shape
number 1

Shape
number 2

Shape
number 3

Shape
number 4

(a) Work out the number of matchsticks in shape number 5 and in shape number 6.

(b) Find an expression for the number of matchsticks in shape number n.

(c) Find the number of matchsticks in shape number 18.

(d) Find the shape number of the shape with 66 matchsticks.

(e) Find the shape number of the largest shape which can be made with 100 matchsticks.

Summary of key points

1 A **sequence** is a succession of numbers formed according to a rule.

2 The numbers in a sequence are called the **terms** of the sequence.

3 The **term to term rule** for a sequence tells you what to do to each term to obtain the next term in the sequence.

4 To find the rule for a sequence, it often helps to find the **differences** between consecutive terms.

5 The **position to term rule** for a sequence tells you what to do to the term number to obtain that term in the sequence.

6 Sequences of shapes can lead to number sequences.

7 You can use the nth term to generate any term in a sequence. Substitute the number of the term you want for n.

8 A sequence where the differences between terms are all the same (the same number is added or subtracted each time to obtain the next term) is called an **arithmetic series**.

9 When the differences between terms are all d, the nth term includes dn.

> d is a positive or negative number.

10 You can find an expression for the nth term of a shape sequence.

> Find the nth term of the number sequence generated by the shapes.

6 Linear graphs

6.1 Straight lines parallel to the axes

- Lines parallel to the x-axis have equation y = a constant.
- Lines parallel to the y-axis have equation x = a constant.

A **constant** is a fixed number value.

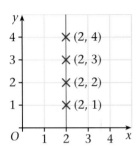

The x-coordinate for all points on this line is 2.
The equation of this line is $x = 2$.

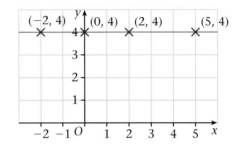

The y-coordinate for all points on this line is 4.
The equation of this line is $y = 4$.

Example 1

(a) Write down the equations of the lines marked
(i) P (ii) Q (iii) R

(b) Draw the line with equation $y = -2$.

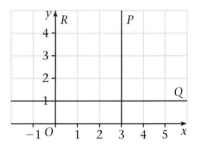

(a) (i) The equation of P is $x = 3$.

> All points on P have 3 as the x-coordinate.

   (ii) The equation of Q is $y = 1$.

> All points on Q have 1 as the y-coordinate.

   (iii) The equation of R is $x = 0$.

> All points on R have 0 as the x-coordinate.

(b)

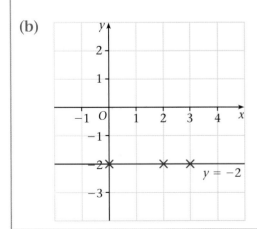

> To draw the line with equation $y = -2$ mark any three points with y-coordinate -2.

> Two points is enough but mark three to be sure.

> Join the points.

Exercise 6A

1 Write down the equations of the lines shown on the grid.

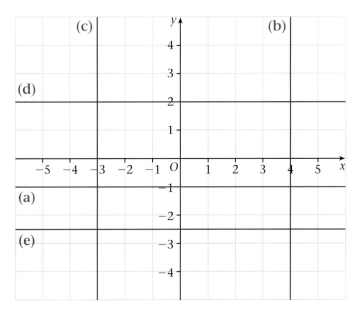

2 On a grid, draw lines with the equations

(a) $y = 2$ (b) $y = 5$ (c) $y = 0$ (d) $y = -1\frac{1}{2}$

What do you notice about these lines?

6.2 Straight lines passing through the origin

> The **origin** is the point $(0, 0)$.

- The equation of the straight line passing through $(0, 0)$, such that for each point on the line the x-coordinate equals the y-coordinate, is

$$y = x$$

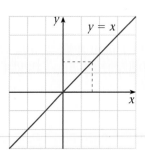

- The equation of the straight line passing through $(0, 0)$, such that for each point on the line the x-coordinate equals the negative of the y-coordinate, is

$$y = -x$$

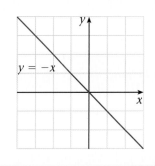

- The equation of any straight line passing through (0, 0) is always either

    $y =$ a positive number times x ($y = ax$)

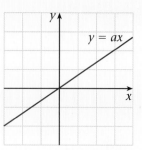

or

    $y =$ a negative number times x ($y = -ax$)

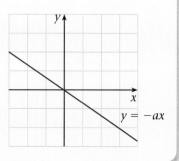

Example 2

Write down the equation of this line.

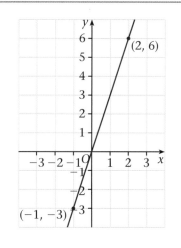

> Look for a relationship between the x- and y-coordinates for each point.

The equation is $y = ax$ for some value of a.

The line passes through $(-1, -3)$, $(0, 0)$ and $(2, 6)$.

For each point the y-coordinate is 3 times the x-coordinate.

The equation is $y = 3x$.

Exercise 6B

1 (a) Plot the points with coordinates
    $(0, 0)$ $(1, 1)$ $(2, 2)$ $(3, 3)$ $(-5, -5)$

(b) Join these points with a straight line.

(c) Write down the equation of the straight line.

> Draw a grid from -6 to 6 on both axes.

2

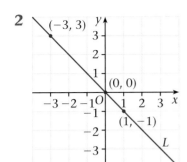

Write down the equation of the line marked L.

3 Draw a coordinate grid with both axes from -10 to 10. Draw the line with equation $y = 5x$.

> When $x = 1$, $y = 5 \times 1 = 5$.

4 (a) Choose at least three different positive values of a and draw the graphs of $y = ax$.
   Write down anything you notice about your lines.

(b) Choose at least three different negative values of a and draw the graphs of $y = ax$.
   How are these different from your graphs in part **(a)**?

5 (a) Plot the points with coordinates
   $(0, 0)$ $(3, 6)$ $(-2, -4)$

(b) Join these points with a straight line.

(c) Find the equation of this straight line.

6 (a) Plot the points with coordinates
   $(0, 0)$ $(1, -3)$ $(-2, 6)$

(b) Join these points with a straight line.

(c) Find the equation of this straight line.

6.3 Graphs of linear functions

16 Plotting linear graphs

- To draw a graph, you can draw up a table of values for x and y. Plot the points from the table on a grid.
- Equations like $y = 2x + 3$, $y = -2x + 1$ and $y = \frac{1}{2}x - 5$ are equations of straight lines.
- The coordinates of any point on the straight line satisfy its equation.

Example 3

Draw the graph of $y = 2x + 3$, taking values of x from -3 to 2.

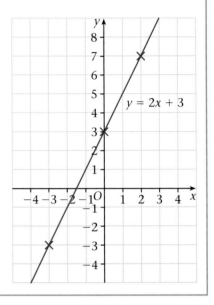

Table of values:

x	-3	-2	-1	0	1	2
y	-3	-1	1	3	5	7

When $x = -3$
$y = (2 \times -3) + 3$
$= -6 + 3$
$= -3$

This gives coordinates $(-1, 1)$

- In general, $y = mx + c$ is the equation of a straight line. m may be positive or negative, and a whole number or a fraction.

For example, $y = -2x + 1$ and $y = \frac{1}{2}x - 5$ are equations of straight lines.

Example 4

Draw the graph of $y = -2x + 1$, taking values of x from -2 to 3.

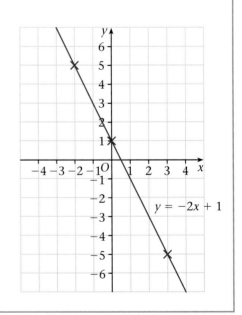

Table of values:

x	-2	-1	0	1	2	3
y	5	3	1	-1	-3	-5

The equation $y = -2x + 1$ may also be written as $y = 1 - 2x$ or $2x + y = 1$.

- You only need to plot two points on a line to be able to draw it, but a third point is a useful check.

Choose numbers which make your working out as easy as possible!

Example 5

Draw the graph of $x + y = 3$, for values of x from -2 to 5.

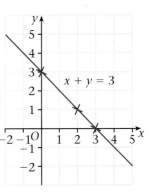

x + y = 3

Extend the line to $x = -2$ and $x = 5$.

Table of values:

x	0	2	3
y	3	1	0

For every point on the line $x + y = 3$, the sum of the x-coordinate and the y-coordinate is 3.
So,
when $x = 0$, $y = 3$
when $x = 2$, $y = 1$
when $y = 0$, $x = 3$

The equation $x + y = 3$ may also be written as $y = -x + 3$ or $y = 3 - x$.

Choose values that make the calculation easy. Include $x = 0$ and $y = 0$.

Example 6

Draw the graph of $2x + 3y = 12$ for values of x from -2 to 8.

Table of values:

x	0	3	6
y	4	2	0

The equation $2x + 3y = 12$ may also be written as $y = \frac{2}{3}x + 4$.

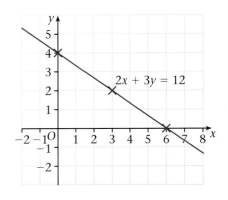

2x + 3y = 12

- Equations like $x + y = 3$ and $2x + 3y = 12$ are also equations of straight lines, as they can be written in the form $y = mx + c$.

Exercise 6C

1 Copy and complete the table of values for $y = 3x - 2$ and draw its graph.

x	−3	−2	−1	0	1	2	3
y		−8					7

When $x = -3$,
$y = (3 \times -3) - 2$
$= -11$

2 Copy and complete the table of values for $y = -2x + 3$ and draw its graph.

x	-3	-2	-1	0	1	2	3
y		7					-3

3 Complete the table of values for $y = \frac{1}{2}x + 2$ and draw its graph.

x	-6	-4	-2	0	2	4	6
y			1				5

4 Complete the table of values for $x + y = 5$ and draw its graph.

x	-2	-1	0	1	2	3	4	5	6
y		6							

5 Complete the table of values for $x - y = 1$ and draw its graph.

x	-2	-1	0	1	2	3	4	5	6
y		-2							

6 Complete the table of values for $x + 2y = 6$ and draw its graph.

x	-4	-2	0	2	4	6	8	10
y		4						

7 Complete the table of values for $3x + 4y = 12$ and draw its graph.

x	-4	0	4	8	12
y					-6

8 Complete the table of values for $2x - 3y = 18$ and draw its graph.

x	-3	0	3	6	9	12
y			-4			

9 Complete the table of values for $y = -\frac{3}{4}x + 1$ and draw its graph.

x	-8	-4	0	4	8
y	7				

10 By finding the coordinates of three points on the line, draw each of the following lines between $x = -4$ and $x = 4$.

(a) $y = 4x + 1$ (b) $y = -3x + 4$ (c) $y = \frac{1}{3}x + 2$

(d) $y = 5 - \frac{1}{2}x$ (e) $x + y = 2$ (f) $2x + y = 4$

(g) $x - y = 3$ (h) $3x + 2y = 6$ (i) $3x - 2y = 6$

11 For each line in question **10**, write down the coordinates of the point where it crosses the *y*-axis.
How are your answers to **(g)** and **(i)** different from the others?

6.4 Straight line graphs in real life

- A function such as
    ax + *b* (where *a* and *b* are numbers)
  gives a straight line graph and is called a **linear function**.
- Many linear functions and straight line graphs occur in real-life situations.

Example 7

This graph can be used for converting between pounds sterling (£) and euros (€).

(a) Use the graph to convert £150 to euros.

Alicia came back from holiday in Tenerife with €48.

(b) Using the conversion graph, or otherwise, convert €48 to pounds sterling.

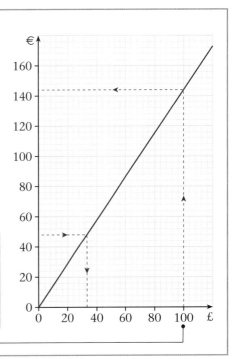

(a) From the graph
    £100 = €144   £50 = €72
  so
    £150 = €144 + €72 = €216

> Draw a line up from £100 to the graph, then across to the euros axis.

(b) From the graph €48 = £33

Example 8

The instructions for cooking a turkey are:

> *Allow 45 minutes per kilogram, then add an extra 30 minutes.*

(a) Work out the time, in minutes, to cook a turkey weighing 4 kg.
(b) Find a formula for the time *t* (minutes) to cook a turkey weighing *x* kilograms.

(c) Complete the table below for cooking times.

Weight (kg)	2	4	6	8	10	12
Time (min)						

(d) Draw the graph of cooking time against weight.

(e) Comment on the graph.

(a) Time is $45 \times 4 + 30 = 180 + 30 = 210$ minutes

(b) Time = 45 × weight + 30, so
$$t = 45 \times x + 30 \quad \text{or} \quad t = 45x + 30$$

> Write the formula in words first. Use x to stand for weight and t for time.

(c) The times for the weights are

$45 \times 2 + 30 = 120 \qquad 45 \times 4 + 30 = 210$

$45 \times 6 + 30 = 300 \qquad 45 \times 8 + 30 = 390$

$45 \times 10 + 30 = 480 \qquad 45 \times 12 + 30 = 570$

So the completed table is:

Weight (kg)	2	4	6	8	10	12
Time (min)	120	210	300	390	480	570

(d)

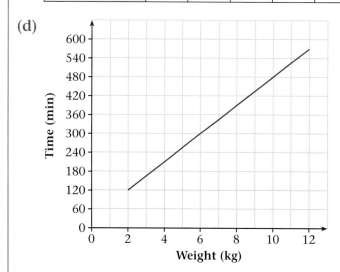

(e) The graph is of a linear function, so it is a straight line graph.

The weight cannot be negative.

You can extend the graph line in either direction to find the cooking time for turkeys less than 2 kg or more than 12 kg.

It would be pointless to extend the line back to where it crosses the vertical axis because a turkey of zero weight doesn't exist.

Exercise 6D

1 This graph can be used for converting between kilometres and miles.

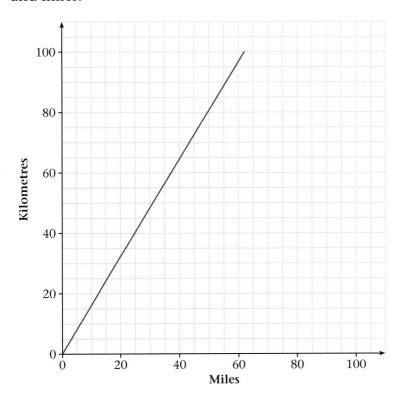

(a) Use the graph to convert 100 km to miles.

(b) Use the graph to convert 240 miles to kilometres.

The maximum speed limit in the United Kingdom is 70 miles per hour.

The maximum speed limit in France is 130 kilometres per hour.

(c) Which of these two speed limits is the greater, and by how much?

2 The cost of hiring a limo from Alpha Limos is £100 per day plus 40 pence per mile.

(a) Work out the cost of hiring the limo for a day and travelling 100 miles.

(b) Complete the table below for the total cost of hiring a limo for a day and travelling different numbers of miles.

Miles	20	30	50	100	150	200
Total cost (£)						

(c) Draw the graph of the total cost against distance travelled.

Alan hires a limo from Alpha Limos for a day. He travels x miles. The total cost to Alan is £y.

(d) Write down a formula connecting x and y.

The cost of hiring a limo from Betta Limos for the day is fixed at £140 per day, with no extra costs for the miles travelled.

(e) Using your graph, or otherwise, find the distance for which the total cost with Alpha Limos is equal to the cost with Betta Limos.

3 This graph can be used to convert between litres and gallons.

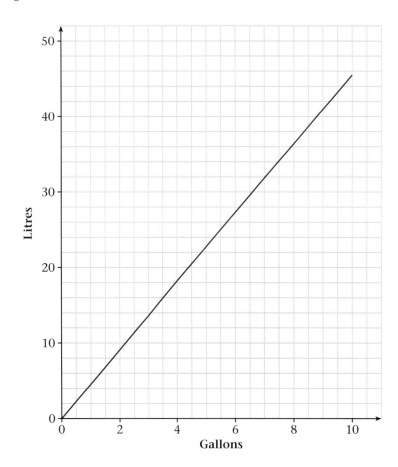

(a) Convert 6 gallons to litres.

(b) Convert 40 litres to gallons.

An oil tank holds 1760 litres.

(c) Convert 1760 litres to gallons.

4 Jamal works as a plumber. He charges a fixed call-out fee of £30 plus £25 for each hour he works.

(a) Copy and complete the table for his total charge.

Hours	1	2	3	4	5	6	7	8
Total charge (£)								

(b) Draw the graph of total charge against hours.

(c) Using y to represent total charge and x to represent the number of hours find the equation of the graph.

Jamal worked at Sunita's house. The total charge to Sunita was £142.50.

(d) Using your graph, or otherwise, find the number of hours Jamal worked at Sunita's house.

Mixed exercise 6

1

Match each equation to a line on the graph.

(a) $x = 3$ (b) $y = -2x$ (c) $y = 3$ (d) $y = 2x$

2 Copy and complete the table of values for $y = 4x + 5$ and draw the graph.

x	-3	-2	-1	0	1	2	3
y		-3					17

3 Draw the graph of $y = 2x - 1$ for values of x from -2 to 3.

4 Draw the graph of $y = -3x + 5$ for values of x from -2 to 4.

5 Draw the graph of $x + y = 2$ for values of x from -2 to 4.

6 By finding the coordinates of three points on the line, draw the graph of $x + 2y = 4$ between $x = -2$ and $x = 6$.

7 By finding the coordinates of three points on the line, draw the graph of $5x + 2y = 10$ between $x = -2$ and $x = 4$.

8 This graph can be used to convert between gallons and litres.

(a) Convert to litres
  (i) 20 gallons
  (ii) 18 gallons
  (iii) 28 gallons.

(b) Convert to gallons
  (i) 50 litres
  (ii) 160 litres
  (iii) 110 litres.

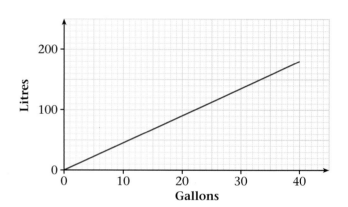

Summary of key points

1 Lines parallel to the x-axis have equation $y =$ a constant.

2 Lines parallel to the y-axis have equation $x =$ a constant.

3 The equation of the straight line passing through $(0, 0)$, such that for each point on the line the x-coordinate equals the y-coordinate, is

$y = x$

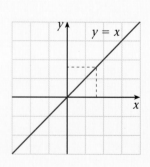

4 The equation of the straight line passing through $(0, 0)$, such that for each point on the line the x-coordinate equals the negative of the y-coordinate, is

$y = -x$

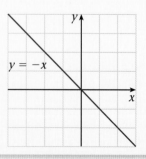

5 The equation of any straight line passing through (0, 0) is always either

y = a positive number times x ($y = ax$)

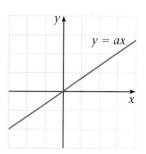

or

y = a negative number times x ($y = -ax$)

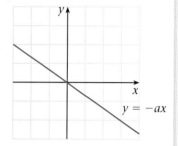

6 Equations like $y = 2x + 3$, $y = -2x + 1$ and $y = \frac{1}{2}x - 5$ are equations of straight lines.

7 The coordinates of any point on a straight line satisfy its equation.

8 To draw a graph, you can draw up a table of values for x and y. Plot the points from the table on a grid.

9 In general, $y = mx + c$ is the equation of a straight line. m may be positive or negative, and a whole number or a fraction.

10 You only need to plot two points on a line to be able to draw it, but a third point is a useful check.

11 Equations like $x + y = 3$ and $2x + 3y = 12$ are also equations of straight lines, as they can be written in the form $y = mx + c$.

12 A function such as
$ax + b$ (where a and b are numbers)
gives a straight line graph and is called a **linear function**.

13 Many linear functions and straight line graphs occur in real-life situations.

7 Properties of shapes

7.1 Polygons

- A **polygon** is a 2-D shape with any number of straight sides.
  The table shows the special names for polygons with different numbers of sides.

Number of sides	Name of polygon
3	triangle
4	quadrilateral
5	pentagon
6	hexagon
7	heptagon
8	octagon
9	nonagon
10	decagon

- A polygon is **regular** if all its sides and all its angles are equal.
- The point where two sides meet is called a **vertex**.
- The angle at a vertex is a measure of the turn between the two sides that meet there. Angles are usually measured in degrees.

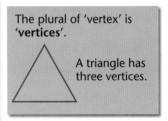

The plural of 'vertex' is **'vertices'**.

A triangle has three vertices.

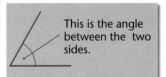

This is the angle between the two sides.

Exercise 7A

Write down the names of these polygons.

1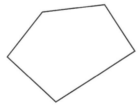

2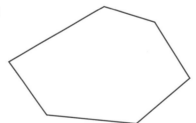

3

4

5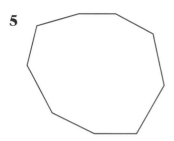

6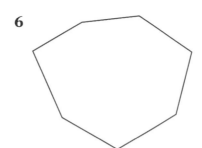

7

8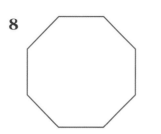

7.2 Parallel and perpendicular lines

- Lines which have a right angle between them are called **perpendicular lines**.
- Lines which are always the same distance apart are called **parallel lines**.

These marks are used to show parallel and perpendicular lines.

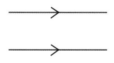 

Exercise 7B

1 Write down the names of lines that are

(a) parallel

(b) perpendicular.

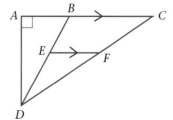

> *AB* is the line from *A* to *B*.

2 Write down the names of lines that are

(a) parallel

(b) perpendicular.

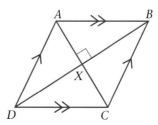

7.3 Properties of triangles

- A **triangle** is a polygon with three sides.

You need to recognise these special types of triangle.

Name	Shape	Properties
Scalene triangle		no sides equal no angles equal
Isosceles triangle		two sides equal two angles equal
Equilateral triangle		three sides equal three angles equal and 60°
Right-angled triangle		one angle 90°
Obtuse triangle		one angle greater than 90°
Acute triangle		all angles less than 90°

> The dashes show the equal sides.

> Matching arcs show equal angles.

> For more on obtuse and acute angles see Section 8.1.

> Scalene and isosceles triangles can be acute or obtuse. Equilateral triangles are always acute.

Exercise 7C

Write down the names of these special types of triangle.
The first one is done for you.

1
right-angled triangle
scalene triangle

2

3

4 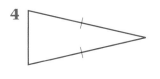   **5**    **6**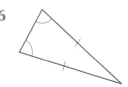

7   **8**

7.4 Properties of quadrilaterals

- A **quadrilateral** is a four-sided polygon.

You need to know these quadrilaterals and their properties.

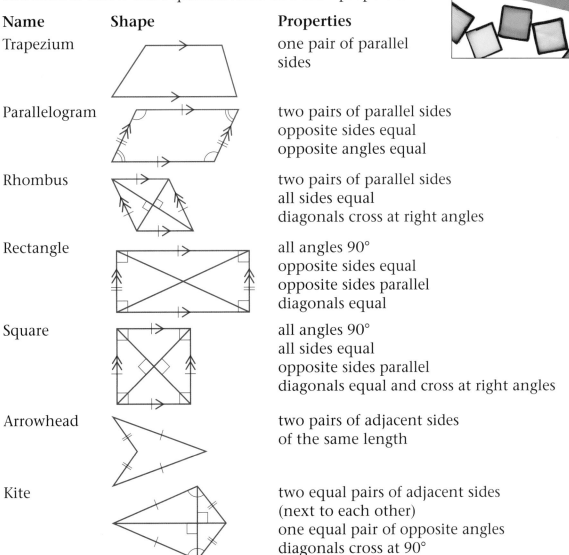

Name	Shape	Properties
Trapezium		one pair of parallel sides
Parallelogram		two pairs of parallel sides opposite sides equal opposite angles equal
Rhombus		two pairs of parallel sides all sides equal diagonals cross at right angles
Rectangle		all angles 90° opposite sides equal opposite sides parallel diagonals equal
Square		all angles 90° all sides equal opposite sides parallel diagonals equal and cross at right angles
Arrowhead		two pairs of adjacent sides of the same length
Kite		two equal pairs of adjacent sides (next to each other) one equal pair of opposite angles diagonals cross at 90°

Example 1

Complete the sentence with a word or number from the box.

| equal | parallel | opposite | sides | angles | 90 | 180 |

A rhombus has four equal _____; the diagonals cross at _____ degrees.

A rhombus has four equal <u>sides</u>; the diagonals cross at <u>90</u> degrees.

Example 2

Name these special quadrilaterals.

(a)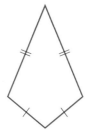

(b)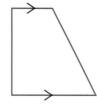

(a) Kite   (b) Trapezium

Example 3

On squared paper draw
(a) a trapezium with parallel sides 5 cm and 3 cm
(b) a square of side 4 cm.

There are other possible trapezia for part (a).

(a)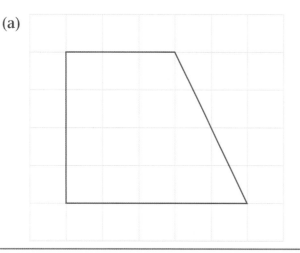

(b)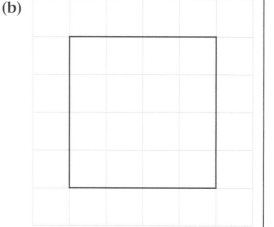

Exercise 7D

1 Copy and complete the sentences using numbers and words from the box.

| equal parallel opposite sides angles four 90 |

(a) Opposite _____ of a square are _____; all sides are _____.

(b) A quadrilateral is a _____ sided shape.

(c) _____ sides of a rectangle are _____ and _____.

(d) The diagonals of a kite cross at _____ degrees.

(e) Opposite sides of a rhombus are _____ and all _____ are _____; the diagonals cross at _____ degrees.

(f) A trapezium has _____ sides.

(g) _____ sides of a parallelogram are _____ and _____.

2 Name these special quadrilaterals.

(a)  (b)   (c)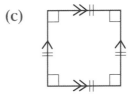

(d) 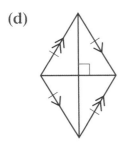 (e) 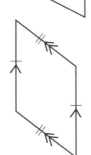 (f)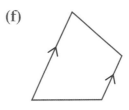

(g)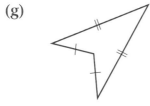

3 On squared paper draw

(a) a parallelogram with longest side 6 cm

(b) a rhombus with side 4 cm

(c) a trapezium with parallel sides 3 cm and 7 cm

(d) a rectangle with opposite sides 2 cm and 5 cm

(e) a kite with adjacent sides 4 cm and 6 cm

(f) an arrowhead with two pairs of sides 6 cm and 4 cm.

> Use centimetre squared paper.

7.5 Angle properties of triangles

- In an **equilateral** triangle all angles are 60°.

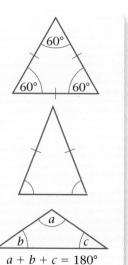

- In an **isosceles** triangle two angles and two sides are equal.

- The **interior angles** of a triangle always add up to 180°.

$a + b + c = 180°$

Example 4

Work out the missing angles in these isosceles triangles.

(a)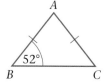

(b)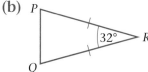

(a) angle $B = 52°$
   angle $C = 52°$

   angle $A = 180 - 52 - 52$
   $= 76°$

(b) angle $R = 32°$
   angle $P +$ angle $Q = 180 - 32$
   $= 148°$
   angle $P =$ angle $Q = 74°$

Example 5

Find the angles in this triangle.

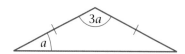

Because the triangle is isosceles, the unmarked angle must be a.

So $a + a + 3a = 180$
   $5a = 180$
   $a = 36°$

The angles must be 36°, 36° and 108°.

Exercise 7E

In questions **1–8** work out the marked angles.

1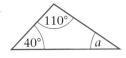

2

3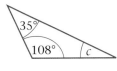

4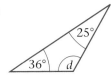

5

6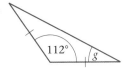

7

8

Find the angles in these triangles.

9

10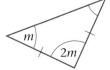

11

7.6 Properties of circles

- A **circle** is the shape enclosed by a curve which is everywhere the same distance from the centre.

 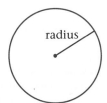  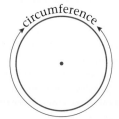 

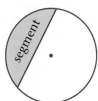 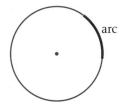 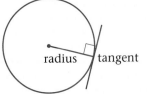 

- The **circumference** of a circle is the distance measured around the curve which makes the circle.
- A **chord** is a straight line drawn across a circle.
- A **tangent** to a circle touches the circle at one point only. The radius is at 90° to the tangent.

Exercise 7F

1 Draw a diagram to show a radius, diameter and circumference of a circle.

2 Draw a diagram to show an arc, circumference and tangent.

3 Draw a diagram to show a chord, sector and segment.

4 Use a pair of compasses to draw a circle.
   Mark an arc on the circumference.
   At each end of the arc, *P* and *Q*, draw a tangent to the circle.
   T is the point where the tangents meet.

   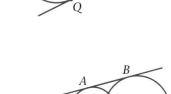

   Join *PQ*, *PT* and *QT*.
   What is the mathematical name for *PQ*?
   What can you say about triangle *PQT*?

5 Draw two circles of different size as shown in the diagram.
   Draw the common tangents to meet at *O*.
   What can you say about *AX* and *BY*?

   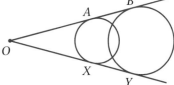

6 Repeat question **5** with non-intersecting circles.

7.7 Exploring cubes and cuboids

⊙ **13** Euler's formula

- On a solid shape
  - a **face** is a flat surface
  - an **edge** is where two faces meet
  - a **vertex** is where two or more edges meet.
- A **cube** is a solid shape whose faces are all squares.
- A **cuboid** is a solid shape whose faces are all rectangles.

Example 6

How many vertices, edges and faces are in this cube?

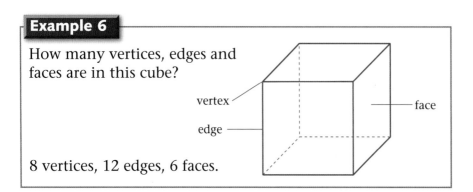

8 vertices, 12 edges, 6 faces.

A Swiss mathematician called Euler worked out that there was a relationship between the numbers of vertices, faces and edges in a solid shape.

Euler (pronounced 'oiler') lived from 1707 to 1783.

This relationship is   vertices + faces = edges + 2

For a cube this means that   vertices (8) + faces (6) = 14
                       and   edges (12) + 2 = 14

Exercise 7G

1 Work out the numbers of vertices, edges and faces in this cuboid.

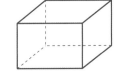

2 Here is another drawing of a cuboid.
   Are the numbers of vertices, edges and faces the same as in question **1**? Explain why.

3 Check that Euler's relationship works for a cuboid.

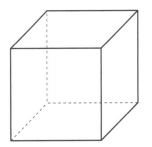

4 Copy this diagram of a cube.
   (a) Mark on your diagram a diagonal of a face.
   (b) Mark on your diagram a diagonal that crosses the cube.

5 Repeat question **4** for a cuboid.

A diagonal must join two vertices.

6 Check whether Euler's relationship works for these shapes.

(a)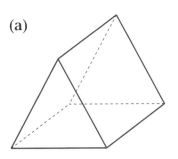

(b)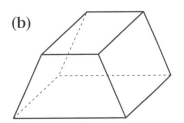

(c)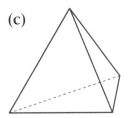

7.8 Drawing on isometric grids

- You can draw 3-D solids on an isometric grid.

Example 7

Sketch a 1 cm cube on an isometric grid.

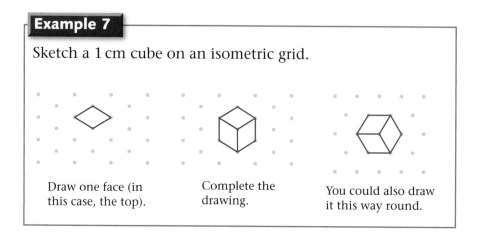

Draw one face (in this case, the top).

Complete the drawing.

You could also draw it this way round.

Exercise 7H

The diagram shows three possible ways of drawing the letter L on an isometric grid.

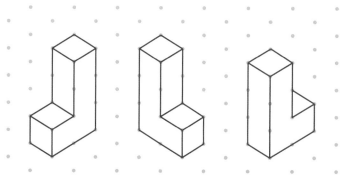

In the following questions one drawing is given.
In each case, draw two other representations of the shape on isometric paper.

1

2

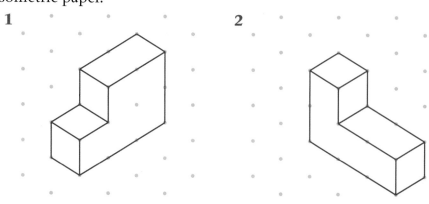

3

4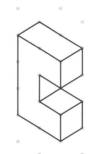

5 On isometric paper draw a sketch of

   (a) a cuboid with length 4 cm, width 3 cm, height 2 cm

   (b) this stair shape.

   (c) Draw another representation of the shape in part (b).

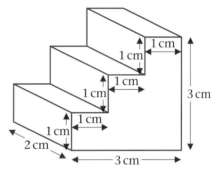

Mixed exercise 7

1 Write down the names of these special quadrilaterals and triangles.
Copy the diagrams and show their properties.

> Show parallel lines, equal sides, etc.

(a)

(b)

(c)

(d)

(e)

(f)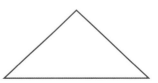

2 Write down the names of these polygons.

(a)

(b)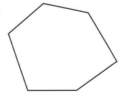

(c)

3 **(a)** List sets of lines which are parallel.

(b) List pairs of lines which are perpendicular.

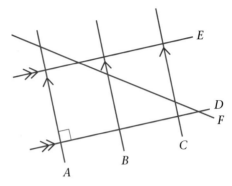

4 Draw a circle radius 5 cm.
Label a radius, circumference and diameter.

5 Draw a diagram to show a chord, segment and arc of a circle.

6 Write down the names of all quadrilaterals with
(a) all angles 90°
(b) opposite sides parallel
(c) one angle greater than 180°
(d) diagonals that bisect each other
(e) two pairs of adjacent sides equal.

7 Write down the number of
(i) vertices
(ii) edges
(iii) faces
on these 3-D shapes.

(a)
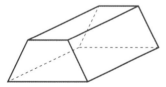

(b)
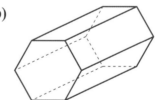

8 Find the value of the letter in these triangles.

(a)
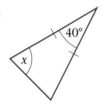

(b)
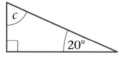

(c)
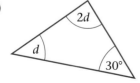

(d)

Summary of key points

1 A **polygon** is a 2-D shape with any number of straight sides.

2 A polygon is **regular** if all its sides and all its angles are equal.

3 The point where two sides meet is called a **vertex**.

The plural of vertex is vertices.

4 The angle at a vertex is a measure of the turn between the two sides that meet there. Angles are usually measured in degrees.

5 Lines which have a right angle between them are called **perpendicular lines**.

6 Lines which are always the same distance apart are called **parallel lines**.

7 A **triangle** is a polygon with three sides.

8 A **quadrilateral** is a four-sided polygon.

9 In an **equilateral triangle** all angles are 60°.

10 In an **isosceles triangle** two angles and two sides are equal.

11 The **interior angles** of a triangle always add up to 180°.

12 A **circle** is the shape enclosed by a curve which is everywhere the same distance from the centre.

13 The **circumference** of a circle is the distance measured around the curve which makes the circle.

14 A **chord** is a straight line drawn across a circle.

15 A **tangent** to a circle touches the circle at one point only. The radius is at 90° to the tangent.

16 On a solid shape
  ○ a **face** is a flat surface
  ○ an **edge** is where two faces meet
  ○ a **vertex** is where two or more edges meet.

17 A **cube** is a solid shape whose faces are all squares.

18 A **cuboid** is a solid shape whose faces are all rectangles.

19 You can draw 3-D solids on an isometric grid.

8 Angles and bearings

8.1 Describing angles

- An angle which is a quarter turn or 90° is called a **right angle**.

- An angle which is less than a quarter turn is called an **acute angle**.

- An angle which is more than a quarter turn but less than a half turn is called an **obtuse angle**.

- This diagram shows angle *ABC*.

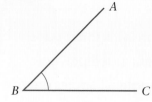

> Angles are named using the three letters of the lines that make the angle.

> Angle *ABC* is sometimes written ∠*ABC*.

Example 1

Use letters to describe the marked angle.
Write down the mathematical name for this angle.

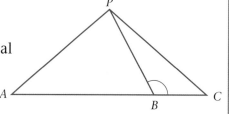

The marked angle is angle *PBC*.
Angle *PBC* is an obtuse angle.

> It is between a quarter turn and a half turn.

Example 2

Estimate the size of angle *XYZ*.

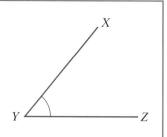

Angle *XYZ* is less than 90°.
It is just over half a right angle.
Estimate: Angle *XYZ* = 50°.

- An angle which is more than a half turn is called a **reflex angle**.

Example 3

Label and describe the angles marked at *A* and *C*.

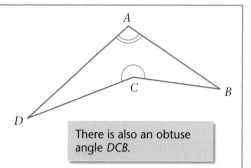

The angle at *A* is angle *DAB*. It is an obtuse angle.
The marked angle at *C* is the reflex angle *DCB*.

> There is also an obtuse
> angle *DCB*.

Example 4

Copy the diagram on the right and mark angle *C*,
angle *APB* and angle *PBC*.

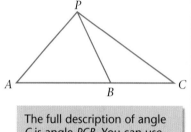

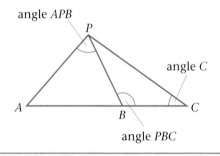

> The full description of angle
> *C* is angle *PCB*. You can use
> the single letter if there is
> only one angle at the point.

Exercise 8A

In each of questions **1–6** use letters to describe the marked angle.
Say whether each angle is acute or obtuse.

1

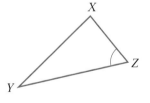

2

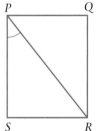

3

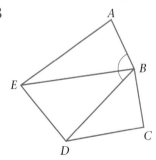

4

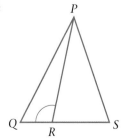

5

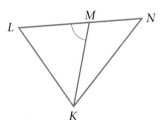

6

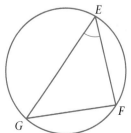

In questions **7–9** estimate the size of the angles.

7    **8**    **9**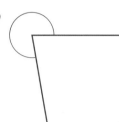

In each of questions **10–15** copy the diagram and mark the named angles.

10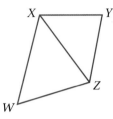

Angle *W*, angle *YXZ* and angle *XZW*

11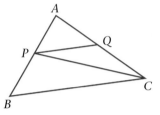

Angle *B*, angle *AQP* and angle *APC*

12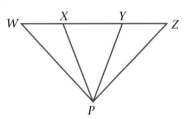

Angle *PXY*, angle *ZPY* and angle *WYP*

13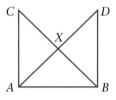

Angle *C*, angle *AXB* and angle *CBA*

14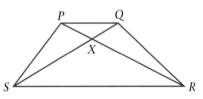

Angle *SPQ*, and reflex angle *SXR*

15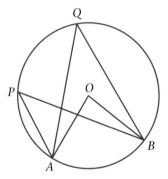

Reflex angle *AOB*, angle *PAQ* and angle *QBP*

8.2 Angles on a straight line

• Angles on a straight line add up to 180°.

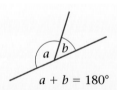

$a + b = 180°$

> **6** Angles on a straight line
> **21** Angles on a straight line (algebraic)

Example 5

Work out the value of *x*.

$$x + 15 + 32 = 180$$
$$x + 47 = 180$$
$$x = 180 - 47 = 133$$

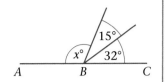

ABC is a straight line.

Exercise 8B

In these questions work out the size of the marked angles.

1

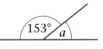

153° *a*

2

b 76°

3

c 32°

4

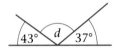

43° *d* 37°

5

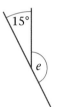

15° *e*

6

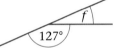

f 127°

7

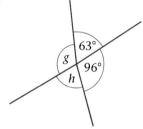

63° *g* 96° *h*

8

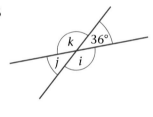

k 36° *j* *i*

8.3 Angles meeting at a point

- Angles meeting at a point add up to 360°.

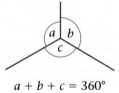

a *b* *c*

$a + b + c = 360°$

- Where two straight lines cross, the opposite angles are equal. They are called **vertically opposite angles**.

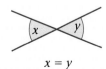

x *y*

$x = y$

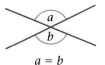

a *b*

$a = b$

6 Angles around a point
21 Angles around a point (algebraic)

Example 6

Work out the values of p and q.

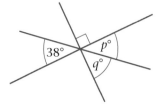

$$p = 38 \text{ (vertically opposite angles)}$$
$$90 + p + q = 180 \text{ (angles on a straight line)}$$
$$90 + 38 + q = 180$$
$$q = 180 - 90 - 38 = 52$$

Always explain your reasoning in angle problems.

Exercise 8C

In these questions, work out the angles marked by letters.

1
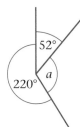

2
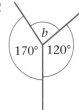

3
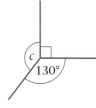

4
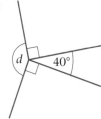

5
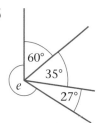

6

7
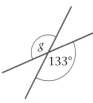

8
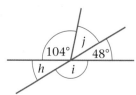

9
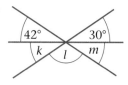

10
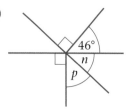

8.4 Angles in parallel lines

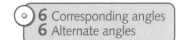
6 Corresponding angles
6 Alternate angles

- The shaded angles are equal.
  They are called **alternate angles**.
  They make a Z shape.

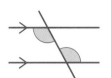

- The shaded angles are equal.
  They are called **corresponding angles**.
  They make an F shape.

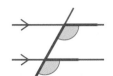
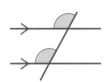

Example 7

Work out the marked angles
in the diagram.
Give reasons for your answers.

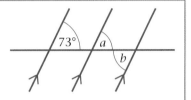

$a = 73°$ (corresponding angles)
$b = a = 73°$ (alternate angles)

Exercise 8D

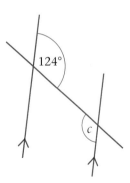
6 Testing the relations
between angles

In questions **1–8** work out the size of the marked angles.
Give reasons for your answers.

1

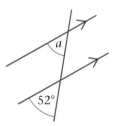

2

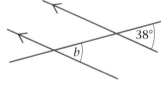

3

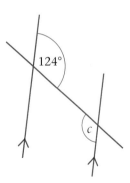

4

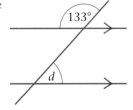

5

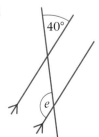

6

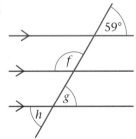

7

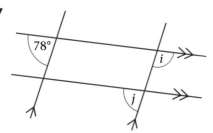

8

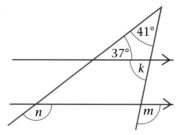

9 *PQRS* is a parallelogram.
Angle *QSP* = 47°
Angle *QSR* = 24°
PST is a straight line.

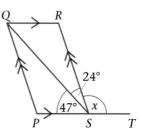

(a) Find the size of the angle marked *x*.
Give a reason for your answer.

(b) Work out the size of angle *PQS*.
Give a reason for your answer. [E]

10

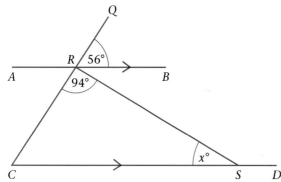

In the diagram the lines *AB* and *CD* are parallel.
CRQ is a straight line.
Angle *CRS* = 94°
Angle *QRB* = 56°
Angle *RSC* = *x*°
Find the value of *x*. [E]

8.5 Proofs

- Proof 1 Opposite angles in a parallelogram are equal.

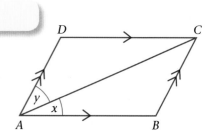

x = angle *BAC* = angle *ACD* (alternate angles)
y = angle *CAD* = angle *BCA* (alternate angles)
x + *y* = angle *A* = angle *C*

Opposite angles of a parallelogram are equal.

- Proof 2   Angles in a triangle add up to 180°.

Draw a line *XAY* parallel to the base *BC*. Then

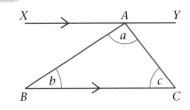

angle *XAB* = angle *ABC* = *b* (alternate angles)
angle *YAC* = angle *ACB* = *c* (alternate angles)
and angle *BAC* = *a*

The angles in the triangle are *a*, *b* and *c*.
The angles which make straight line *XAY* are *a*, *b* and *c*.

Therefore the angles in a triangle add up to 180°.

- Proof 3   The exterior angle of a triangle is equal to the sum
  of the interior and opposite angles.

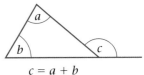

Draw *CE* parallel to *BA*. Then

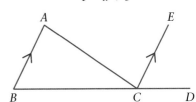

angle *BAC* = angle *ACE* (alternate angles)
angle *ABC* = angle *ECD* (corresponding angles)

Adding these together:

angle *BAC* + angle *ABC* = angle *ACD*

Exercise 8E

1 *ABC* is a straight line.
Show that angle *ABD* = *a* + *b*.
Give reasons.

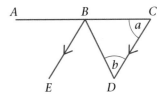

2 *XBC* and *ZBA* are straight lines.
Show that angle *YBZ* = *b* + *c*.
Give reasons.

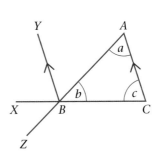

3 *AB* = *BC*
Angle *BCA* = *x*
(a) Write down angle *BAC* in terms of *x*.
(b) Show that *AC* bisects angle *BCX*.

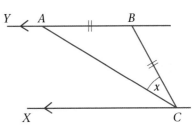

4 *ABCD* is a parallelogram.
Show that angle *A* = angle *C*.

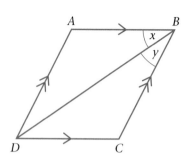

5 *ABC* is a straight line.
Explain why angle *CBY* = 54°.

Hint: There are two steps.

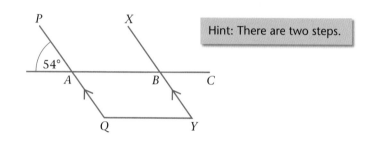

6 *PQ* is parallel to *RS*.
AD is parallel to *WZ*.
Explain why angle *RCD* = 48°.

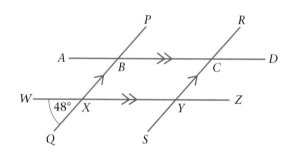

7 *ABCD* is a parallelogram.
XC = *BC*
Explain why angle *BXC* = angle *D*.

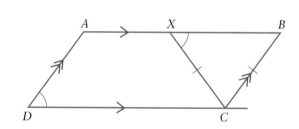

8 *ABCD* is a straight line.
PQ is parallel to *RS*.
CD = *CS*
Show, with reasons, that
angle *CSD* = 20°.

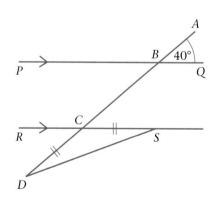

8.6 Bearings

6 Geometry set

- A three-figure bearing gives a direction in degrees. It is an angle measured clockwise from the North.

Example 8

Give the three-figure bearing of
(a) *A* from *B*
(b) *C* from *D*.

The 'bearing of *A* from *B*' means: if you stand at *B*, which direction is *A*?

(a) The angle measured clockwise from North gives the bearing 065°.

For a bearing like this add a zero to give it three figures.

(b) The angle 53° is measured anticlockwise from North.
So the angle measured clockwise is
360° − 53° = 307°.
The bearing is 307°.

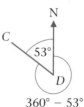

360° − 53°

Example 9

The bearing of Witney from Oxford is 283°.
What is the bearing of Oxford from Witney?

At Oxford, looking towards Witney

To face Oxford from Witney you
have to make a half turn.
This is a change of direction of 180°.
So the bearing of Oxford from Witney is
283° − 180° = 103°.

At Witney, make a half turn to face Oxford.

Exercise 8F

In questions **1–10**, write down (a) the bearing of *B* from *A*
(b) the bearing of *A* from *B*.

1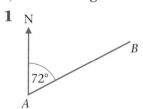

2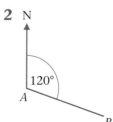

3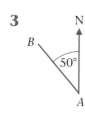

4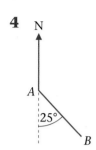

5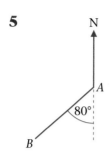

6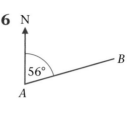

7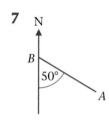

8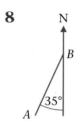

9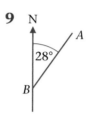

10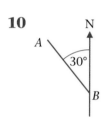

11 *A*, *B* and *C* are three towns. The bearing of *B* from *A* is 070°. The bearing of *B* from *C* is 125°. The bearing of *C* from *A* is 330°. Draw a sketch to show the relative positions of the towns.

> Label the angles on your sketch.

12 The bearing of Charlbury from Oxford is 310°. What is the bearing of Oxford from Charlbury?

13 The bearing of Bicester from Woodstock is 055°. What is the bearing of Woodstock from Bicester?

Mixed exercise 8

1 Use letters to describe the marked angles. Write down the mathematical name for each angle.

(a)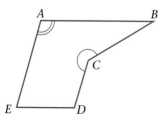

(b)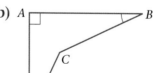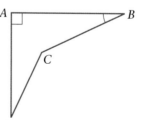

(c)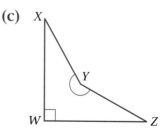

2 Copy the diagrams and mark on them the named angles.

(a)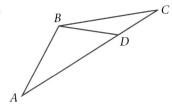

Angle C, angle CBD and
angle BDA

(b)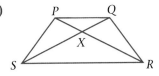

Reflex angle QXR, angle XSP
and angle PQS

3

Diagram **NOT**
accurately drawn

(a) (i) Work out the size of the angle marked x.

(ii) Give a reason for your answer.

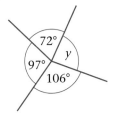

Diagram **NOT**
accurately drawn

(b) Work out the size of the angle marked y.　　　[E]

4 Work out the size of the marked angles.
Give reasons for your answers.

(a)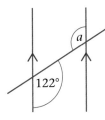

(b)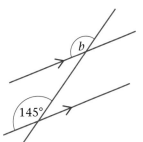

(c)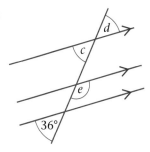

5 Work out the size of angle ADB.

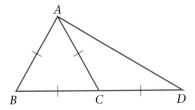

6 In each of these diagrams work out the size of the marked angles. You must also give reasons.

(a)

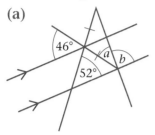

(b)

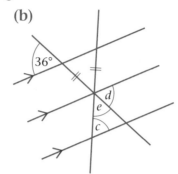

(c)

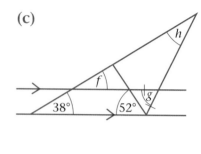

(d)

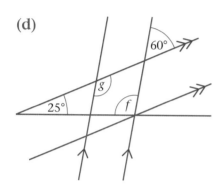

(e)

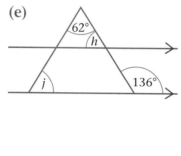

(f)

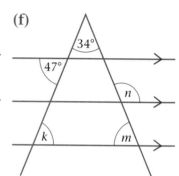

7 The diagram shows the position of each of three buildings in a town.

The bearing of the Hospital from the Art gallery is 072°.

The Cinema is due East of the Hospital.

The distance from the Hospital to the Art gallery is equal to the distance from the Hospital to the Cinema.

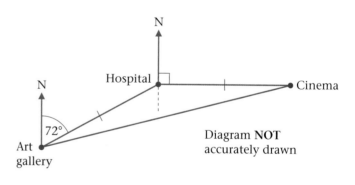

Diagram **NOT** accurately drawn

Work out the bearing of the Cinema from the Art gallery.   [E]

8 The bearing of Cambridge from Colchester is 300°.
The bearing of Cambridge from Luton is 040°.
The bearing of Colchester from Luton is 095°.

(a) Draw a sketch to show the relative positions of Luton, Cambridge and Colchester.

(b) Work out the bearing of Colchester from Cambridge.

(c) Work out the bearing of Luton from Colchester.

Punting on the Cam is a popular summertime activity in Cambridge

9 (a) Find angle *XBA*.

(b) Explain why triangle *CEB* is isosceles.

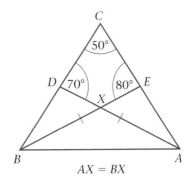

Diagram **NOT** accurately drawn.

AX = BX

Summary of key points

1 An angle which is a quarter turn or 90° is called a **right angle**.

2 An angle which is less than a quarter turn is called an **acute angle**.

3 An angle which is more than a quarter turn but less than a half turn is called an **obtuse angle**.

4 This diagram shows angle *ABC*. The angle is described as it is drawn.

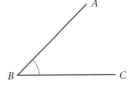

5 An angle which is more than a half turn is called a **reflex angle**.

6 Angles on a straight line add up to 180°.

7 Angles meeting at a point add up to 360°.

8 Where two straight lines cross, the opposite angles are equal. They are called **vertically opposite angles**.

9 **Alternate angles** are equal. They make a Z shape.

10 **Corresponding angles** are equal. They make an F shape.

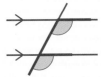

11 Opposite angles in a parallelogram are equal.

12 Angles in a triangle add up to 180°.

13 The exterior angle of a triangle is equal to the sum of the interior and opposite angles.

$c = a + b$

14 A three-figure bearing gives a direction in degrees. It is an angle measured clockwise from the North.

9 Measures

9.1 Time

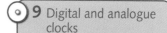
9 Digital and analogue clocks

Example 1

Write these 24-hour clock times as 12-hour clock times.
(a) 08 20   (b) 11 52   (c) 15 30   (d) 22 10

(a) 08 20 is 8:20 am
(b) 11 52 is 11:52 am
(c) 15 30 is 3:30 pm | 15 − 12 = 3 |
(d) 22 15 is 10:15 pm | 22 − 12 = 10 |

> 08 20 and 11 52 are both before 12 noon, so they are am times.

> 15 30 and 22 15 are both after 12 noon so they are pm times.

Example 2

Change these times to decimal fractions of hours.
(a) 2 hours 30 minutes   (b) 5 hours 10 minutes

(a) 2 hours 30 minutes $= 2$ hours $+ \frac{30}{60}$ hours
$$= 2 \text{ hours} + \frac{1}{2} \text{ hour}$$
$$= 2.5 \text{ hours}$$

> 60 minutes = 1 hour

(b) 5 hours 10 minutes $= 5 + \frac{10}{60}$ hours
$$= 5 + 0.166\,66\ldots \text{ hours}$$
$$= 5.17 \text{ hours (to 2 d.p.)}$$

Exercise 9A

1   Write down the times shown by these clocks as you would say them.

(a)    (b)    (c)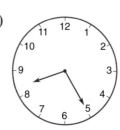

(d) 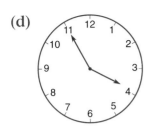 **(e)** 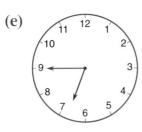 **(f)**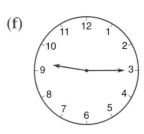

2 Draw clock faces and mark on them
  (a) eight o'clock
  (b) five minutes to six
  (c) a quarter past five
  (d) half past seven
  (e) a quarter to twelve
  (f) ten minutes past four.

3 Write these times as you would say them.
  (a) 4:30   (b) 10:05   (c) 3:15
  (d) 7:45   (e) 12:35   (f) 8:50

4 Write these times as they would appear on a digital display.
  (a) two o'clock   (b) five past three
  (c) a quarter past eight   (d) half past midnight
  (e) twenty to seven   (f) five to three

5 Change these times to 24-hour clock times.
  (a) 2:15 am   (b) 3:20 pm
  (c) 12:40 pm   (d) 11:30 pm
  (e) 9:55 am   (f) three forty-five pm
  (g) ten past eight am   (h) seven fifty pm
  (i) twenty to ten pm   (j) ten past midnight

6 Write these 24-hour clock times as 12-hour clock times
  (am or pm).
  (a) 15 20   (b) 07 15   (c) 23 30   (d) 12 30   (e) 18 45
  (f) 10 05   (g) 19 20   (h) 13 50   (i) 20 20   (j) 03 25

7 Use your calculator to change these times to decimal
  fractions of hours.
  The first one has been done for you.
  (a) 1 hour 15 minutes = 1.25 hours
  (b) 3 hours 30 minutes
  (c) 5 hours 12 minutes
  (d) 4 hours 16 minutes
  (e) 11 hours 57 minutes

8 Use your calculator to change these times into hours and minutes.

(a) 2.25 hours (b) $3\frac{1}{2}$ hours (c) $5\frac{3}{4}$ hours (d) 4.7 hours

9.2 Time calculations

Example 3

Add these times together.
(a) 2 hours 30 minutes and 4 hours 5 minutes
(b) 1 hour 35 minutes and 5 hours 40 minutes

(a) 2 h 30 min + 4 h 5 min = (2 h + 5 h) + (30 min + 5 min) = 7 h 35 min
(b) 1 h 35 min + 5 h 40 min = (1 h + 5 h) + (35 min + 40 min)

= 6 h + 75 min

> Add the hours (h) and minutes (min) separately.

= 6 h + 1 h + 15 min

= 7 h 15 min

> 60 min = 1 hour

Example 4

How long is it from
(a) 3:35 pm to 8:15 pm (b) 09 15 to 13 25?

(a) 3:35 pm to 8:15 pm
Count up:
3:35 pm to 4:00 pm is 25 minutes
4:00 pm to 8:00 pm is   4 hours
8:00 pm to 8:15 pm is 15 minutes
_____
Total   4 hours 40 minutes

> Check: Add 4 hours 40 minutes to 3:35 pm and you get 8:15 pm.

(b) 09 15 to 13 25
Count up:
09 15 to 10 00 is 45 minutes
10 00 to 13 00 is   3 hours
13 00 to 13 25 is 25 minutes
_____
Total   3 hours 70 minutes
= 4 hours 10 minutes

> 24-hour clock times.

> Check: Add 4 hours 10 minutes to 09 15 and you get 13 25.

Exercise 9B

1 Add these times together.

(a) 3 h 20 min and 2 h 25 min (b) 2 h 45 min and 6 h 40 min
(c) 1 h 30 min and 7 h 25 min (d) 3 h 50 min and 8 h 20 min
(e) 3 h 35 min and 5 h 45 min (f) 2 h 25 min and 2 h 55 min

2 How long is it from
   (a) 15 05 to 19 52
   (b) 01 35 to 23 25
   (c) 1:45 pm to 6:10 pm
   (d) 1:34 pm to 10:40 pm
   (e) 3:50 am to 8:40 am?

3 A sports programme started at 21 05 and finished at 23 50.
   How long was the programme on for?

4 Jeremy left home at 8:40 am and arrived at the end of his
   journey at 3:45 pm.
   How long was his journey?

5 Jane arrived at a bus stop at 10:25 am and waited until
   11:50 am for a bus.
   How long did she wait?

6 A train left Manchester at 07 05 and arrived in London at
   09 11.
   How long did the journey take?

7 Here is part of a train timetable from Crewe to London.

Station	Time of leaving
Crewe	08 00
Wolverhampton	08 40
Birmingham	09 00
Coventry	09 30
Rugby	09 40
Milton Keynes	10 10

   (a) What time should the train leave Coventry?

   (b) The train should arrive in London at 10 45.
       How long should the train take to travel from Crewe
       to London?

   (c) Verity arrived at Milton Keynes station at 09 53.
       How many minutes should she have to wait before the
       10 10 train leaves?   [E]

9.3 Reading scales

There is rarely room to number all the marks on a scale. Scales do not always go up in 1s. Sometimes they go up in 2s or 5s or steps of another number.

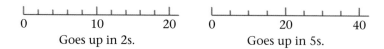

Goes up in 2s.   Goes up in 5s.

> • To read a scale, work out what each division on the scale represents.

Exercise 9C

1 Give the readings on these scales.

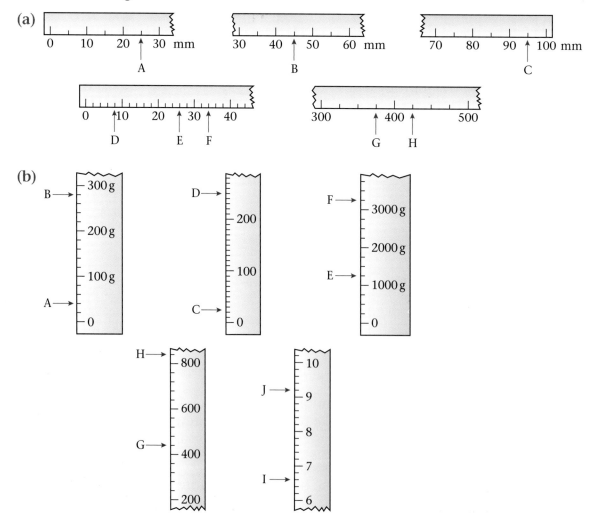

(c)

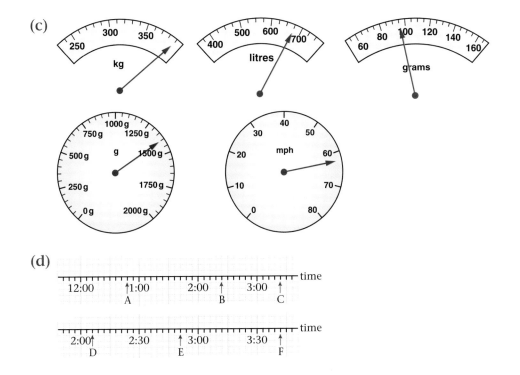

(d)

9.4 Choosing suitable units

- Length
  metric: kilometres (km), metres (m), centimetres (cm), millimetres (mm)
  Imperial: miles, yards, feet (ft), inches (in)

- Weight
  metric: tonnes (t), kilograms (kg), grams (g), milligrams (mg)
  Imperial: tons, hundredweight (cwt), stones, pounds (lb), ounces (oz)

- Capacity
  metric: litres (*l*), centilitres (*cl*), millilitres (*ml*)
  Imperial: gallons, pints (pt)

Example 5

Choose suitable metric units for
(a) the length of a tennis court
(b) the weight of a blackbird
(c) the capacity of a cup.

(a) Metres
(b) Grams
(c) Millilitres

Length can be mm, cm, m or km.
A tennis court is nowhere near 1 km long.
mm and cm are too small.

The weight of a blackbird must be much less than 1 kg.

You cannot get a litre of water into a cup.

Exercise 9D

Copy and complete the table, giving suitable units for each measurement. Give both metric and Imperial units.

		Metric	Imperial
1	The weight of an exercise book.		
2	The height of a tree.		
3	The length of a window cleaner's ladder.		
4	The capacity of a milk jug.		
5	The distance between Bristol and London.		
6	The weight of a packet of biscuits.		
7	The capacity of a water butt.		
8	The weight of a hippopotamus.		
9	The height of a daffodil.		
10	The thickness of a pane of glass.		
11	The weight of a person.		
12	The capacity of a can of soft drink.		
13	The length of a corridor in a hospital.		
14	The weight of a sack of coal.		
15	The weight of iron in a portion of breakfast cereal.		

9.5 Estimating

- To estimate a measurement, compare with a measurement you know.

1 cm is about the width of a fingernail.

2 m is the height of a standard door.

1 kg is the weight of the usual size bag of sugar.

165 m*l* is about a cupful.

Exercise 9E

1 Use the picture below to help you make a sensible estimate for each of these.

  (a) The length of the whiteboard.

  (b) The height of the teacher's desk.

  (c) The height of the filing cabinet.

  (d) The thickness of the textbook.

  (e) The width of the keyboard.

  (f) The height of the seat of the chair.

  (g) The length of the keyboard.

  (h) The height of the top of the whiteboard.

2 Put these sets of three in order of weight.
Put the smallest first. Choose the most suitable weight
from the list for each.

  (a) Canary, crow, swan.   5 g, 50 g, 0.5 kg, 5 kg, 50 kg

  (b) Labrador, Corgi, St Bernard. 600 g, 6 kg, 20 kg, 60 kg, 200 kg

  (c) Elephant, bear, wolf.   2000 g, 30 kg, 100 kg, 1000 kg, 4000 kg

  (d) Shark, whale, carp.   800 g, 8 kg, 80 kg, 250 kg, 800 kg, 8000 kg

  (e) Pig, horse, sheep.   20 kg, 80 kg, 500 kg

3 Use the picture to help you estimate the capacity of each of these.

    (a) The watering can.   **(b)** The flower pot.

    (c) The water butt.   **(d)** The bucket.

    (e) The wheelbarrow.   **(f)** The swimming pool.

    (g) The weedkiller spray.   **(h)** The small bottle (root hormone).

9.6 Converting between metric units

• You need to know these conversions.

Length	Weight	Capacity
10 mm = 1 cm 100 cm = 1 m 1000 mm = 1 m 1000 m = 1 km	1000 mg = 1 g 1000 g = 1 kg 1000 kg = 1 tonne (t)	100 cl = 1 litre 1000 ml = 1 litre 1000 l = 1 cubic metre

• When you change from small units to large units you divide.

• When you change from large units to small units you multiply.

Example 6

Convert

(a) 0.062 m into cm   **(b)** 23 200 g into kg.

(a) 100 cm = 1 m

    0.062 m = 0.062 × 100 = 6.2 cm

> Centimetres are smaller than metres so you get more of them.

(b) 1000 g = 1 kg

    23 200 g = 23 200 ÷ 1000 = 23.2 kg

> Kilograms are larger than grams so you get fewer of them.

Exercise 9F

1 Convert these measurements into mm.
(a) 3 cm   (b) 8 cm   (c) 2.9 cm
(d) 4.7 cm   (e) 5.26 cm   (f) 6.21 cm

2 Convert these measurements into cm.
(a) 129 mm   (b) 630 mm   (c) 2 m
(d) 3.47 m   (e) 0.021 km

3 Convert these measurements into grams.
(a) 3 kg   (b) 4.1 kg   (c) 2.97 kg
(d) 0.132 kg   (e) 0.0057 kg   (f) 230 mg
(g) 8000 mg   (h) 7550 mg

4 Convert these amounts into kg.
(a) 15 000 g   (b) 6500 g   (c) 2 t
(d) 3.72 t   (e) 0.013 t   (f) 20 000 mg
(g) 1 million milligrams

5 Convert these measurements into m*l*.
(a) 5 litres   (b) 22.6 litres   (c) 3.712 litres
(d) 50 c*l*   (e) 26 c*l*   (f) 200 c*l*

6 Convert these measurements into litres.
(a) 23 000 m*l*   (b) 3700 m*l*   (c) 500 c*l*   (d) 632 c*l*
(e) 10 500 c*l*   (f) 500 m*l*   (g) 850 m*l*

9.7 Metric equivalents

- You need to know these rough metric–Imperial conversions.

Metric	Imperial
8 km	5 miles
1 kg	2.2 pounds (lb)
1 litre (*l*)	1.75 pints
4.5 *l*	1 gallon
30 cm	1 foot

- These conversions may also be useful.

Metric	Imperial
25 g	1 ounce (oz)
1 m	39 inches
2.5 cm	1 inch

Example 7

1 yard = 36 inches
How many centimetres are there in a yard?

    1 inch = 2.5 cm
    1 yard = 36 inches = 36 × 2.5 cm = 90 cm

Exercise 9G

1 Change these weights into pounds (lb).
   (a) 7 kg   (b) 22 kg   (c) 39.2 kg
   (d) 4.07 kg   (e) 600 g

2 Change these weights into kilograms.
   (a) 3 lb   (b) 150 lb   (c) 96.5 lb
   (d) 24.2 lb   (e) 1 lb

3 There are 14 lb in a stone.
   Bill weighs 12 stone 10 lb.
   What is his weight in kilograms?

4 The distance from Doncaster to Edinburgh is 237 miles.
   How far is this in kilometres?

5 The horizon is approximately 21 kilometres away.
   How far is this in miles?

6 Change 28 miles to kilometres.   [E]

7 Mary measures out 15 litres of water using a 1 pint milk bottle.
   How many full bottles would she need?

8 Petrol costs 98.4p per litre.
   How much is this per gallon?

9 There are 16 ounces (oz) in a pound (lb).
   A laptop computer weighs 7 lb 3 oz.
   How much does this laptop computer weigh in grams?

10 A plank of wood is 1.8 metres long.
   What is its length in feet?

11 There are 12 inches in a foot.
   Ajay is 5 feet 7 inches tall.
   How tall is he in centimetres?

9.8 Accuracy

- Measurements of time, length, weight, capacity and temperature are **continuous**. They can never be measured exactly.
- If you make a measurement correct to a given unit the true value lies in a range that extends half a unit above and half a unit below that measurement.
- Measures expressed to a given unit have a maximum possible error of half a unit.

Example 8

The length of a piece of string is 53 cm to the nearest cm.
What is **(a)** the shortest **(b)** the longest it could be?
(c) What is the maximum error possible?

(a) The shortest it could be is 52.5 cm.
(b) The longest it could be is 53.5 cm.
(c) The maximum error possible is 0.5 cm.

Exercise 9H

In questions **1–4** all measurements are given correct to the nearest unit. In each question, give the maximum and minimum values that the exact measurement could be.

1 (a) 72 cm   (b) 16 mm   (c) 5 km   (d) 100 m

2 (a) 50 kg   (b) 125 g   (c) 3 tonnes   (d) 82 mg

3 (a) 4 hours   (b) 23 minutes   (c) 7 seconds   (d) 65 years

4 (a) 26 °C   (b) 55 °F   (c) 750 m*l*   (d) 8 litres

5 In this question the measurements are to the nearest cm. Write down the maximum and minimum values that the exact length could be.
  (a) 260 cm   (b) 5.28 m   (c) 600 mm   (d) 2000 mm

6 In this question write down the maximum error possible in an answer given to the nearest
  (a) hour   (b) 10 g   (c) 15 minutes
  (d) second   (e) 50 cm   (f) 0.2 seconds
  (g) 25 m*l*   (h) 5 °C

9.9 Speed

- Speed = $\dfrac{\text{distance}}{\text{time}}$

- Average speed = $\dfrac{\text{total distance}}{\text{total time}}$

You can use this triangle to help you remember the formulae.

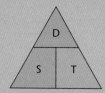

Cover the value you wish to find with your thumb: e.g. to find speed, cover S. You are left with

D over T, that is $\dfrac{\text{distance}}{\text{time}}$.

Common units for speed are

    m/s (metres per second)
    km/h (kilometres per hour)
    mph (miles per hour).

Example 9

The average speed for a journey of 273 km was 57.2 km/h. How long did the journey take?

$$\text{Time} = \frac{\text{distance}}{\text{speed}}$$

$$\text{Time} = \frac{273}{57.2} = 4.772\,727\,3 \text{ hours}$$

$$0.772\,727\,3 \text{ hours} = 0.772\,727\,3 \times 60$$
$$= 46 \text{ minutes (to the nearest minute)}$$

So the journey took 4 hours 46 minutes.

Using the triangle above
speed = $\dfrac{\text{distance}}{\text{time}}$

Notice that the answer is in **hours** because the speed is in km per **hour**.

One hour is 60 minutes. To change hours into minutes multiply by 60.

Exercise 9I

1 Copy and complete the table.

	Distance	Time	Average speed
(a)	128 km	2 hours	
(b)	58 miles		8 mph
(c)		20 s	30 m/s
(d)	2.3 km	50 s	
(e)		$3\frac{1}{2}$ hours	50 mph
(f)	165 km	$2\frac{1}{2}$ hours	
(g)	750 m		25 m/s
(h)		$2\frac{1}{2}$ minutes	40 m/s

(i)	100 km	50 minutes	
(j)	254 miles	1 hour 15 minutes	
(k)	76 km		15 km/h
(l)	27.15 km	16 minutes 10 s	
(m)	127 miles		55 mph
(n)		3 hours 18 minutes	30 mph
(o)	2350 km	$1\frac{1}{2}$ days	

2 A car travels for 3 hours at an average speed of 43 mph.
How far does it travel?

3 According to the railway timetable the distance between
Edinburgh and Glasgow is 57 miles and the journey takes
1 hour 7 minutes.
What is the average speed for this journey?

4 The winner of a 100 m race took 9.3 seconds.
What was his average speed?

5 How long does it take to do a journey of 190 kilometres at
55 km/h?

6 A skier averages 20 m/s for 6 minutes.
How far does he travel?

7 How far would you travel in 13 minutes if your average
speed was 28 km/h?

8 How long does it take to travel 185 km at 40 km/h?

9 How long does it take to travel the 335 miles from London
to Cornwall at an average speed of 37 mph?

10 A 26 mile race is completed in 2 hours 6 minutes by the
winner.
What was her average speed?

11 Myfanwy drives the 120 km from her home in Bristol in
3 hours. Work out her average speed.

12 Errol cycles for $2\frac{1}{2}$ hours at an average speed of
18 km/h. How far does he travel?

13 The distance from London to York by rail is 300 km.
The fastest train takes 1 hour 50 minutes for the journey.
What is the average speed of this train?

14 The speed of a shell fired from a gun is 1800 m/s.
How far does it travel in 1 minute?

Speed skiers can reach
speed of over 100 mph.

9.10 Changing units

* You need to be able to change units of speed between kilometres per hour, metres per second and miles per hour.

Example 10

Change 20 metres per second to kilometres per hour.

There are $60 \times 60 = 3600$ seconds in an hour.

In   1 second the distance travelled is 20 metres

and in 1 hour the distance travelled is $20 \times 3600 = 72\,000$ metres

> First find how many metres are travelled in 1 hour.

In   1 hour distance travelled $= \dfrac{72\,000}{1000} = 72$ kilometres

$20 \, \text{m/s} = 72 \, \text{km/h}$

> There are 1000 metres in 1 kilometre so you divide by 1000 to turn metres into kilometres.

Example 11

Change 30 miles per hour to metres per second.
(Use 5 miles = 8 kilometres)

$5 \text{ miles} = 8 \text{ kilometres}$

$1 \text{ mile} = (8 \div 5) \text{ kilometres}$

$30 \text{ miles} = 30 \times \frac{8}{5} = 48 \text{ kilometres}$

$1 \text{ kilometre} = 1000 \text{ metres}$

so $48 \, \text{km} = 48\,000$ metres

In 1 hour 48 000 metres is travelled

and in 1 second $\frac{48\,000}{3600} = \frac{40}{3} = 13\frac{1}{3}$ metres is travelled.

$30 \text{ mph} = 13\frac{1}{3} \, \text{m/s}$

> Change miles to kilometres.

> Change km to metres.

> 1 hour = 3600 seconds

Example 12

Ben travels 7.3 km in 8.5 minutes.
What is his average speed in
(a) metres per second   (b) kilometres per hour?

(a) Average speed $= \dfrac{\text{total distance}}{\text{total time}}$

Speed $= \dfrac{7.3 \, \text{km}}{8.5 \, \text{minutes}}$

For an answer in metres per second change the units.

$7.3 \, \text{km} = 7300 \, \text{m}$ and $8.5 \text{ minutes} = 510 \text{ seconds}$

Speed $= \dfrac{7300 \, \text{m}}{510 \, \text{seconds}}$

       $= 14.3 \, \text{m/s}$ (1 d.p.)

(b) For an answer in kilometres per hour, change the units for time.

8.5 minutes $= \dfrac{8.5}{60}$ hours $= 0.141\,66\ldots$

Speed $= \dfrac{7.3 \text{ km}}{0.141\,66 \ldots \text{ hours}}$

$= 51.5294\ldots$ km/h

$= 52$ km/h (to the nearest km/hour)

Do not round until the end of the calculation.

Exercise 9J

Use 5 miles = 8 km and 1 gallon = 4.5 litres, where necessary.

1 Change 30 metres per second to kilometres per hour.

2 Change 72 km/h to metres per second.

3 Change 120 miles per hour to miles per minute.

4 Change 48 kilometres per hour to miles per hour.

5 Change 150 miles per hour to kilometres per hour.

6 An electron travels at 600 000 metres per second.
   What is this speed in miles per hour?

7 Change 120 miles per hour into metres per second.

8 Change 40 miles per gallon to kilometres per litre.

9 Change 40 kilometres per litre to miles per gallon.

10 A pipe delivers 20 litres of water per second.
   What is this in gallons per hour?

11 A pump removes 280 gallons of water in 5 minutes.
   What is the rate in litres per second?

12 A Formula 1 racing car completes a 6.3 km lap in 1 minute
   16.2 seconds. Work out the average speed in
   (a) m/s   (b) km/h.

13 The time gap between the first and second cars in a Grand
   Prix was 3.146 seconds. Assuming the cars were travelling at
   305 km/h at the finish, work out how far apart they were.

9.11 Density

- Density = $\dfrac{\text{mass}}{\text{volume}}$

Common units are g/cm³ (grams per cubic centimetre) and kg/m³ (kg per cubic centimetre).

Example 13

The density of wood is 0.8 g per cubic centimetre. What is the mass of a wooden post with volume 10 125 cm³?

Mass = density × volume
= 0.8 × 10 125 = 8100 grams
= 8.1 kg

> Rearranging
>
> Density = $\dfrac{\text{mass}}{\text{volume}}$

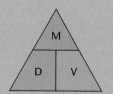

You can use this triangle to help you remember the formulae.

Cover the value you wish to find with your thumb: e.g. to find density, cover D. You are left with M over V, that is $\dfrac{\text{mass}}{\text{volume}}$.

m/s can also be written m s⁻¹, g/cm³ can also be written g cm⁻³, and so on.

Exercise 9K

1 The density of iron is 7.86 g per cm³. An iron bar has a mass of 6.32 kg. What is its volume?

2 A decorative lamp is to be filled with glycerine. Its volume is 72 cm³ and the density of the glycerine is 1.27 g per cm³. What mass of glycerine is required?

3 Copy and complete the table.

Substance	Mass	Volume	Density
Hydrogen		1 km³	0.0009 g/cm³
Air	20 kg		0.0013 g/cm³
Aluminium	15 kg	5556 cm³	

4 The density of silver is 10.5 g/cm³. To check whether a dish is solid silver it is weighed and its volume found by immersing the dish in water and measuring the water displaced. The volume is 52.3 cm³ and its mass is 611 g. Is the dish likely to be solid silver?

5 A ring is made from gold with a diamond. The ring has volume 0.95 cm³. The gold is known to have a mass of 15 g. The density of the gold is 19.3 g/cm³. Work out the volume of the diamond.

6 A rectangular sheet of glass measures 500 mm by 400 mm by 6 mm. It has a mass of 3 kg. What is the density of the glass?

> Volume of cuboid = length × width × height

7 The mass of 5 m³ of copper is 44 800 kg.
(a) Work out the density of copper.

> Give your answer in kg/m³.

The density of zinc is 7130 kg/m³.
(b) Work out the mass of 5 m³ of zinc. [E]

> Give your answer in kg.

9.12 Comparing measurements

- To work out which is the better buy, compare the prices for equal amounts.

Example 14

Which is the better buy,
  a 1 kilogram tin costing £3.25
  or a 450 gram packet costing £1.44?

1 1000 grams cost £3.25
   This is 32.5p per 100 grams
2 450 grams cost £1.44
   50 grams cost £1.44 ÷ 9 = 16p
   100 grams cost 32p
3 The 450 gram packet is the better buy.

> Work out the cost of 100 g for each.

- To compare measurements they need to be in the same units.

Example 15

One car is travelling at 40 mph.
Another car is travelling at 50 km/h.
Which car is travelling the faster?

$$40 \times \frac{8}{5} = 64 \text{ km}$$
So 40 mph = 64 km/h
The car travelling at 40 mph is travelling faster.

> Change 40 miles to km.
> (5 miles = 8 km)

Exercise 9L

1 One car is travelling at 65 mph.
Another car is travelling at 105 km/hour.
Which car is travelling the faster?

2 Which is the better buy, 3 for £1.19 or 5 for £1.99?

3 Which is the better value,

a 330 m*l* can costing 45p
or a 1 litre bottle costing £1.35?

Give a reason.

4 A small 50 g jar of coffee costs £1.35.
A medium 100 g jar of coffee costs £2.75.
A large 200 g jar of coffee costs £5.20.
Find the cost per 100 g to decide the best buy.

5 One car travels the 40 miles from London to Wycombe
in $1\frac{1}{4}$ hours. Another car travels the 15 km from
Whitechapel to Wanstead in 18 minutes.
Which car had the faster average speed?

6 Petrol is priced at a garage at

£4.20 per gallon
or 95p per litre.

Are these prices the same? If not, which is cheaper?

7 A swift flies at 50 metres per second.
An inter-city train travels at 120 miles per hour.
Which is travelling the faster?
What is the distance between them after 10 minutes?

> Assume they both start from the same point at the same time.

Mixed exercise 9

1 Write down the time shown by these clocks, as you would
say them.

(a)

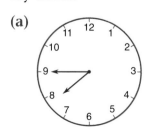

(b)

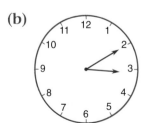

(c)

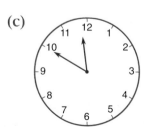

2 Write these times as you would say them.
  (a) 04:45   (b) 12:30   (c) 09:05   (d) 01:35

3 Write these times as they would appear on a digital display.
  (a) a quarter past seven   (b) ten to nine
  (c) a quarter to eleven

4 Write these times as 24-hour clock times.
  (a) 3:50 am   (b) 1:20 pm
  (c) 10:15 pm   (d) 5 past midnight

5 Amanda left the house at 10:30 am to go shopping.
  She returned at 3:40 pm.
  For how long was she out?

6 Chertsey village had a power cut from 06 15 to 22 35.
  How long did the power cut last?

7 Derek watched a film for 2 h 20 min and then a programme for 50 min.
  How long did he spend watching television?

8 Read these scales.
  (a) 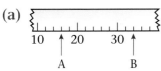   (b)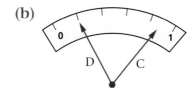

9 Convert
  (a) 2.03 metres to centimetres
  (b) 1500 grams to kilograms
  (c) 5000 cl into (i) litres (ii) millilitres
  (d) 0.04 kilometres into (i) metres (ii) millimetres.

10 The distance between London and Exeter is 170 miles.
  How far is this in kilometres?

11 A car's petrol tank holds 25 gallons.
  How many litres is this?

12 Work out the weight, in kilograms, of a 56 lb sack of potatoes.

13 A running track is 400 metres to the nearest metre.
  Write down the greatest and least distance this can be.

14 A gold necklace has a mass of 127 grams, correct to the nearest gram.

   (a) Write down the **least** possible mass of the necklace.

   (b) Write down the **greatest** possible mass of the necklace. [E]

15 How long does it take to travel 160 km at 50 km/h?

16 A runner sprints 400 metres in 48 seconds.
   What is his speed in metres per second?

17 A cyclist plans to cycle the 870 miles from Land's End to John O'Groats in six days.
   Work out the average speed.

The cyclist travels for 12 hours per day.

18 Daniel leaves his house at 07 00.
   He drives 87 miles to work.
   He drives at an average speed of 36 miles per hour.

   At what time does Daniel arrive at work? [E]

19 A doorstop in the shape of a cuboid with volume 150 cm³ is made from plastic with a density of 3.1 g/cm³.
   Work out the mass of the doorstop.

20 The mass of a glass paperweight is 236 grams. The density of the glass is 2.7 grams per cubic centimetre.
   Work out the volume of the paperweight.

21 Change 36 miles per hour into metres per second.

22 1966 cm³ of iron weighs 34 lb.
   1500 cm³ of steel weighs 11 550 grams.

   (a) Which metal has the greater density?

   (b) What is the difference in weight between 10 000 cm³ of iron and 10 000 cm³ of steel?

23

   These two metal blocks each have a volume of 0.5 m³.
   The density of the copper block is 8900 kg per m³.
   The density of the nickel block is 8800 kg per m³.

   Calculate the difference in the masses of the blocks. [E]

24 A 1 kg box of washing powder costs £6.50.
   A 3.5 kg tub of washing powder costs £23.00.
   Which is the better buy?

Summary of key points

1 To read a scale, work out what each division on the scale represents.

2 Length
metric: kilometres (km), metres (m), centimetres (cm), millimetres (mm)
Imperial: miles, yards, feet (ft), inches (in)

3 Weight
metric: tonnes (t), kilograms (kg), grams (g), milligrams (mg)
Imperial: tons, hundredweight (cwt), stones, pounds (lb), ounces (oz)

4 Capacity
metric: litres (l), centilitres (cl), millilitres (ml)
Imperial: gallons, pints (pt)

5 To estimate a measurement, compare with a measurement you know.

6 You need to know these conversions.

Length	Weight	Capacity
10 mm = 1 cm 100 cm = 1 m 1000 mm = 1 m 1000 m = 1 km	1000 mg = 1 g 1000 g = 1 kg 1000 kg = 1 tonne (t)	100 cl = 1 litre 1000 ml = 1 litre 1000 l = 1 cubic metre

7 When you change from small units to large units you divide.

8 When you change from large units to small units you multiply.

9 You need to know these rough metric–Imperial conversions.

Metric	Imperial
8 km	5 miles
1 kg	2.2 pounds (lb)
1 litre (l)	1.75 pints
4.5 l	1 gallon
30 cm	1 foot

10 These conversions may also be useful.

Metric	Imperial
25 g	1 ounce (oz)
1 m	39 inches
2.5 cm	1 inch

11 Measurements of time, length, weight, capacity and temperature are **continuous**. They can never be measured exactly.

12 If you make a measurement correct to a given unit the true value lies in a range that extends half a unit above and half a unit below that measurement.

13 Measures expressed to a given unit have a maximum possible error of half a unit.

14 Speed $= \dfrac{\text{distance}}{\text{time}}$

15 Average speed $= \dfrac{\text{total distance}}{\text{total time}}$

16 You need to be able to change units of speed between kilometres per hour, metres per second and miles per hour.

17 Density $= \dfrac{\text{mass}}{\text{volume}}$

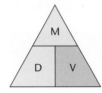

18 To work out which is the better buy, compare the prices for equal amounts.

19 To compare measurements they need to be in the same units.

10 Perimeter, area and volume

10.1 Perimeter

- The **perimeter** of a shape is the distance around the edge of the shape.

Example 1

Work out the perimeter of this shape.
All the corners are right angles.

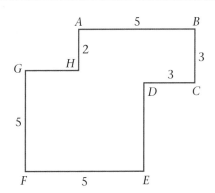

You do not know the length of *GH* or *DE*.

$GH + AB = EF + CD$ (the width of the shape)
$GH + 5 = 5 + 3$
$GH = 3$

Also $FG + AH = DE + BC$ (the height of the shape)
$5 + 2 = DE + 3$
$DE = 4$

Perimeter $= 5 + 3 + 3 + 4 + 5 + 5 + 3 + 2 = 30$

> Start at *A* and work round in alphabetical order to *B*, *C*, *D*, etc.

Exercise 10A

Work out the perimeter of these shapes.

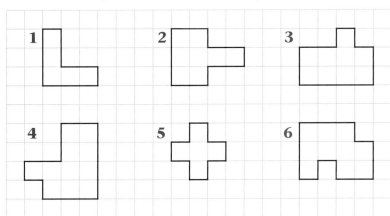

Width of each
square = 1

7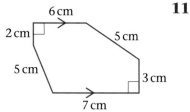

8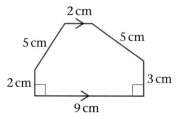

9

10

11

mm, cm, m, km are units of length.

12 A swimming pool measures 10 m by 4 m. It is surrounded by a path made from square slabs 50 cm by 50 cm. The path goes all the way round and is 1 m wide. How many slabs are used?

13 Fencing panels are 2 m long and cost £12.99 each. Work out the cost for the fencing panels to surround three sides of a garden as shown.

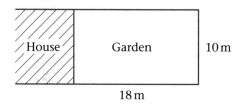

10.2 Area

- The **area** of a shape is a measure of the amount of space it covers. Typical units of area are square centimetres (cm²), square metres (m²) and square kilometres (km²).

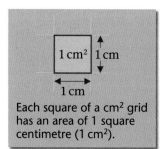

Each square of a cm² grid has an area of 1 square centimetre (1 cm²).

Example 2

Estimate the area of the shape drawn on this grid of centimetre squares.

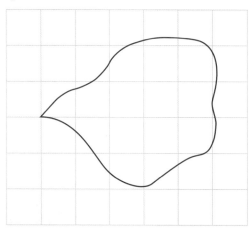

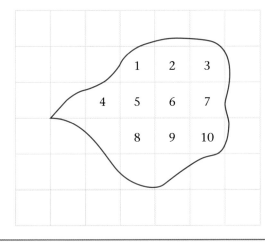

There are 10 complete or almost complete squares. The other pieces are enough to make about three squares.

Area is approximately 13 cm²

Exercise 10B

For questions **1–6**, work out the area of the shapes in Exercise 10A, questions **1–6**.

In the following questions estimate the area of each shape.

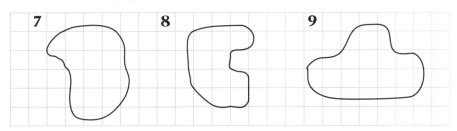

10 A shaded shape is shown on the grid of centimetre squares.

(a) Work out the perimeter of the shaded shape.

(b) Work out the area of the shaded shape. [E]

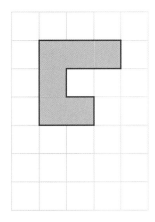

10.3 Area of rectangles

• Area of a rectangle = length × width

$$A = lw$$

The formula still works when length and width are not whole numbers.

Example 3

Work out the area of this rectangle.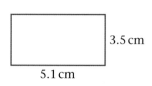

In centimetres: In millimetres:
5.1 × 3.5 = 17.85   51 × 35 = 1785
    area = 17.85 cm²   area = 1785 mm²

Example 4

The area of a rectangle is 240 m².
Its length is 15 m.
Work out its width.

        Area = length × width
        240 = 15 × width
So, width = 240 ÷ 15 = 16 m

Exercise 10C

Work out the area of these rectangles.

1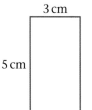

2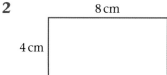

3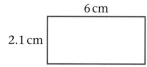

4

5

6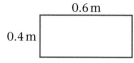

7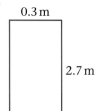

8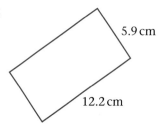

Work out the length of these rectangles.

9

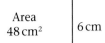

Area
48 cm²   6 cm

10

Area
50 cm²   5 cm

11

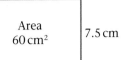

Area
60 cm²   7.5 cm

12

Area
42.7 cm²   3.5 cm

13

Area
27.6 cm²   6.2 cm

14

Area
0.0105 m²   0.21 m

10.4 Area of triangles, parallelograms, trapezia and composite shapes

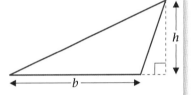

- Area of a triangle
  $= \frac{1}{2} \times$ base $\times$ vertical height
  $A = \frac{1}{2}bh$

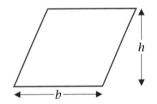

- Area of a parallelogram
  $=$ base $\times$ vertical height
  $A = bh$

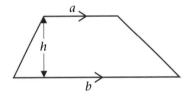

- Area of a trapezium
  $= \frac{1}{2} \times$ sum of parallel sides
  $\times$ vertical height
  $A = \frac{1}{2}(a + b)h$

Example 5

Work out the area
of this trapezium.

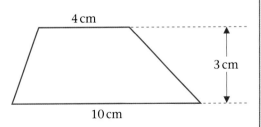

Using the formula
$A = \frac{1}{2}(4 + 10) \times 3 = 21 \text{ cm}^2$

- To find the area of a composite shape, split it into simple shapes and find the area of each separately.

Example 6

Find the area of this shape.

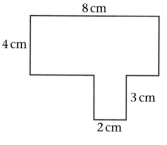

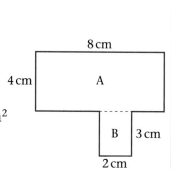

Area of A = 8 × 4 = 32 cm²
Area of B = 2 × 3 = 6 cm²
Total area of shape = 32 + 6 = 38 cm²

Divide the shape into two rectangles A and B.

Exercise 10D

Find the areas of these triangles.

1
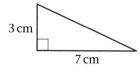

2
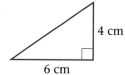

3
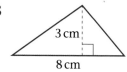

4
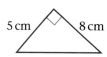

Find the areas of these parallelograms.

5
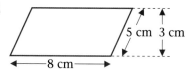

6
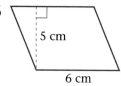

7
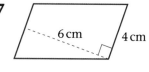

Find the areas of these trapeziums.

8
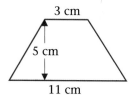

9
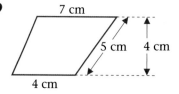

10
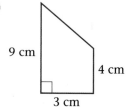

Find the areas of these composite shapes.

11

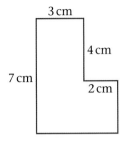

12

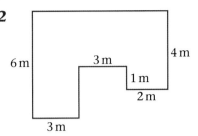

13

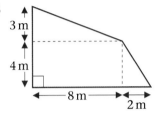

14

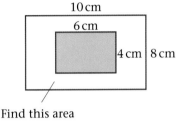

15

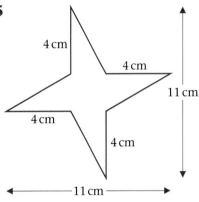

16 Carpet tiles measure 60 cm by 60 cm. They are sold in packs of 10. How many packs are required to cover the floor of a room which measures 4.8 m by 4.2 m?

10.5 Surface area of cuboids

- The **surface area** of a solid shape is the total area of all its faces.

Example 7

Find the surface area of this cuboid.

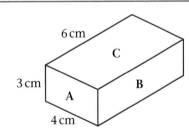

Area of end face   **A** = 3 × 4 = 12 cm²
Area of front face   **B** = 6 × 3 = 18 cm²
Area of top face   **C** = 6 × 4 = 24 cm²
Two ends = 24 cm²
   front and back = 36 cm²
  top and bottom = 48 cm²
Total surface area = 24 + 36 + 48 = 108 cm²

> Opposite faces have the same area.

Exercise 10E

1 Work out the surface area for these cuboids.

	Length	Width	Height	Surface area
(a)	4	7	2	
(b)	16	8	3	
(c)	21	4	5	
(d)	16	3	2	
(e)	10	5	3	

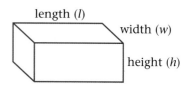

length (*l*)
width (*w*)
height (*h*)

2 A CD case is a cuboid 14 cm long, 12 cm wide and 1 cm high.
Work out its surface area.

3 An MP3 player is a cuboid 9 cm long, 6 cm wide and 2 cm high.
Work out its surface area.

4

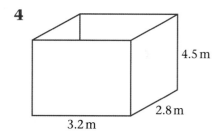

4.5 m
2.8 m
3.2 m

Diagram **NOT**
accurately drawn

The diagram represents a large tank in the shape of a cuboid.
The tank has a base.
It does not have a top.
The width of the tank is 2.8 metres.
The length of the tank is 3.2 metres.
The height of the tank is 4.5 metres.

The outside of the tank is going to be painted.
1 litre of paint will cover 2.5 m² of the tank.
The cost of the paint is £2.99 per litre.

Calculate the cost of the paint needed to paint the
outside of the tank.   [E]

10.6 Volume of cuboids

19 Volume of cuboids

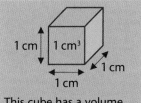

- The **volume** of a 3-D shape is a measure of the amount of space it occupies. Typical units of volume are cubic centimetres (cm^3) and cubic metres (m^3).

This cube has a volume of one cubic centimetre ($1\ cm^3$).

Example 8

Work out the volume of this cuboid. Each small cube is $1\ cm \times 1\ cm \times 1\ cm$.

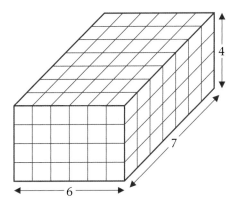

Counting the cubes:

Number of cubes in the bottom layer = $6 \times 7 = 42$

The cuboid has 4 layers, so number of cubes = $4 \times 42 = 168$

Volume = $168\ cm^3$

Volume = $6 \times 7 \times 4$
        = $168\ cm^3$
        = length × width
          × height

- Volume of a cuboid = length × width × height
$$V = lwh$$

- Volume of a cube is $V = l^3$.

Exercise 10F

1 Work out the number of cubes in each of these cuboids.

(a)

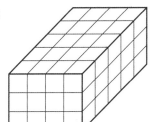

(b)

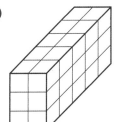

(c)

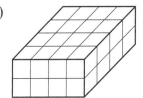

2 Work out the volume of these cuboids.

(a)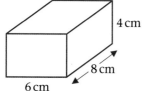

(b)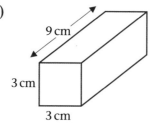

(c)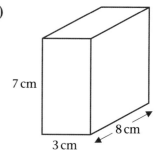

3 Work out the volume of these cuboids.

(a)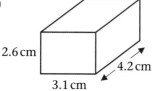

(b)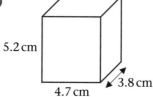

(c)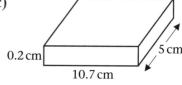

4 A packet of tea has the dimensions shown. What is the volume of the packet?

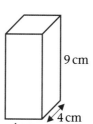

5 Work out the volume of a cube with side 4 cm.

6 A crate has volume 5.25 m³. It is in the shape of a cuboid with length 5 m and width 3.5 m. What is the height of the crate?

7 Copy and complete the table for these cuboids.

	Length	Width	Height	Volume
(a)	2 m	3 m	5 m	
(b)	2 m	4 m		40 m³
(c)		6 m	3 m	72 m³
(d)	5 m		8 m	200 m³
(e)		4 m	5 m	30 m³
(f)	8 m	3 m		60 m³
(g)	50 cm		4 cm	40 cm³
(h)		6 cm	0.5 cm	1.2 cm³

8 Find the volumes of these shapes made from cuboids.

(a)

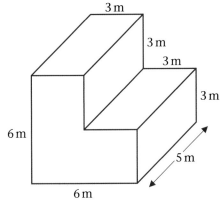

(b)

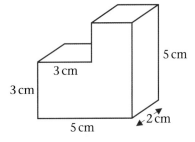

(c)

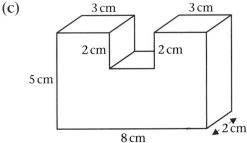

9 (a) Work out the volume of water in a full fish tank which measures 45 cm by 20 cm by 25 cm.

(b) 1 cm³ of water weighs 1 g. What is the weight of the water in the tank?

10 A drink dispenser is in the shape of a cuboid with base 40 cm by 18 cm. Each drink served is 220 m*l*. During the morning the level drops from 23 cm to 12 cm. How many drinks have been served?

1 cm³ of liquid is 1 m*l*.

10.7 Volume of prisms

26 Volume of prisms

- A **prism** is a 3-D shape with the same cross-section all along its length.

- Volume of a prism = area of cross-section × length

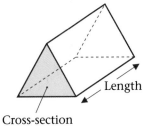

Length

Cross-section

Example 9

Work out the volume of this triangular prism.

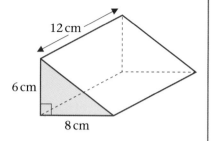

Volume of prism = area of cross-section × length
Area of cross-section = $\frac{1}{2}$ × base × height
$= \frac{1}{2} \times 8 \times 6$
$= 24 \text{ cm}^2$
So volume of prism $= 24 \times 12$
$= 288 \text{ cm}^3$

> Remember: area of triangle = $\frac{1}{2}bh$

Exercise 10G

1 Work out the volumes of these triangular prisms.

(a)

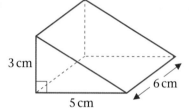

(b)

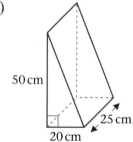

2 Work out the volumes of these prisms.

(a)

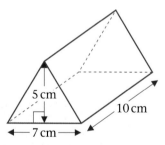

(b)

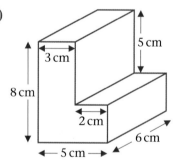

(c)

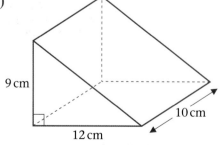

(d)

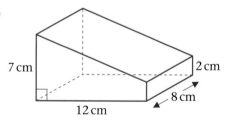

3 The cross-section of a garden shed is shown.
The garden shed is 8 metres long.
Calculate the volume of the shed.

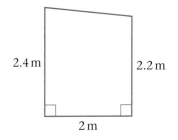

2.4 m   2.2 m

2 m

4 A square fence post is 3.2 m high.
The volume of the post is 32 000 cm³.
Calculate the length of the square side of the post.

Hint: Change the height to cm.

10.8 Fitting boxes into larger boxes

Example 10

The diagram shows a box measuring $30\,\text{cm} \times 50\,\text{cm} \times 20\,\text{cm}$
which is to be filled with packets measuring $5\,\text{cm} \times 4\,\text{cm} \times 10\,\text{cm}$.
How many packets are needed to completely fill the box?

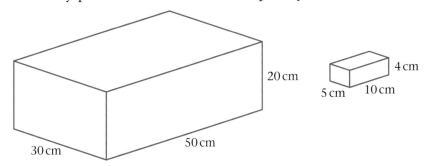

20 cm   4 cm
5 cm   10 cm
50 cm
30 cm

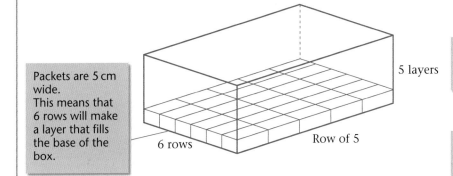

5 layers

Packets are 4 cm high so the box has room for 5 layers.

Packets are 5 cm wide.
This means that 6 rows will make a layer that fills the base of the box.

6 rows   Row of 5

Packets are 10 cm long.
A row of 5 packets will fit the 50 cm length.

$5 \times 6 = 30$ packets form a layer.

There are 5 layers.

Total number of packets to fill the box = $30 \times 5 = 150$

Exercise 10H

1 Work out how many boxes measuring $2\,cm \times 3\,cm \times 5\,cm$ will fit into a container measuring $20\,cm \times 30\,cm \times 50\,cm$.

2 Work out how many matchboxes measuring $1.5\,cm \times 4\,cm \times 6\,cm$ will exactly fill a packet measuring $15\,cm \times 20\,cm \times 30\,cm$.

3 Work out how many cereal packets measuring $9\,cm \times 20\,cm \times 32\,cm$ will fill a container measuring $36\,cm \times 96\,cm \times 1\,m$.

4 The diagrams show a packet and a box. Find out how many packets will completely fill the box.

> The packet may not be facing the best way.

(a)

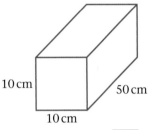

(b)

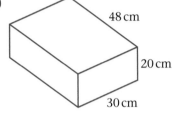

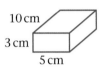

(c)

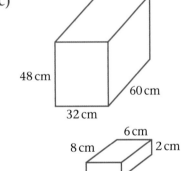

5 A box of matches measures $5\,cm$ by $3\frac{1}{2}\,cm$ by $1\frac{1}{2}\,cm$. How many boxes of matches can be packed into a container which measures $25\,cm$ by $35\,cm$ by $15\,cm$?

> Hint: A row of 5 matchboxes is 25 cm long.

6 A DVD cover measures $19\,cm$ by $13.5\,cm$ by $1.5\,cm$. How many DVDs will fit into a carton which measures $19\,cm$ by $40.5\,cm$ by $4.5\,cm$?

7 A mobile phone is packed in a box which measures $15\,cm$ by $21\,cm$ by $6\,cm$. How many mobile phones can be packed into a carton which measures $75\,cm$ by $42\,cm$ by $60\,cm$?

Mixed exercise 10

1 Work out the perimeter of each shape.

> All corners are right angles.

(a)

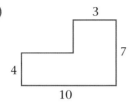

(b)

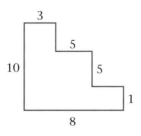

(c)

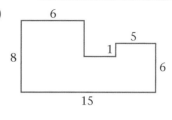

2 Find the area and perimeter of these composite shapes.

(a)

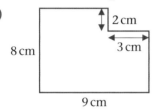

(b)

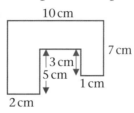

(c)

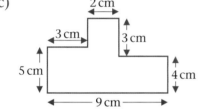

3 Find the area of these shapes.

(a)

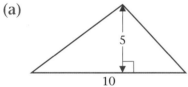

(b)

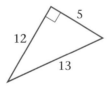

(c)

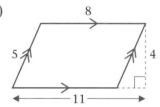

(d)

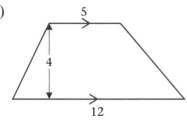

(e)

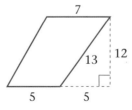

4 Work out the surface area of these cuboids.

(a)

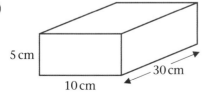

(b)

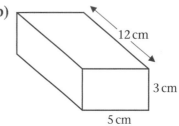

5 A box of counters has length 4 cm, width 3 cm and height 10 cm.
What is the volume of the box?

6 A cuboid-shaped packet has volume 97.5 cm³.
Its length is 5 cm and its width is 3 cm. What is its height?

7 Work out the volume of these prisms.

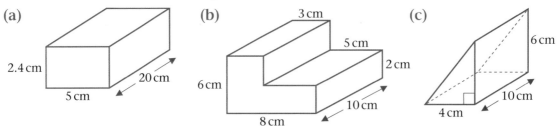

(a) 2.4 cm 20 cm 5 cm

(b) 3 cm 5 cm 2 cm 6 cm 10 cm 8 cm

(c) 6 cm 10 cm 4 cm

8 A mirror measuring 75 cm by 60 cm is made from square
mirror tiles with side 15 cm.
How many tiles are there in this mirror?

9 Kerb stones are 45 cm long and cost £2.20 each.
How much does it cost to put a kerb along each side of a
road 144 metres long?

10 The diagram shows a shape.
Work out the area of the shape.

[E]

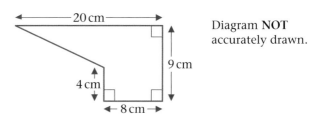

Diagram **NOT**
accurately drawn.

20 cm
9 cm
4 cm
8 cm

11 The diagram shows the dimensions of a box of chocolates.
What is the volume of the box?

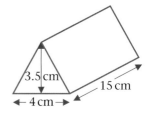

3.5 cm 15 cm 4 cm

12 A cornflake packet measures 7 cm by 23 cm by 29 cm.
How many packets will fit into a carton which measures
58 cm by 46 cm by 63 cm?

13 A packet of pencils measures 14 cm by 5 cm by 1 cm.
What would be a sensible size for a box to contain 144
packets?

14 A box of chocolates measures 3 cm by 18 cm by 12 cm.
How many can be packed into a carton which measures
30 cm by 36 cm by 54 cm?

15 Metric bricks are 20 cm long by 10 cm high.
How many bricks are required to build a wall 6 m long and
1.2 m high?

Summary of key points

1 The **perimeter** of a shape is the distance around the edge of the shape.

2 The **area** of a shape is a measure of the amount of space it covers. Typical units of area are square centimetres (cm^2), square metres (m^2) and square kilometres (km^2).

3 Area of a rectangle = length × width
$$A = lw$$

4 Area of a triangle
$= \frac{1}{2} \times$ base × vertical height
$A = \frac{1}{2}bh$

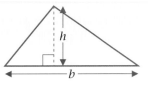 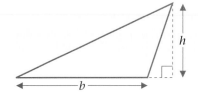

5 Area of a parallelogram
= base × vertical height
$A = bh$

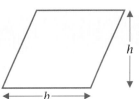

6 Area of a trapezium
$= \frac{1}{2} \times$ sum of parallel sides
  × vertical height
$A = \frac{1}{2}(a + b)h$

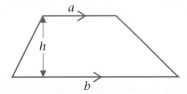

7 To find the area of a composite shape, split it into simple shapes and find the area of each separately.

8 The **surface area** of a solid shape is the total area of all its faces.

9 The **volume** of a 3-D shape is a measure of the amount of space it occupies. Typical units of volume are cubic centimetres (cm^3) and cubic metres (m^3).

10 Volume of a cuboid = length × width × height
$$V = lwh$$

11 Volume of a cube is $V = l^3$.

12 A **prism** is a 3-D shape with the same cross-section all along its length.

13 Volume of a prism = area of cross-section × length

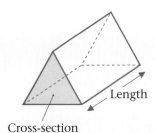

Length

Cross-section

Examination practice paper
Stage 1 (multiple choice)

1 Here is a list of numbers.

    2104   2203   2359   2207   2512

These numbers are written in order, smallest first.
Which one of the numbers would be the 4th in order?

A 2203   **B** 2359   **C** 2104   **D** 2512   **E** 2207

2 Here is a sequence of numbers.

    7, 10, 13, 16, ...

What is the next number in the sequence?

A 17   **B** 18   **C** 19   **D** 20   **E** 21

3 The diagram shows a reading of mass on a scale.

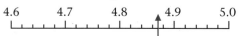

What is the reading indicated by the arrow?

A 4.8 kg   **B** 4.9 kg   **C** 4.83 kg

D 4.87 kg   **E** 4.8 kg

4 The fraction $\frac{15}{20}$ can be written in a simpler form.

Which fraction is equivalent to $\frac{15}{20}$?

A $\frac{3}{5}$ **B** $\frac{3}{4}$ **C** $\frac{5}{4}$ **D** $\frac{10}{15}$ **E** $\frac{3}{10}$

5 This is a series of diagrams made from sticks.

  Diagram   Diagram   Diagram
    1   2   3

How many sticks are needed for diagram 4?

A 18   **B** 19   **C** 20   **D** 21   **E** 22

6 A farmer has 400 eggs for sale.
In one day he sells 282 eggs.
How many eggs has he left?

A 118   **B** 228   **C** 128   **D** 222   **E** 182

7 This is a rectangle on a centimetre grid.

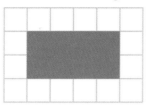

What is the perimeter of the shaded shape?

A 8 cm   **B** 6 cm   **C** 10 cm
D 12 cm   **E** 14 cm

8 Here is a list of temperatures.

4°C   −5°C   2°C   −8°C   6°C

What is the lowest temperature?

A 4°C   **B** −5°C   **C** 2°C   **D** −8°C   **E** 6°C

9 Here are the first 5 terms of a sequence of numbers.

4, 7, 10, 13, 16

What is the 10th term in this sequence?

A 31   **B** 32   **C** 33   **D** 34   **E** 35

10 Which of these angles is a **reflex** angle?

A   B   C   D   E

11 Work out 63.8×3

A 189.24   **B** 19.14   **C** 1914
D 1892.4   **E** 191.4

12 What are the coordinates of point P?

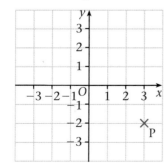

A (3, 2)   **B** (−3, 2)   **C** (3, −2)
D (−2, 3)   **E** (−2, −3)

13

Diagram NOT accurately drawn

What is the size of angle x?

A 225°   B 45°   C 90°   D 35°   E 165°

14 Shelley is working out the answer to $3 \times 4 + 20 \div 2$.
What is the correct answer?

A 22   B 54   C 16   D 52   E 120

15 A single calculator costs £3.95.
How much would is cost to buy 25 of these calculators for a class?

A £27.65   B £276.50   C £987.50

D £95.00   E £98.75

16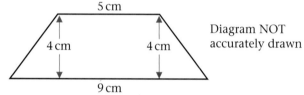

Diagram NOT accurately drawn

Work out the area of this shape.

A 24 cm²   B 28 cm²   C 30 cm²

D 36 cm²   E 40 cm²

17 There are 28 eggs in a box.
Work out the total number of eggs in 128 boxes.

A 1110   B 1280   C 3584   D 1270   E 3900

18 25 notebooks have been bought for a class.
The total cost was £48.
How much does each notebook cost?

A £23.00   B 19p   C 20p

D £12.00   E £1.92

19 The cost of a pencil is 15 pence.
The cost of a pen is 20 pence.
Atiq buys x pencils and y pens.
What expression best describes the total cost?

A $x + y + 15 + 20$ B $20x + 15y$

C $20x15y$ D $15x + 20y$

E $35xy$

20

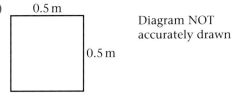

Diagram NOT accurately drawn

The diagram shows the dimensions of a board.
The board is to be covered with plastic tiles.
Each tiles is square, with a side of length 2 cm.
Work out the number of tiles needed to completely cover the board.

   A   6.25   **B**   50   **C**   625

   D   100   **E**   125

21 Given that $23 \times 337 = 7751$
Find the value of $7751 \div 2.3$.

   A   0.337   **B**   3.37   **C**   33.7

   D   0.0377   **E**   3370

22

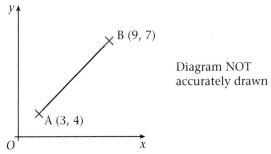

Diagram NOT accurately drawn

Work out the coordinates of the midpoint of the line AB.

   A $(6, 5\frac{1}{2})$ **B** $(6, 5)$ **C** $(6, 6)$

   D $(7, 5\frac{1}{2})$ **E** $(5, 5)$

23

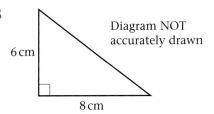

Diagram NOT accurately drawn

Work out the area of the triangle.

   A   48 cm²   **B**   12 cm²   **C**   24 cm²

   D   36 cm²   **E**   20 cm²

24 Here is an arithmetic sequence.

      5, 8, 11, 14, 17

What is an expression for the nth term of this sequence?

A $n + 2$ **B** $2n$ **C** $2n + 3$

D $3n$ **E** $3n + 2$

25 Find the Highest Common Factor (HCF) of 18 and 63.

   A   6   **B**   9   **C**   18   **D**   21   **E**   1134

Practice questions
Stage 1 (multiple choice)

1 Which diagram has been shaded by $\frac{1}{4}$?

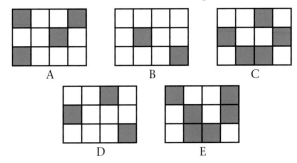

2 Which of these is an equilateral triangle?

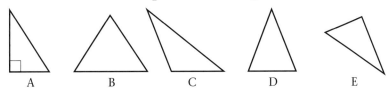

3 This is a series of diagrams made from dots.

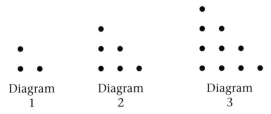

How many dots are needed for diagram 4?

  A   11   **B**   12   **C**   13   **D**   14   **E**   15

4 Here is a list of numbers: 5, 6, 7, 8, 9
Which number is a factor of 12?

  A   5   **B**   6   **C**   7   **D**   8   **E**   9

5 Here is a sequence of numbers: 20, 23, 26, 29, 32
Find the next number in the sequence.

  A   33   **B**   34   **C**   35   **D**   36   **E**   37

6 Sally buys three notepads. Each pad costs 65p.
She has a £5 note.
Work out how much change she should get.

   A £4.35   **B** £3.05   **C** £4.95

   D £3.70   **E** £1.95

7 Which of these shapes is a trapezium?

8 Shirley bought a bag for £8.95 and a brooch for £9.35.
Work out her total bill.

   A £18.50   **B** £18.30   **C** £18.20

   D £17.30   **E** £18 120

9

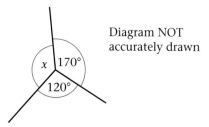

Work out the coordinates of point P.

   A (1, 3)   **B** (3, 3)   **C** (2, 3)

   D (1, 1)   **E** (3, 1)

10 Work out the value of 64.8 ÷ 8

   A 8 r 8   **B** 7.1   **C** 8.1   **D** 8.8   **E** 81

11

Diagram NOT
accurately drawn

x   170°

120°

What is the size of angle x?

   A 10°   **B** 90°   **C** 120°   **D** 80°   **E** 70°

12 Here is a list of numbers: 4, −3, 2, −6, 9
These numbers are written in order, largest first.
Which number will be 4th in order?

A 4   B −3   C 2   D −6   E 9

13 A town has a population of 14 637.
What is the population written to the nearest hundred?

A 15 000   B 14 000   C 600
D 14 600   E 14 500

14 Here are the first 5 terms of a sequence of numbers.

2, 6, 10, 14, 18

What is the 9th term of this sequence?

A 34   B 328   C 30   D 28   E 22

15

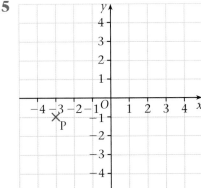

What are the coordinates of point P?

A (−3, −3)   B (−1, −3)   C (−3, −1)
D (−3, 0)   E (−1, −1)

16 What is the value of $10 - 2 \times 4$?

A 2   B 32   C 48   D 36   E 40

17 Here is a list of numbers.

4, 6, 9, 15, 19

Which of these numbers is a prime number?

A 4   B 6   C 9   D 15   E 19

18 Which fraction is equivalent to the decimal 0.479?

A $4\frac{79}{100}$ B $\frac{479}{10}$ C $\frac{479}{100}$ D $\frac{479}{1000}$ E $\frac{479}{10000}$

19 Work out the value of $-5 - 3$

   A -2 **B** -8 **C** $+2$ **D** $+8$ **E** $+3$

20 In a shop a T-shirt costs £5, and a pair of sports socks costs £2.
Jamie buys 9 items for a total of £36.
He buys 6 T-shirts. How many pairs of sports socks did he buy?

   A 1   **B** 2   **C** 3   **D** 4   **E** 5

21 A football costs £T to buy from a shop.
Jojo buys x footballs from the shop.
What expression, in terms of x, best describes the total amount he paid?

   A £T $+ x$ **B** £x **C** £$\frac{x}{T}$ **D** £$\frac{T}{x}$ **E** £Tx

22 Pens are packed into boxes, each containing 32 pens.
How many boxes can be packed from 8192 pens?

   A 270   **B** 272   **C** 256
   D 263   **E** 265

23 A book costs £13.50 to buy. How much would it cost to buy 25 of these books?

   A £337.50   **B** £702.00   **C** £94.50
   D £72.00   **E** £69.12

24 Given that $23 \times 347 = 7981$
find the value of 2.3×34.7

   A 798.1   **B** 79.81   **C** 7.981
   D 0.7981   **E** 0.07981

25 Here is an arithmetic sequence.

     8, 13, 18, 23, 28

Work out an expression, in terms of n, for the nth term of the sequence.

   A $5n - 3$ **B** $5n$ **C** $5n + 3$
   D $n + 3$ **E** $3n$

26

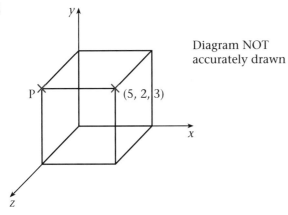

Diagram NOT
accurately drawn

Work out the coordinates of the point P.

A (5, 0, 3)   B (5, 2, 0)   C (5, 2, 3)

D (0, 2, 3)   E (5, 0, 0)

Formulae sheet

Area of trapezium $= \frac{1}{2}(a + b)h$

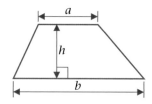

Volume of prism = area of cross-section × length

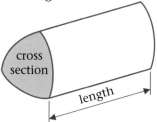

Answers

Exercise 1A

1

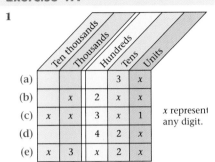

	Ten thousands	Thousands	Hundreds	Tens	Units
(a)				3	x
(b)		x	2	x	x
(c)	x	x	3	x	1
(d)			4	2	x
(e)	x	3	x	2	x

x represent any digit.

2 (a) 500   (b) 50   (c) 50 000
    (d) 5   (e) 5000   (f) 50

Exercise 1B

1 (a) Two hundred and thirty-seven
   (b) Six thousand five hundred and two
   (c) Ten thousand three hundred and two
   (d) Three hundred and twenty-one
   (e) Fifteen

2 (a) 323   (b) 6204   (c) 42
    (d) 16 732   (e) 999

3 (a) 3450, 324, 67, 18
   (b) 2681, 963, 256, 234
   (c) 10 002, 9999, 9460, 6554
   (d) 59 342, 56 762, 56 745, 56 321

4 (a) Seven thousand nine hundred and ninety-five pounds
    Eleven thousand four hundred and ninety-five pounds
    Four thousand eight hundred and thirty-five pounds
    Six thousand five hundred and forty-nine pounds
    Thirteen thousand two hundred and five pounds

   (b)

Sharan	£13 205
Focus	£11 495
Peugeot	£7995
Mini	£6549
Ka	£4835

5 37 992, 39 042, 39 681, 43 621, 43 845

Exercise 1C

1

2 (a) 9:

   (b) 8:

   (c) 18:

(d) 25:

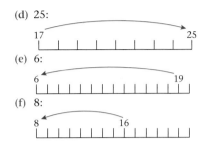

   (e) 6:

   (f) 8:

3 (a) decrease by 4
   (b) increase by 6
   (c) decrease by 7
   (d) increase by 5
   (e) decrease by 8
   (f) increase by 6

Exercise 1D

1 12

2 (a) 100   (b) 100   (c) 100
    (d) 100   (e) 100   (f) 100

3 (a) 16   (b) 39   (c) 36
    (d) 18   (e) 3   (f) 59

4 11   **5** 26
6 11   **7** 151
8 67   **9** £1.13
10 218   **11** 147
12 369   **13** 1437
14 126   **15** 226
16 404

Exercise 1E

1 (a) 48   (b) 8   **2** 95
3 9   **4** 5
5 492   **6** 150
7 23 400   **8** 80
9 27   **10** 424
11 25 m   **12** 208
13 £1958   **14** 12 192

Exercise 1F

1 (a) 12   (b) 2
   (c) 3   (d) 2
   (e) 7   (f) 13
   (g) 9   (h) 8
   (i) 6   (j) 31

2 (a) $7 \times 3 = 21$ (b) $2 \times (3 + 4) = 14$
   (c) $3 \times (5 + 2) = 21$ or $2 + 3 \times 4 = 14$
   (d) $(10 - 4) \div 2 = 3$

Exercise 1G

1 (a) 10   (b) 20   (c) 10   (d) 70
   (e) 80   (f) 110   (g) 300   (h) 1060
   (i) 2010   (j) 3150

2 (a) 200   (b) 600   (c) 100   (d) 900
   (e) 700   (f) 3700   (g) 6000   (h) 9000
   (i) 10 100   (j) 50 400

3 (a) 8000   (b) 6000   (c) 3000
   (d) 4000   (e) 14 000   (f) 16 000
   (g) 157 000   (h) 1000   (i) 1000
   (j) 372 000

4 (a) 10   (b) 30
   (c) 80   (d) 400
   (e) 5000   (f) 190 000
   (g) 364 600   (h) 3000

5 1500

6 48 000

7 50 000

Exercise 1H

1 (a) 1, 2, 3, 6
   (b) 1, 2, 5, 10
   (c) 1, 3, 5, 15
   (d) 1, 17
   (e) 1, 3, 9, 27
   (f) 1, 2, 3, 4, 6, 9, 12, 18, 36
   (g) 1, 2, 3, 5, 6, 9, 10, 15, 18, 30, 45, 90
   (h) 1, 2, 3, 4, 5, 6, 8, 10, 12, 15, 20, 24, 30, 40, 60, 120

2 (a) 1, 2
   (b) 1, 5
   (c) 1, 2, 3, 4, 6, 12
   (d) 1, 3
   (e) 1, 5

3 (a) 3, 6, 9, 12, 15
   (b) 7, 14, 21, 28, 35
   (c) 4, 8, 12, 16, 20
   (d) 10, 20, 30, 40, 50
   (e) 13, 26, 39, 52, 65

4 (a) 1, 4, 6, 12
   (b) 5, 15, 20
   (c) 1, 4, 8, 16
   (d) 6, 9, 12, 15
   (e) 1, 4, 8
   (f) 1, 5

Exercise 1I

1 (a) 1, 2, 3, 4, 6, 8, 12, 16, 24, 48
   (b) 1, 2, 3, 4, 5, 6, 8, 9, 10, 12, 15, 18, 20, 24, 30, 36,
      40, 45, 60, 72, 90, 120, 180, 360
   (c) 1, 29
   (d) 1, 2, 4, 5, 10, 20, 25, 50, 100
   (e) 1, 71
   (f) 1, 3, 5, 15, 43, 129, 215, 645

2 29, 71

3 (a) 5, 10, 15, 20, 25
   (b) 8, 16, 24, 32, 40
   (c) 11, 22, 33, 44, 55
   (d) 20, 40, 60, 80, 100

4 (a) $2 \times 5 \times 5, 2 \times 5^2$
   (b) $2 \times 2 \times 2 \times 3 \times 3, 2^3 \times 3^2$
   (c) $2 \times 3 \times 3 \times 5 \times 5, 2 \times 3^2 \times 5^2$
   (d) $2 \times 2 \times 2 \times 3 \times 5 \times 7, 2^3 \times 3 \times 5 \times 7$

5 (a) 3   (b) 2   (c) 4   (d) 3   (e) 4

6 (a) 24   (b) 35   (c) 12   (d) 12   (e) 30

Exercise 1J

1 (a) 5, −8   (b) 10, −6   (c) 8, −9
   (d) −1, −18   (e) 0, −11

2 (a) 2   (b) −4
   (c) −1   (d) 5
   (e) −1   (f) −8
   (g) 4   (h) −3
   (i) −10   (j) −3

3 (a) −10   (b) −40
   (c) −200   (d) −100
   (e) −220   (f) −250
   (g) −350   (h) −170
   (i) −330   (j) −520

4 (a) Thursday
   (b) Monday
   (c) Tuesday

5 −5 °C

Exercise 1K

1 (a) −7   (b) 4   (c) 10   (d) 9
   (e) −1   (f) 2   (g) −2   (h) −10

2 (a) 24   (b) −15   (c) −8   (d) 3
   (e) −40   (f) −6   (g) −30   (h) 10

3 11 metres

4 −12 °C

5 (a)

	1st number		
×	−2	6	−7
5	−10	30	−35
−3	6	−18	21
8	−16	48	−56

2nd number (rows 5, −3, 8)

(b)

	1st number		
−	2	−3	8
−4	6	1	12
5	−3	−8	3
−1	3	−2	9

2nd number (rows −4, 5, −1)

(c)

	1st number		
+	−3	−4	2
5	2	1	7
1	−2	−3	3
−6	−9	−10	−4

2nd number (rows 5, 1, −6)

(d)

	1st number		
÷	16	−24	−36
−2	−8	12	18
4	4	−6	−9
−8	−2	3	4.5

2nd number (rows −2, 4, −8)

Mixed exercise 1

1 (a) 20   (b) 3   (c) 70
   (d) 700   (e) 9000

2 (a) two hundred and four
     three thousand one hundred and seventy-five
     eight hundred and forty-five
     one thousand and ninety-six
     two thousand and fifty-two

   (b)

Athens	3175 km
Lisbon	2052 km
Hanover	1096 km
Bordeaux	845 km
Brussels	204 km

3 (a)

ans. 9

(b)

7 12   ans. 7

(c)

8 14   ans. 14

(d)

8 20   ans. 8

(e)

9 13   ans. 9

(f)

2 15   ans. 15

4 (a) 10 (b) 14 (c) 52 (d) 9
5 (a) 39 (b) 124 (c) 144 (d) 1056 (e) 160
6 287
7 774 g
8 £14 896
9 119 trips
10 (a) 13 (b) 17 (c) 14 (d) 2 (e) 32
11 (a) 240 (b) 6900 (c) 9800
  (d) 6000 (e) 2000 (f) 6400
12 (a) 6, 9 (b) 7, 14
  (c) 6, 9, 12, 15 (d) 6, 12
  (e) 6, 12 (f) 7
13 (a) $2 \times 2 \times 3 \times 3 \times 5, 2^2 \times 3^2 \times 5$
  (b) $2 \times 2 \times 7 \times 7, 2^2 \times 7^2$
  (c) $2 \times 2 \times 2 \times 3 \times 5 \times 5, 2^3 \times 3 \times 5^2$
14 (a) 6 (b) 6 (c) 3
15 (a) 20 (b) 24 (c) 24
16 (a) 2 (b) −5 (c) 11 (d) 7
  (e) −6 (f) −40 (g) −125 (h) −190
17 (a) −9 (b) 10 (c) 4 (d) 2
18 (a) −16 (b) 2 (c) −2 (d) 35

Exercise 2A

1 (a) $1\frac{1}{4}$ (b) $1\frac{1}{2}$ (c) $1\frac{2}{5}$
  (d) $1\frac{2}{7}$ (e) $1\frac{2}{11}$ (f) $2\frac{1}{2}$
  (g) $2\frac{1}{5}$ (h) $2\frac{3}{5}$ (i) $2\frac{3}{7}$
  (j) $2\frac{4}{8} = 2\frac{1}{2}$ (k) $4\frac{1}{2}$ (l) $3\frac{1}{4}$
  (m) $2\frac{5}{6}$ (n) $4\frac{3}{4}$ (o) $7\frac{2}{3}$
2 (a) $\frac{6}{5}$ (b) $\frac{10}{7}$ (c) $\frac{7}{4}$
  (d) $\frac{3}{2}$ (e) $\frac{13}{10}$ (f) $\frac{14}{5}$
  (g) $\frac{8}{3}$ (h) $\frac{9}{4}$ (i) $\frac{23}{9}$
  (j) $\frac{20}{7}$ (k) $\frac{10}{3}$ (l) $\frac{15}{4}$
  (m) $\frac{42}{10} (= \frac{21}{5})$ (n) $\frac{16}{3}$ (o) $\frac{57}{10}$

Exercise 2B

1 (a) $\frac{3}{4}$ (b) $\frac{4}{5}$ (c) $\frac{2}{3}$ (d) $\frac{5}{7}$ (e) $\frac{2}{3}$

2

$\frac{1}{5}$ $\frac{5}{8}$
$\frac{3}{4}$ $\frac{12}{16}$
$\frac{15}{24}$ $\frac{3}{7}$
$\frac{5}{10}$ $\frac{3}{15}$
$\frac{6}{14}$ $\frac{1}{2}$
$\frac{2}{5}$ $\frac{8}{20}$

3 (a) $\frac{2}{5} = \frac{4}{10} = \frac{8}{20} = \frac{12}{30} = \frac{40}{100}$
  (b) $\frac{1}{6} = \frac{2}{12} = \frac{4}{24} = \frac{5}{30} = \frac{8}{48}$
  (c) $\frac{3}{8} = \frac{18}{48} = \frac{12}{32} = \frac{9}{24}$
4 (a) $\frac{8}{10}, \frac{12}{15}$ etc.
  (b) $\frac{3}{4}, \frac{6}{8}$ etc.
  (c) $\frac{4}{6}, \frac{2}{3}$ etc.
  (d) $\frac{2}{18}, \frac{3}{27}$ etc.

Exercise 2C

1 (a) $\frac{1}{4}$ (b) $\frac{2}{3}$ (c) $\frac{11}{15}$ (d) $\frac{6}{7}$
2 $\frac{1}{4}, \frac{3}{10}, \frac{2}{5}, \frac{1}{2}$
3 Keith
4 (a) section 2
  (b) section 4
5 $\frac{7}{8}, \frac{13}{16}, \frac{2}{3}, \frac{1}{4}$

Exercise 2D

1

	Tens	Units	.	Tenths	Hundredths	Thousandths
(a)		5	.	8	2	
(b)		7	.	8	0	1
(c)	1	9	.	1		
(d)	2	0	.	0	2	
(e)	1	3	.	3	8	1
(f)		0	.	7	6	
(g)		0	.	5		
(h)		0	.	0	0	1

2 (a) 3 tenths (b) 2 thousandths
  (c) 7 tenths (d) 1 thousandth
  (e) 1 unit (f) 9 tenths
  (g) 1 thousandth (h) 2 thousandths
  (i) 1 ten (j) 8 tenths
3 (a) 6 hundredths (b) 6 tenths
  (c) 6 units (d) 6 tens
  (e) 6 thousandths

Exercise 2E

1 (a) 3.68, 2.1, 0.20, 0.03 (b) 0.76, 0.75, 0.07, 0.001
  (c) 9.08, 9.009, 0.98, 0.09 (d) 6.01, 1.06, 0.61, 0.016
  (e) 9.0, 0.9, 0.09, 0.009 (f) 30.0, 0.303, 0.30, 0.03

2

Ben	10.87 s
Ameet	10.93 s
Alex	10.96 s
Jack	11.02 s
Tom	11.13 s

3

Niacin	0.89 mg
Pantothenic acid	0.30 mg
B6	0.10 mg
B2	0.08 mg

4 2.15 m, 2.10 m, 2.06 m, 1.96 m, 1.92 m

Exercise 2F

1. (a) 7.9   (b) 5.2
   (c) 5.27   (d) 0.81
   (e) 2.78   (f) 7.64
   (g) 33.59   (h) 23.33
   (i) 5.811   (j) 21.32
2. (a) 4.2   (b) 3.2
   (c) 17.5   (d) 7.43
   (e) 3.86   (f) 2.54
   (g) 13.59   (h) 13.81
   (i) 5.38   (j) 0.324
3. 2.575 kg
4. 6.35 kg
5. 40.3 seconds
6. No, they need a length of 4.13 m.
7. Yes, the total weight is 19.9 kg.

Exercise 2G

1. (a) 21   (b) 10
   (c) 23   (d) 1.7
   (e) 280   (f) 31
   (g) 460   (h) 360
   (i) 314   (j) 3140
2. (a) 2.81   (b) 0.369
   (c) 0.689   (d) 0.1231
   (e) 0.231   (f) 0.023
   (g) 0.013   (h) 0.314
   (i) 0.0314   (j) 0.000 02
3. (a) 21   (b) 0.62
   (c) 162   (d) 0.0389
   (e) 30   (f) 0.002 38
   (g) 35   (h) 0.0002
4. (a) 33.2   (b) 15
   (c) 55.5   (d) 12.44
   (e) 18.48   (f) 9.1
   (g) 7.1   (h) 13.1
   (i) 0.81   (j) 1.01

Exercise 2H

1. (a) £43.60   (b) £40.95   (c) £61.36
   (d) £1.61   (e) £54.46
2. (a) 0.28   (b) 0.48   (c) 4.48
   (d) 56.95   (e) 40.95   (f) 2.46
3. (a) 1.5   (b) 0.42
   (c) 0.468   (d) 0.3303
   (e) 7.62   (f) 4.716
   (g) 59.94   (h) 0.227 84
4. (a) 2.6   (b) 52.3
   (c) 7.125   (d) 17.6
   (e) 2.95   (f) 23.44
   (g) 7.3125   (h) 20.375
5. 4.68 m
6. 3 kg
7. 5 glasses
8. 146.2 km
9. 18 stamps

Exercise 2I

1. (a) 0.2   (b) 0.6
   (c) 0.625   (d) 0.45
   (e) 0.75   (f) $0.\dot{3}$
   (g) $0.\dot{4}$ (h) $0.58\dot{3}$
   (i) $0.31\dot{8}$ (j) $0.\dot{2}5\dot{9}$
2. (a) $\frac{7}{10}$ (b) $\frac{1}{2}$ (c) $\frac{3}{25}$ (d) $\frac{13}{20}$
   (e) $\frac{5}{6}$ (f) $\frac{181}{500}$ (g) $\frac{137}{1000}$ (h) $\frac{137}{200}$

3. (a) exact
   (b) recurring
   (c) exact
   (d) recurring
   (e) recurring

Exercise 2J

1. (a) 30   (b) 330   (c) 500   (d) 2800
   (e) 3000   (f) 5000   (g) 5820   (h) 500
2. (a) 300   (b) 5000   (c) 300   (d) 40
   (e) 5000   (f) 70 000   (g) 30   (h) 30 000
3. (a) 5   (b) 2   (c) 8   (d) 7
   (e) 9   (f) 10   (g) 2   (h) 3
4. (a) 0.3   (b) 0.7   (c) 0.08   (d) 0.06
   (e) 0.003   (f) 0.003   (g) 0.08   (h) 1
5. 1000
6. 30 000
7. £20 000

Exercise 2K

1. (a) (i) 400×40 (ii) 16 000
   (b) (i) $1000 \div 40$ (ii) 25
   (c) (i) $\dfrac{800 \times 5000}{3000}$ (ii) $1333\frac{1}{3}$
   (d) (i) 600×3 (ii) 1800
   (e) (i) $400 \div 5$ (ii) 80
   (f) (i) 7×2 (ii) 14
   (g) (i) $9 \div 2$ (ii) 4.5
   (h) (i) $\dfrac{4 \times 5}{10}$ (ii) 2
   (i) (i) $\dfrac{2 \times 8}{4 \times 2}$ (ii) 2
2. (a) (i) 15 709   (ii) $700 \times 20 = 14\,000$
   (b) (i) 126.9   (ii) $50 \times 3 = 150$
   (c) (i) 29.14   (ii) $3 \times 9 = 27$
   (d) (i) 11   (ii) $400 \div 40 = 10$
   (e) (i) 39   (ii) $300 \div 9 = 33\frac{1}{3}$
   (f) (i) 3   (ii) $10 \div 3 = 3\frac{1}{3}$
   (g) (i) 7.76 (3 s.f.)   (ii) $\dfrac{900 \div 20}{5} = 9$
   (h) (i) 0.362 (3.s.f.)   (ii) $\dfrac{3 \times 3}{20} = 0.45$

Exercise 2L

1. £13.09
2. 12 books
3. 9 egg boxes
4. £6.66
5. £7.80
6. 42 g
7. It is not possible to measure 9.549 cm; 9.5 cm is more sensible.
8. Shoe sizes are only in whole or half sizes.
9. 16 cars
10. He cannot be paid exactly £38.933 333 (£38.93 is more sensible).

Exercise 2M

1. 4 went swimming, 2 played squash
2. 5 ballpoint pens and 2 gel pens
3. 2 wins, 1 draw and 1 defeat
4. 96 days
5. 4 tea and 4 coffee

Exercise 2N

1 (a) 24%   (b) 19%
  (c) 57%   (d) $\frac{24}{100}, \frac{19}{100}, \frac{57}{100}$

2 (a) 63%   (b) 3%
  (c) 16% $\frac{16}{100} \left(= \frac{4}{25}\right)$

3 (a) 82%   (b) 8%
  (c) 9%   (d) $\frac{82}{100}, \frac{8}{100}, \frac{9}{100}$

4 See illustration (a) (b) below.
  (c) 62%

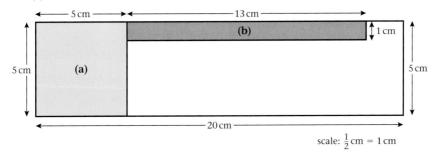

scale: $\frac{1}{2}$ cm = 1 cm

Exercise 2O

1 (a)

Team	Percentage won
Greenfield FC	40%
Millbrook Utd	60%
Carrbrook Town	45%

  (b) Millbrook Utd

2 (a) 30%, 26%, 29%
  (b) Packet 2
  (c) Packet 2

Exercise 2P

1 (a) 3   (b) 3
  (c) 10.5   (d) 9
  (e) 36   (f) 20 pence or £0.20
  (g) £1.35   (h) £2.40
  (i) £18   (j) £130.50

2 45 marks
3 13 passengers
4 43 games
5 (a) £16   (b) £64
6 £30.60

Mixed exercise 2

1 (a) $1\frac{1}{8}$ (b) $1\frac{2}{3}$
  (c) $3\frac{1}{3}$ (d) $3\frac{1}{8}$

2 (a) $\frac{5}{4}$ (b) $\frac{5}{3}$
  (c) $\frac{12}{5}$ (d) $\frac{26}{7}$

3 (a) $\frac{3}{4}$ (b) $\frac{3}{5}$
  (c) $\frac{8}{9}$ (d) $\frac{4}{5}$

4 (a) $\frac{3}{4} = \frac{\mathbf{9}}{12}$ (b) $\frac{5}{8} = \frac{\mathbf{10}}{16}$
  (c) $\frac{\mathbf{3}}{4} = \frac{24}{32}$ (d) $\frac{\mathbf{2}}{7} = \frac{6}{21}$
  (e) $\frac{3}{\mathbf{5}} = \frac{12}{20}$ (f) $\frac{3}{8} = \frac{\mathbf{15}}{40}$

5 (a) eat at the desk
  (b) eat no lunch

6 $\frac{3}{10}, \frac{1}{3}, \frac{3}{5}, \frac{5}{6}$

7 (a) 8 hundredths
  (b) 1 thousandth
  (c) 3 hundredths
  (d) 6 tenths

8 0.087, 0.8, 0.87, 0.878, 8.078

9 (a) 9.26   (b) 5.53
  (c) 7.13   (d) 1.06
  (e) 34.25   (f) 7.02
  (g) 16.48   (h) 7.07

10 (a) 63   (b) 0.09
  (c) 3200   (d) 1791
  (e) 0.11   (f) 0.002 36

11 (a) 14.4   (b) 39.3
  (c) 12.1   (d) 5.3
  (e) 11.2   (f) 0.61

12 (a) 3.13   (b) 43.8   (c) 0.0256
  (d) 20   (e) 0.0056   (f) 2130

13 (a) 37.5 kg   (b) 0.0068 kg, 68 g

14 (a) 4.264   (b) 4.4
  (c) 83.46   (d) 3.6

15 15 servings
16 £96.25

17 (a) 0.8   (b) 0.875   (c) $0.\dot{5}$

18 (a) $\frac{4}{25}$ (b) $\frac{3}{5}$ (c) $\frac{97}{200}$

19 5 packs
20 It is not possible to measure 6.6666 cm; 6.7 cm is more sensible.

21 (a) 30   (b) 50   (c) 200
  (d) 6000   (e) 4   (f) 0.02

22 20 000 people

23 (a) (i) 400 × 50   (ii) 20 000
  (b) (i) $\frac{200 \div 40}{5}$ (ii) 1
  (c) (i) $\frac{4 \times 8}{8 \div 2}$ (ii) 8

24 (a) (i) 16 436   (ii) 18 000
  (b) (i) 24.96   (ii) 24
  (c) (i) 4.82 (3 s.f.)   (ii) 4
  (d) (i) 78.8 (3 s.f.)   (ii) 80

25 £4.56
26 4 biscuits and 1 cake
27 (a) 35%   (b) 23%

28

(c) 42%

29 Biology: 65%
Chemistry: 62%
Physics: 64%
She did best in Biology.

30 (a) 3   (b) 9   (c) 9
    (d) £1.50   (e) £3   (f) £1.80

31 12 g

32 1248

33 £68

Exercise 3A

1 1, 4, 9, 16, 25

2 1, 8, 27, 64, 125

3 (a) 4.41   (b) 35.937
    (c) ±2.4   (d) 3.5
    (e) 196   (f) 1000
    (g) 31   (h) 4913
    (i) 4   (j) 23 104
    (k) ±25   (l) −6
    (m) 225   (n) 453.69
    (o) ±0.6   (p) −0.9
    (q) 1   (r) 1
    (s) −1   (t) −1

Exercise 3B

1 (a) 9   (b) 64   (c) 49   (d) 64
    (e) 100   (f) 4   (g) 36   (h) 27
    (i) 1000   (j) 16   (k) 125   (l) 144
    (m) 169   (n) 8   (o) 25   (p) 81
    (q) 121   (r) 196   (s) 225

2 (a) ±8   (b) ±3   (c) ±5   (d) ±12
    (e) ±13   (f) ±15   (g) ±2   (h) ±10
    (i) ±6   (j) ±11   (k) ±7   (l) ±9
    (m) ±4   (n) ±14

3 (a) ±7   (b) ±6   (c) ±11   (d) ±5

Exercise 3C

1 (a) 32   (b) 256   (c) 1
    (d) 10 000   (e) 625   (f) 7776

2 (a) 2^4 (b) 4^5 (c) 1^6
    (d) 8^3 (e) 6^2 (f) 7^4
    (g) $3^2 \times 8^4$ (h) $2^3 \times 4^4$

3 (a) 16   (b) 243   (c) 216   (d) 25
    (e) 512   (f) 11 664   (g) 65 536   (h) 10 125
    (i) 31 104   (j) 256

4

Power of 10	Index	Value	Value in words
10^3	3	1000	A thousand
10^2	2	100	A hundred
10^6	6	1 000 000	A million
10^1	1	10	Ten
10^5	5	100 000	A hundred thousand

5 (a) 6400   (b) 400   (c) 6000
    (d) 4   (e) 125   (f) 16

6 (a) $x = 3$ (b) $x = 4$ (c) $x = 6$ (d) $x = 4$
    (e) $x = 2$ (f) $x = 3$ (g) $x = 4$ (h) $x = 2$

Exercise 3D

1 (a) 33   (b) 4
    (c) 24   (d) 16
    (e) 2.7   (f) 81
    (g) ±3   (h) 16
    (i) ±1   (j) ±6
    (k) 77   (l) 11

2 (a) $3 \times (4 + 5) = 27$
    (b) $(2 + 3) \times (2 + 3) = 25$
    (c) $(6 − 7) \div (8 − 9) = 1$
    (d) $10 + 9 + 8 + 7 = 34$
    (e) $(3 − 3) \times 3 = 0$
    (f) $3 − (3 \div 3) = 2$

Exercise 3E

1 (a) 8   (b) 0.6   (c) 5

2 (a) 22.09   (b) 9.261
    (c) 1055.6001   (d) 2.985 984
    (e) 2.5   (f) 2.3

3 (a) ±3.6   (b) ±2.5
    (c) ±17.986   (d) ±26.042 (3 d.p.)
    (e) ±8.875 (3 d.p.)

4 (a) 11.014 (3 d.p)   (b) ±2.2
    (c) ±5.707 (3 d.p.)   (d) ±0.970 (3 d.p.)

5 (a) 0.05   (b) ±0.2
    (c) 12.5   (d) ±3.333 (3 d.p.)

Exercise 3F

1 8^6 **2** 3^6 **3** 2^9 **4** 5^3
5 3^2 **6** 7^2 **7** 8^2 **8** 10^3
9 8^9 **10** 2^9 **11** 4^4 **12** 6^2
13 2^{-1} **14** 4^{10} **15** 9   **16** 1
17 x^7 **18** y^2 **19** a^3 **20** z

Exercise 3G

1 (a) 8×10^2 (b) 7×10^3 (c) 9×10^4
    (d) 8.72×10^2 (e) 9.2×10^3 (f) 8.7×10^3
    (g) 9.84×10^4 (h) 8.34×10^5 (i) 1.2×10^6

2 (a) 300   (b) 50 000   (c) 8 000 000
    (d) 25 000   (e) 3 800 000   (f) 23 600
    (g) 4 780 000   (h) 294 000   (i) 38 400 000

3 (a) 8×10^{-1} (b) 7.2×10^{-1} (c) 4×10^{-2}
    (d) 2×10^{-2} (e) 5.3×10^{-3} (f) 8.9×10^{-3}
    (g) 3.2×10^{-3} (h) 4.85×10^{-2} (i) 4.1×10^{-5}

4 (a) 0.2   (b) 0.03
    (c) 0.000 5   (d) 0.021
    (e) 0.000 034   (f) 0.000 58
    (g) 0.000 002 38   (h) 0.000 000 043 9
    (i) 0.000 000 026 1

5 (a) 7.8×10^5 (b) 3.6×10^{-2}
    (c) 9.8×10^{10} (d) 5.7×10^{-6}

6 (a) 1.15×10^5 (b) 9.4×10^{-3}
    (c) 1.53×10^7 (d) 3.28×10^{-3}

Mixed exercise 3

1 (a) 6^3 (b) 11^2 (c) 2^6

2 (a) 625   (b) 128
    (c) 1000   (d) 100 000

3 (a) 144   (b) 784
    (c) 400   (d) 30 000

4 (a) 3.351 (3 d.p.)
(b) ±10.153 (3 d.p.)
(c) ±3.818 (3 d.p.)
(d) ±1.429 (3 d.p.

5 (a) 16 (b) 144
(c) 64 (d) 169
(e) ±7 (f) ±14
(g) ±15 (h) 64
(i) 125 (j) 1000

6 (a) $2^2 \times 3^3$ (b) $5^2 \times 7^2$
(c) $4^2 \times 8^4$ (d) $2^3 \times 6^3$

7 (a) 512 (b) 10 000 (c) 125
(d) 144 (e) 800

8 (a) $x = 4$ (b) $x = 5$ (c) $x = 3$

9 (a) 25 (b) 100
(c) 64 (d) 4
(e) ±6 (f) 8
(g) 39.69 (h) 13.824
(i) 2.4 (d) −2

10 (a) 32 (b) 5
(c) 7 (d) 2

12 (a) 2^7 (b) 5^5
(c) 3^5 (d) 7^3
(e) 9^4 (f) 8^2
(g) 7^3 (h) 6

13 (a) 3×10^3 (b) 5.8×10^3
(c) 7.89×10^5 (d) 8.63×10^4
(e) 5×10^{-1} (f) 6.1×10^{-2}
(g) 2.1×10^{-4} (h) 3.81×10^{-4}

14 (a) 20 000 (b) 2300
(c) 384 000 (d) 89 700 000
(e) 0.0003 (f) 0.000 002 1
(g) 0.007 92 (h) 0.0826

14 (a) 5.6×10^{-2} (b) 3.9×10^7

15 (a) 8.04×10^4 (b) 1.528×10^{-4}

Exercise 4A

1
A	(4, 2)	F	(9, 8)
B	(7, 3)	G	(5, 0)
C	(7, 6)	H	(4, 8)
D	(0, 7)	I	(1, 2)
E	(3, 5)	J	(10, 1)

2
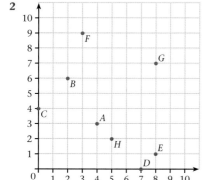

Exercise 4B

1
A	(−2, 3)	F	(6, 2)
B	(5, −1)	G	(−6, 4)
C	(−5, 0)	H	(−5, −3)
D	(−2, −2)	I	(−3, −4)
E	(0, −4)	J	(3, −2)

2
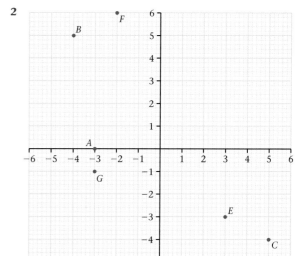

Exercise 4C

1 For example

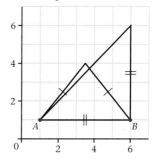

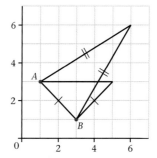

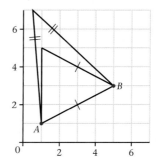

2

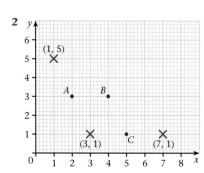

(3, 1), (7, 1) or (1, 5)

3

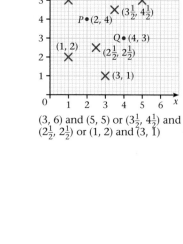

(3, 6) and (5, 5) or $(3\frac{1}{2}, 4\frac{1}{2})$ and $(2\frac{1}{2}, 2\frac{1}{2})$ or (1, 2) and (3, 1)

4

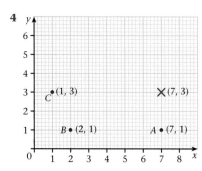

(7, 3) is one example of D that will make a trapezium

5

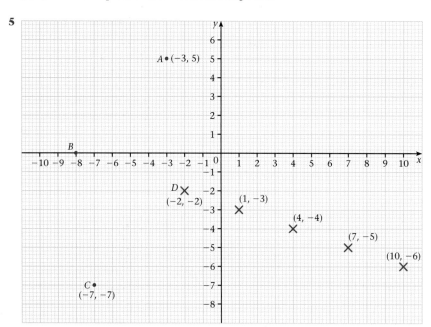

(a) $D(-2, -2)$

(b) For a kite the points could be:
$(1, -3)(4, -4)(7, -5)(10, -6)$

Exercise 4D

1 (a) (i) (7, 1)   (ii) (0, 3)   (iii) (7,5)
  (b) (14, 3)
  (c) (i) (7, 3)   (ii) (10.5, 4)

2

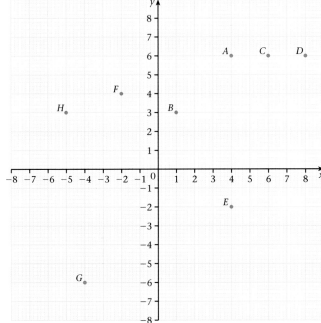

Mid-points of *AC* (5, 6), *AE*(4, 2), *EF*(1, 1),
FH(−3.5, 3.5), *EG*(0, −4), *EH*(−0.5, 0.5), *BH*(−2, 3)

3 (a) (−0.5, 0.5)   (b) (0.5, −0.5)
4 (8, 11)

Exercise 4E

1

Two-dimensional	Three-dimensional
pentagon	pyramid
hexagon	cylinder
triangle	cone
trapezium	cuboid
rectangle	sphere
square	
circle	

2 (1, 4, 2), (2, 3, 4), (4, 5, 0), (6, 0, 7), (−3, 0, 0)

3 (0, 0, 0), (0, 2, 0), (4, 2, 0), (4, 0, 0), (0, 0, 7), (4, 0, 7),
    (4, 2, 7), (0, 2, 7)

Exercise 4F

1 (a) *x* − 6   (b) *y* + 4   (c) 3*a*
    (d) *c* + 7   (e) 8*p*   (f) *q* − 2
    (g) 9 + *t*   (h) 5 − *n*   (i) 2*p*
    (j) *d* + *c*   (k) *n* − *m*   (l) *pq*
    (m) $\frac{a}{3}$ (n) $\frac{b}{4}$ (o) $\frac{x}{y}$

2 *m* + *w*   **3** 20 − *n*
4 £8*c*   **5** *xy*
6 *y* − 3   **7** 7*w*
8 10 − *s*   **9** *cn*

Exercise 4G

1 3*d*   **2** 5*q*
3 3*n*   **4** 10*a*
5 6*c*   **6** 6*d*
7 4*e*   **8** 12*c*

9 5*t*   **10** *x*
11 3*h*   **12** 7*a* + 9*b*
13 6*p* + 8*q*   **14** 5*x* + 4*y*
15 4*t* + 9   **16** 6*m* + 9*n*
17 3*c* + 3*d*   **18** 9*p* + *q*
19 8*x*   **20** 2*a* + 3*b* + 5*c*
21 8*d* − 3*e*   **22** 2*y* − 3
23 9*a* − 2*b*   **24** 8*c* − *d*
25 3*p* − 6*q*   **26** 8 − *x*
27 4*n* − m   **28** 7*x* − 2*y*
29 *d*   **30** 6 − 4*t*
31 4*d*   **32** 2*a* + 2*b*
33 9*d* + 2   **34** 4*t*
35 2*h*

Exercise 4H

1 2*c*   **2** *tu*
3 8*d*   **4** 7*fg*
5 5*xy*   **6** *abc*
7 *pqr*   **8** 3*cde*
9 20*xy*   **10** 21*fg*
11 6*pq*   **12** 24*d*
13 20*y*   **14** 2*mn*
15 7*pq*   **16** 24*stu*
17 60*abc*   **18** 24*def*
19 12*xyz*   **20** 40*bcd*

Exercise 4I

1 42   **2** 27
3 18   **4** 6
5 2   **6** 6
7 10   **8** 10
9 0   **10** 6
11 6   **12** 10
13 2   **14** 1
15 1   **16** 21
17 11   **18** 5
19 24   **20** 13

21 1
22 $(8 - 5) \times 6 = 18$
23 $7 - (5 - 1) = 3$
24 $3 \times (5 + 3) \times 2 = 48$
25 $5 - 2 = 3$
26 $6 \times 3 = 18$
27 $3 + 2 - 4 = 1$
28 $(5 - 2) \times 7 = 21$
29 $5 \times 2 + 7 = 17$
30 $5 + 2 \times 7 = 19$

Exercise 4J

1 $6c + 6d$
2 $5p - 5q$
3 $2x + 6$
4 $4y - 8$
5 $21a + 14$
6 $24p - 30$
7 $10c + 15d$
8 $24p - 32q$
9 $ab + 2a$
10 $cd - 2c$
11 $xy + xz$
12 $pq - pr$
13 $mn - m$
14 $10 - 2x$
15 $10fg + 2fh$
16 $3pq - 12pr$
17 $20xy + 12xz$
18 $30bc - 25b$
19 $21de + 7d$
20 $24ab - 16ac$

Exercise 4K

1 $5x + 14$
2 $20x + 17$
3 $23x + 14$
4 $-8x + 12$ or $12 - 8x$
5 $9 - 21x$
6 $15 - 23x$
7 $12x - 22y$
8 $22y - 2x$
9 $-4x - 21y$
10 $x + 4y$
11 $7y + 2$
12 27
13 $x - 3$
14 $7y - 16x + 6$
15 $21x - 19y$
16 $21y - 27x$
17 $10x - 7y$
18 $20x - 32y$
19 $8xy + 3x$
20 $8xy + 2x + y$
21 $6x - 4y - 3xy$
22 $10xy - 20x^2 - 6y^2$

Exercise 4L

1 $3(x + 4)$
2 $7(x - 3)$
3 $5(3x + 4)$
4 $3(3x - 4)$
5 $2(2x + 3)$
6 $3(3x - 5)$
7 $6(2x + 3)$
8 $7(3 + 4x)$
9 $7(2 + 3y)$
10 $5(7x - 3)$
11 $3(2x - y)$
12 $7(2x + y)$
13 $5(2x - y)$
14 $5(5a + 3b)$
15 $3(a - 3b)$
16 $17(p + 3q)$
17 $9(4c - d)$
18 $8(3s + 2t)$
19 $x(x + 6y)$
20 $x(2x - 3y)$
21 $y(4x + y)$
22 $a(5b - a)$
23 $b(6c + b)$
24 $b(4b + 5c)$
25 $b(3a - 5c)$
26 $2x(x + 3y)$
27 $3x(x - 3y)$
28 $4p(2p + q)$
29 $7x(2x + 3y)$
30 $5b(2a - 3c)$
31 $2a(2a - 3bc)$
32 $2x^2(x + 2y)$

Exercise 4M

1 (a) $a^2 + 9a + 18$
  (b) $b^2 + 6b + 5$
  (c) $c^2 + 10c + 16$
  (d) $d^2 + 7d + 12$
  (e) $e^2 + 13e + 36$
  (f) $f^2 + 12f + 35$
2 (a) $ab + 5a + 4b + 20$
  (b) $cd - 2c + 6d - 12$
  (c) $pq - 4p - q + 4$
  (d) $xy + 3x - 8y - 24$
  (e) $at - a - 9t + 9$
  (f) $bc - 7b + 3c - 21$
3 (a) $a^2 + 3a - 4$
  (b) $b^2 - 3b - 18$
  (c) $c^2 - 9c + 14$
  (d) $d^2 - 16$
  (e) $e^2 - 12e + 27$
  (f) $f^2 + 2f - 24$
  (g) $g^2 - 3g - 40$
  (h) $x^2 - 36$
  (i) $y^2 + 7y - 18$
4 (a) $3a^2 - 5a - 2$
  (b) $6b^2 - 7b - 20$
  (c) $8c^2 - 34c + 21$
  (d) $2cd + 4c - 3d - 6$

(e) $10e^2 - 51e + 27$
(f) $10ef - 15e + 8f - 12$
(g) $9g^2 - 25$
(h) $12x^2 + 35x + 8$
(i) $16y^2 - 81$
(j) $6a^2 - ab - 2b^2$
(k) $8ac - 20ad + 6bc - 15bd$
(l) $14x^2 - 41xy + 15y^2$
(m) $49p^2 - 4q^2$
5 (a) $a^2 + 10a + 25$
  (b) $b^2 - 2b + 1$
  (c) $c^2 + 16c + 64$
  (d) $d^2 - 14d + 49$
  (e) $4e^2 + 12e + 9$
  (f) $9f^2 - 24f + 16$
  (g) $25g^2 + 10g + 1$
  (h) $49h^2 - 28h + 4$
  (i) $a^2 + 2ab + b^2$
  (j) $9x^2 - 6xy + y^2$
  (k) $9m^2 + 30mn + 25n^2$
  (l) $16p^2 - 56pq + 49q^2$
6 (a) $a^2 + 4a + 2$
  (b) $4b^2 + 6b - 5$
  (c) $2c^2 - 6c - 2$
  (d) $2d^2 + 2d + 25$
  (e) $30e + 25$
  (f) $8f$

Exercise 4N

1 $4pq$
2 $8x^2$
3 $2p$
4 $\frac{5}{3}b$
5 $2b$
6 $3c$
7 $\frac{3}{2}pr$
8 $2y$
9 $\frac{1}{3}bc$
10 $\frac{3}{4}x$

Mixed exercise 4

1 (a)

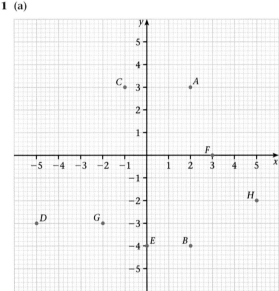

(b) Mid-points of $BE(1, -4)$, $AG(0, 0)$, $AC(0.5, 3)$,
  $DG(-3.5, -3)$, $EH(2.5, -3)$, $CD(-3, 0)$,
  $GH(1.5, -2.5)$, $CE(-0.5, -0.5)$
2 $(5, 1)$, $(7, 5)$ or $(-3, 7)$
3 $(2, 7)$ and $(0, 1)$
4 (a) 1-D
  (b) 2-D
  (c) 2-D
  (d) 1-D
  (e) 3-D
  (f) 2-D
  (g) 3-D
  (h) 3-D
  (i) 1-D
  (j) 2-D
5 $2a + b$
6 (a) $3d$
  (b) mn
  (c) $9de$
  (d) bcd
  (e) $3ab$
  (f) $12pq$
  (g) $10mn$
  (h) $24abc$
7 (a) $5x - 4y$
  (b) $8p - 5q$
  (c) $10s + 2t$
  (d) $-c - 7d$

(e) $5ab$
(f) $3cd$
(g) $5pq$
(h) $a^2 + 4a$
(i) $5b^2 + b$
(j) $5a + 3ab + 4b$
(k) $-x + 5xy$
8 (a) $3p + 3q$
(b) $6a - 6b$
(c) $y^2 + 4y$
(d) $c^2 - c$
(e) $2ax + 3ay$
(f) $5an - 4bn$
(g) $2y^2 - 5y$
(h) $6c^2 + c$
(i) $ap - bp$
9 (a) $9ab - 6a^2 - 4b^2$
(b) $11pq + 18p^2$
(c) $13c^2 + 12cd$
(d) $a^2 + 2ab + b^2$
(e) $5ab + ac - bc$
(f) $-4ab - 4ac - 9bc$
10 (a) $a^2 + 8a + 15$
(b) $b^2 + 2b - 8$
(c) $c^2 - 11c + 30$
(d) $d^2 - 25$
(e) $f^2 + 6f + 9$
(f) $64g^2 - 1$
(g) $9h^2 + 24h + 16$
(h) $24j^2 + 7j - 6$
(i) $12k^2 + 44k + 35$
(j) $12m^2 - 17mn - 5n^2$
(k) $9p^2 - 16q^2$
(l) $25t^2 - 40tu + 16u^2$
11 (a) $5(x + 3y)$
(b) $3(5p - 3q)$
(c) $c(d + e)$
(d) $x(x - 7)$
(e) $t(t + a)$
(f) $x(bx - 1)$
(g) $p(3p + y)$
(h) $a(q^2 - t)$
12 (a) $2q$ (b) $5t$
(c) $2b^2$ (d) $4rs$
13 (a) $2p + 3q$
(b) $2y^2$
(c) $3c + 4d$
(d) $8pq$
14 (a) $x^2 + 3x - 28$
(b) $y^4 + 2y^2$
(c) $p(p + 6)$
(d) $3x(x - 3y)$

Exercise 5A

1 (a) 4, 7, 10
(b) 11, 6, 1
(c) 12, 36, 108
(d) 12, 6, 3
(e) 9, 17, 33
(f) 16, 12, 10
2 (a) Take 2 away
(b) Add 6
(c) Multiply by 3
(d) Multiply by 10
(e) Divide by 10
(f) Divide by 2
3 43
4 7
5 (a) Add 2
(b) 43

Exercise 5B

1 (a) (i) 10, 11, 12
(ii) 19
(b) (i) 7, 14, 21
(ii) 70
(c) (i) 3, 7, 11
(ii) 39
(d) (i) 8, 10, 12
(ii) 26
(e) (i) 11, 17, 23
(ii) 65
2 Twelfth term = 80
3 22nd term = 20

Exercise5C

1 (a) (i)
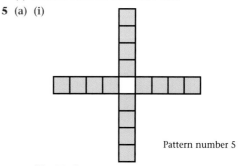
Shape number 5
(ii) 11 matchsticks
(b) (i) Shape number 6 has 13 matchsticks
(ii) Shape number 15 has 31 matchsticks
2 (a) (i) 5   (ii) 23
(b) 100th odd number = $2 \times 100 - 1 = 199$
(c)

● ● ● ●
● ● ● ● ● ●   Pattern number 4
● ● ● ●

(d)

Pattern number	1	2	3	4	5
Number of dots	5	8	11	14	17

3 (a) (i)

Pattern number 5

(ii) 16 tiles
(b) (i) Pattern number 6 has 18 tiles
(ii) Pattern number 17 has 40 tiles
4 (a)

● ● ● ● ●
  ● ● ● ●   Pattern number 4
● ● ● ●

(b)

Pattern number	1	2	3	4	5
Number of dots	5	8	11	14	17

(c) Pattern number 25 has 77 dots
5 (a) (i)

Pattern number 5

(ii) 17 tiles
(b) (i) Patterm number 6 has 21 tiles
(ii) Pattern number 12 has 45 tiles

Exercise 5D

1 (a) (i) 3, 8, 13, 18, 23, ...
(ii) 58
(b) (i) 12, 18, 24, 30, 35, ...
(ii) 78
(c) (i) 11, 19, 27, 35, 43, ...
(ii) 99
(d) (i) 13, 10, 7, 4, 1, ...
(ii) −20
2 (a) $5n - 2$ (b) $6(n + 1)$
(c) $8n + 3$ (d) $16 - 3n$
3 (a) (i) 8, 16, 24, 32, 40, ...
(ii) 96
(b) (i) 3, 5, 7, 9, 11, ...
(ii) 25
(c) (i) 1, 6, 11, 16, 21, ...
(ii) 56
(d) (i) 37, 34, 31, 28, 25, ...
(ii) 4
(e) (i) 13, 7, 1, −5, −11
(ii) −53
4 (a) $9n$ (b) $5n + 4$
(c) $n + 11$ (d) $25 - 4n$
(e) $10n - 7$ (f) $9 - n$
(g) $31 - 8n$ (h) $9n - 21$
5 (a) $2n$ (b) $2n - 1$
(c) $8n$ (d) $2n + 4$
(e) $2n + 7$ (f) $5n + 20$

Exercise 5E

1 $3n + 1$
2 $2n + 6$
3 $3n + 2$
4 $4n - 3$

Mixed exercise 5

1 (a) 20, 27, 34, ...
  (b) 12, 48, 192, ...
  (c) 29, 173, 1037, ...
  (d) 12, 14, 18, ...
2 (a) (i) Each term is 8 more than the precious term
    (ii) 43, 51
  (b) (i) Each term is $\frac{1}{2} \times$ the previous term
    (ii) $\frac{1}{4}, \frac{1}{8}$
  (c) (i) Each term is 4 less than the previous term
    (ii) 0, −4
  (d) (i) Each difference is 2 times the previous one
    (ii) 127, 255
3 (i) (a) 12, 19, 26, 33, 40
    (b) 75
    (c) $7n + 5$
  (ii) (a) 1, 10, 19, 28, 37
    (b) 82
    (c) $9n - 8$
  (iii)(a) 15, 10, 5, 0, −5
    (b) −30
    (c) $20 - 5n$
4 (i) (a) 9, 18, 27, 36, 45, ...
    (b) 180
  (ii) (a) 10, 13, 16, 19, 22, ...
    (b) 67
  (iii)(a) −6, −1, 4, 9, 14, ...
    (b) 89
  (iv) (a) 21, 14, 7, 0, −7
    (b) −112
  (v) (a) −1, −10, −19, −28, −37
    (b) −172
5 (a) $6n + 1$
  (b) $26 - 3n$
  (c) $7n - 7$
  (d) $14 - 9n$
6 13
7 18
8 6
9 35
10 (a) 26, 31
  (b) $5n + 1$
  (c) 91
  (d) 13
  (e) 19

Exercise 6A

1 (a) $y = -1$ (b) $x = 4$
  (c) $x = -3$ (d) $y = 2$
  (e) $y = -2\frac{1}{2}$

2

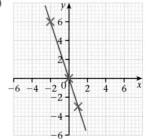

The lines are all parallel.

Exercise 6B

1 (a) (b)

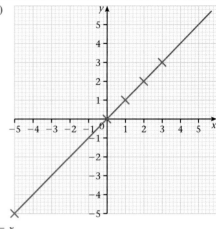

  (c) $y = x$

2 $y = -x$

3

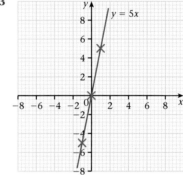

4 (a) The lines all go through the origin and the first and third quadrants.
  (b) The lines all go through the origin and the second and fourth quadrants.

5 (a) (b)

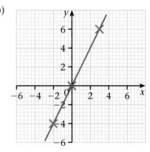

  (c) $y = 2x$

6 (a) (b)   (c) $y = -3x$

Exercise 6C

1

x	−3	−2	−1	0	1	2	3
y	−11	−8	−5	−2	1	4	7

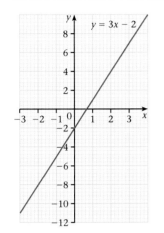

$y = 3x - 2$

2

x	−3	−2	−1	0	1	2	3
y	9	7	5	3	1	−1	−3

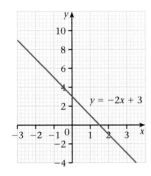

$y = -2x + 3$

3

x	−6	−4	−2	0	2	4	6
y	−1	0	1	2	3	4	5

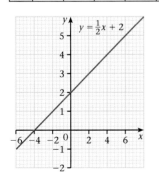

$y = \frac{1}{2}x + 2$

4

x	−2	−1	0	1	2	3	4	5	6
y	7	6	5	4	3	2	1	0	−1

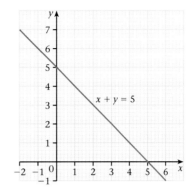

$x + y = 5$

5

x	−2	−1	0	1	2	3	4	5	6
y	−3	−2	−1	0	1	2	3	4	5

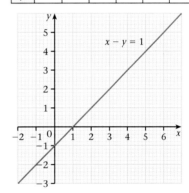

$x - y = 1$

6

x	−4	−2	0	2	4	6	8	10
y	5	4	3	2	1	0	−1	−2

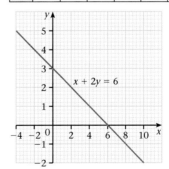

$x + 2y = 6$

7

x	-4	0	4	8	12
y	6	3	0	-3	-6

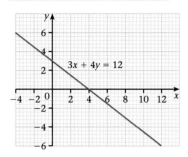

8

x	-3	0	3	6	9	12
y	-8	-6	-4	-2	0	2

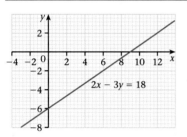

9

x	-8	-4	0	4	8
y	7	4	1	-2	-5

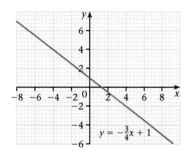

10 (a)

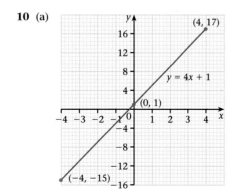

(b)

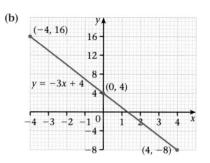

(c)

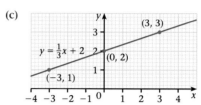

(d)

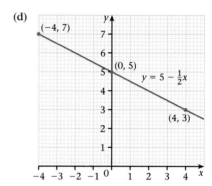

(e)

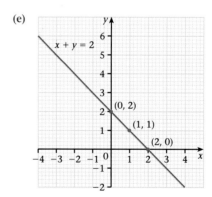

(f)

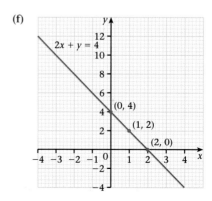

(g)

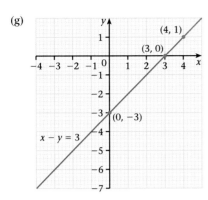

(h)

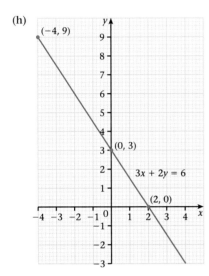

(i)

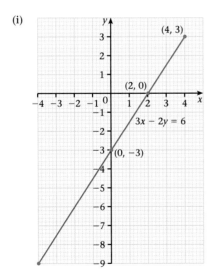

11 (a) (0, 1)   (b) (0, 4)
   (c) (0, 2)   (d) (0, 5)
   (e) (0, 2)   (f) (0, 4)
   (g) (0, −3)   (h) (0, 3)
   (i) (0, −3)

Lines (g) and (i) cross the y-axis below the x-axis.
All the other lines cross the y-axis above the x-axis.

Exercise 6D

1 (a) 62 miles
   (b) 388 km
   (c) France's is greater by 11 miles per hour or 18 kilometres per hour.

2 (a) £140
   (b)

Miles	20	30	50	100	150	200
Total cost (£)	108	112	120	140	160	180

   (c)

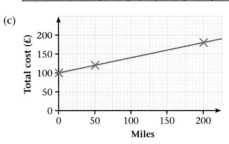

   (d) $y = 100 + 0.4x$
   (e) 100 miles

3 (a) 27 litres
   (b) 8.75 gallons
   (c) 387 gallons

4 (a)

Hours	1	30	3	4	5	6	7	8
Total charge (£)	55	80	105	130	155	180	205	230

   (b)

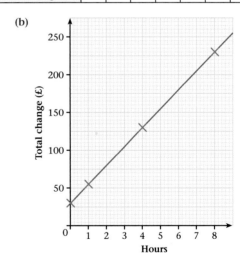

   (c) $y = 25x + 30$
   (d) $4\frac{1}{2}$ hours

Mixed exercise 6

1 (a) B
   (b) D
   (c) A
   (d) C

2

x	-3	-2	-1	0	1	2	3
y	-7	-3	1	5	9	13	17

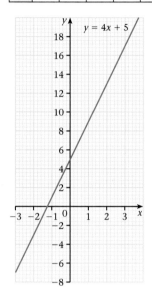

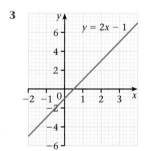

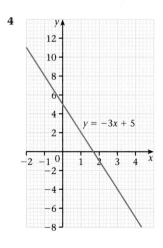

5

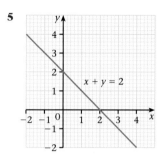

6

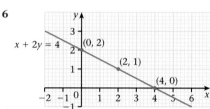

7

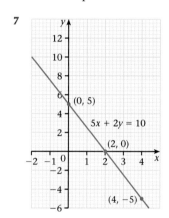

8 (a) (i) 90 litres   (ii) 80 litres   (iii) 125 litres
   (b) (i) 11 gallons   (ii) $35\frac{1}{2}$ gallons   (iii) $24\frac{1}{2}$ gallons

Exercise 7A

1 pentagon   **2** hexagon
3 quadrilateral   **4** triangle
5 nonagon   **6** heptagon
7 regular hexagon   **8** regular octagon

Exercise 7B

1 (a) *BC, EF*
   (b) *AC, AD*

2 (a) *AB, DC* or *AD, BC*
   (b) *AX, XB* or *AX, XD* or *XC, XD* or *XC, XB* or *AC, BD*

Exercise 7C

1 right-angled scalene triangle
2 equilateral triangle
3 isosceles triangle
4 isosceles triangle
5 right-angled scalene triangle
6 isosceles triangle
7 equilateral triangle
8 obtuse scalene triangle

Exercise 7D

1 (a) sides, parallel, equal   (b) 4
   (c) opposite, equal, parallel   (d) 90
   (e) parallel, sides, equal, 90   (f) 4
   (g) opposite, equal, parallel

2 (a) kite   (b) trapezium
   (c) square   (d) rhombus
   (e) parallelogram   (f) trapezium
   (g) arrowhead

3 (a)

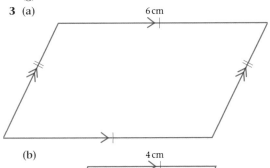

   (b)

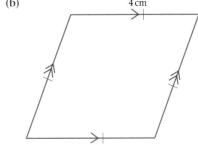

   (c)

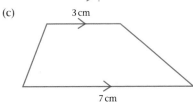

   (d)

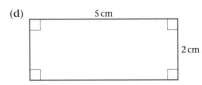

   (e)

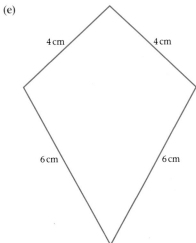

(f)

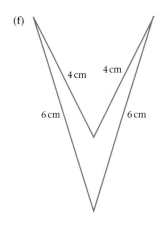

Exercise 7E

1 $a = 30°$ **2** $b = 27°$
3 $c = 37°$ **4** $d = 119°$
5 $e = 63°, f = 54°$ **6** $g = 34°$
7 $h = 45°$ **8** $i = 82°$
9 60°, 60°, 60°   **10** 45°, 45°, 90°
11 30°, 60°, 90°

Exercise 7F

1

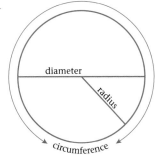

2

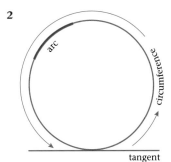

3

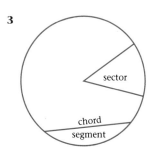

4

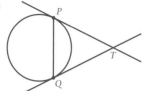

PQ is a chord.
PQT is an isosceles triangle.

5

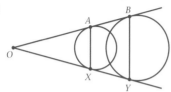

AX and BY are parallel.

6

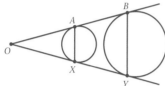

AX and BY are parallel.

Exercise 7G

1 8 vertices, 12 edges, 6 faces
2 All cuboids have 8 vertices, 12 edges and 6 faces.
3 vertices + faces = 8 + 6 = 14
edges + 2 = 12 + 2 = 14

4 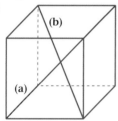 **5**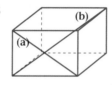

6 (a) vertices + faces = 6 + 5 = 11
edges + 2   = 9 + 2 = 11
(b) vertices + faces = 8 + 6 = 14
edges + 2   = 12 + 2 = 14
(c) vertices + faces = 4 + 4 = 8
edges + 2   = 6 + 2 = 8

Exercise 7H

1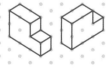

2

3

4

5 (a)

(b), (c)

  or

Mixed exercise 7

1 (a) square   (b) parallelogram
(c) kite   (d) trapezium
(e) equilateral triangle   (f) isosceles triangle
2 (a) regular pentagon   (b) hexagon
(c) regular nonagon
3 (a) A, B, C and D, E
(b) E, A or E, B or E, C or D, A or D, B or D, C
4

radius
5 cm

10 cm
diameter

circumference

5

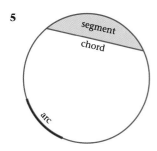

6 (a) rectangle, square
(b) parallelogram, rhombus, rectangle, square
(c) arrowhead
(d) parallelogram, rhombus, rectangle, square
(e) kite, arrowhead
7 (a) (i) 8   (ii) 12   (iii) 6
(b) (i) 12   (ii) 18   (iii) 8
8 (a) $x = 70°$ (b) $c = 70°$
(c) $d = 50°$ (d) $e = 18°$

Exercise 8A

1 angle XZY; acute
2 angle SPR; acute
3 angle ABD; obtuse
4 angle QRP; obtuse
5 angle LMK; acute
6 angle GEF; acute
7 80°
8 120°
9 280°

10

11

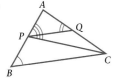

12

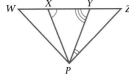

13

14

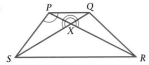

15

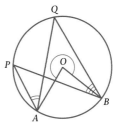

Exercise 8B

1 $a = 27°$ **2** $b = 104°$
3 $c = 58°$ **4** $d = 100°$
5 $e = 238°$ **6** $f = 53°$
7 $g = 133°$
8 $h = 48°, i = 132°, j = 28°$
9 $k = 30°, l = 108°, m = 42°$
10 $n = 44°, p = 46°$

Exercise 8C

1 $a = 88°$ **2** $b = 70°$
3 $c = 140°$ **4** $d = 140°$
5 $e = 238°$ **6** $f = 53°$
7 $g = 133°$
8 $h = 48°, i = 132°, j = 28°$
9 $k = 30°, l = 108°, m = 42°$
10 $n = 44°, p = 46°$

Exercise 8D

1 $a = 52°$ (corresponding angles)
2 $b = 38°$ (corresponding angles)
3 $c = 124°$ (alternate angles)
4 $d = 47°$ (corresponding angles, angles on a straight line)
5 $e = 140°$ (corresponding angles, angles on a straight line)
6 $f = 121°$ (corresponding angles, angles on a straight line)
$g = 59°$ (corresponding angles)
$h = 59°$ (opposite angles)
7 $i = 102°$ (corresponding angles, angles on a straight line)
$j = 78°$ (corresponding angles)
8 $k = 78°$ (angles in a triangle, angles on a straight line)
$m = 102°$ (corresponding angles, angles on a straight line)
$n = 143°$ (corresponding angles, angles on a straight line)
9 (a) $x = 109°$ (angles on a straight line)
(b) angle $PQS = 24°$ (alternate angles)
10 $x = 30$

Exercise 8E

1 Angle ABE = angle $BCD = a$ (corresponding angles)
angle DBE = angle $BDC = b$ (alternate angles)
So, angle ABD = angle ABE + angle $DBE = a + b$
2 Angle XBZ = angle $ABC = b$ (corresponding angles)
angle XBY = angle $ACB = c$ (alternate angles)
So, angle YBZ = angle XBZ + angle $XBY = b + c$
3 (a) angle $BAC = x$
(b) angle ACX = angle $BAC = x$ (alternate angles)
So AC bisects angle BCX
4 Angle BDC = angle $ABD = x$ (alternate angles)
angle ADB = angle $CBD = y$ (alternate angles)
So, angle $A = 180° - x - y$ = angle C (angles in a triangle)
5 Angle $ABX = 54°$ (corresponding angles)
angle $CBY = 54°$ (opposite angles)
6 Angle BCY = angle SYX = angle $QXW = 48°$ (all corresponding angles)
angle RCD = angle $BCY = 48°$ (opposite angles)

7 Angle CBX = angle BXC (equal angles of an isosceles triangle)
angle D = angle CBX (opposite angles of a parallelogram)
So, angle D = angle BXC

8 Angle BCS = angle ABQ = 40° (corresponding angles)
angle DCS = 140° (angles on a straight line)
So, angle CSD = 20° (angles in a triangle and CDS is isosceles)

Exercise 8F

1	(a) 072°	(b) 252°
2	(a) 120°	(b) 300°
3	(a) 310°	(b) 130°
4	(a) 155°	(b) 335°
5	(a) 260°	(b) 080°
6	(a) 056°	(b) 236°
7	(a) 310°	(b) 130°
8	(a) 035°	(b) 215°
9	(a) 208°	(b) 028°
10	(a) 150°	(b) 330°

11

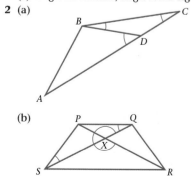

12 130°
13 235°

Mixed exercise 8

1 (a) angle EAB obtuse; angle BCD reflex
  (b) angle ABC acute; angle DAB right angle
  (c) angle XYZ reflex; angle XWZ right angle

2 (a)

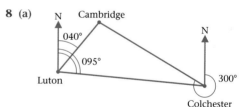

  (b)

3 (a) x = 115° (angles on a straight line)
  (b) y = 85°

4 (a) a = 122° (alternate angles)
  (b) b = 145° (corresponding angles)
  (c) c = 36° (corresponding angles)
    d = 36° (vertically opposite angles)
    e = 144° (corresponding angles, angles on a straight line)

5 $\angle ADB$ = 30°

6 (a) a = 41° (vertically opposite angles, corresponding angles, base angles of an isosceles triangle, angles of a triangle add up to 180°)
    b = 93° (exterior angle of a triangle)
  (b) c = 36° (vertically opposite angles, base angles of an isosceles triangle, alternate angles)
    d = 36° (corresponding angles, vertically oposite angles)
    e = 108° (vertically opposite angles, base angles of an isosceles triangle and angles of a triangle add up to 180°; vertically opposite angles)
  (c) f = 38° (corresponding angles)
    g = 76° (alternate angles, base angles of an isosceles triangle and angles of a triangle add up to 180°)
    h = 38° (angles of a triangle add up to 180°)
  (d) f + 25° + 60° = 180°
    f = 95° (vertically opposite angles, angle of a triangle add up to 180°)
    g = 120° (angles on a straight line, corresponding angles)
  (e) h = 44° (corresponding angles, angles of a straight line)
    j = 74° (angles of a triangle add up to 180°, angles on a straight line)
  (f) k = 47° (alternate angles)
    m = 99° (angles of a triangle add up to 180°)
    n = 81° (alternate angles, angles on a straight line)

7 081°

8 (a)

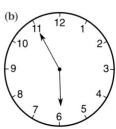

  (b) 120°
  (c) 275°

9 (a) $\angle XBA$ = 10°
  (b) $\angle CBE$ = 180° − 50° − 80° = 50° so $\angle CBE$ = $\angle BCE$ which means triangle CEB is isosceles

Exercise 9A

1 (a) two o'clock
  (b) five minutes past three
  (c) twenty-five minutes past eight
  (d) five minutes to four
  (e) quarter to seven
  (f) quarter past nine

2 (a)   (b)

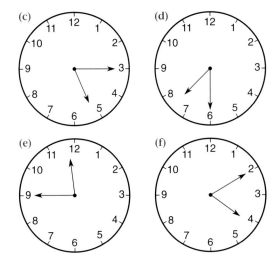

(b) A 40 g
B 280 g
C 25
D 250
E 1250 g
F 3250 g
G 440
H 840
I 6.6
J 9.2
(c) 390 kg
675 litres
95 grams
1400 g
63 mph
(d) A 12:48
B 2:24
C 3:24
D 2:06
E 2:51
F 3:42

3 (a) half past four
(b) five minutes past ten
(c) quarter past three
(d) quarter to eight
(e) twenty-five minutes to one
(f) ten minutes to nine

4 (a) 2:00 (b) 3:05 (c) 8:15
(d) 12:30 (e) 6:40 (f) 2:55

5 (a) 0215 (b) 1520 (c) 1240 (d) 2330
(e) 0955 (f) 1545 (g) 0810 (h) 1950
(i) 2140 (j) 0010

6 (a) 3:20 pm (b) 7:15 am (c) 11:30 pm
(d) 12:30 pm (e) 6:45 pm (f) 10:05 am
(g) 7:20 pm (h) 1:50 pm (i) 8:20 pm
(j) 3:25 am

7 (a) 1.25 hours (b) 3.5 hours
(c) 5.2 hours (d) 4.27 hours
(e) 11.95 hours

8 (a) 2 hours 15 minutes
(b) 3 hours 30 minutes
(c) 5 hours 45 minutes
(d) 4 hours 42 minutes

Exercise 9B

1 (a) 5 h 45 min (b) 9 h 25 min
(c) 8 h 55 min (d) 12 h 10 min
(e) 9 h 20 min (f) 5 h 20 min
2 (a) 4 h 47 min (b) 21 h 50 min
(c) 4 h 25 min (d) 9 h 6 min
(e) 4 h 50 min
3 2 h 45 min
4 7 h 5 min
5 1 h 25 min
6 2 h 6 min
7 (a) 09 30 (b) 2 h 15 min (c) 17 min

Exercise 9C

1 (a) A 25 mm
B 45 mm
C 95 mm
D 8
E 26
F 34
G 375
H 425

Exercise 9D

		Metric	Imperial
1	The weight of an exercise book.	g	oz
2	The height of a tree.	m	ft
3	The length of a window cleaner's ladder.	m	ft
4	The capacity of a milk jug.	ml	pt
5	The distance between Bristol and London.	km	miles
6	The weight of a packet of biscuits.	g	oz
7	The capacity of a water butt.	l	gallons
8	The weight of a hippopotamus.	kg	lb
9	The height of a daffodil.	cm	in
10	The thickness of a pane of glass.	mm	in
11	The weight of a person.	kg	lb
12	The capacity of a can of soft drink.	ml	pt
13	The length of a corridor in a hospital.	m	yards
14	The weight of a sack of coal.	kg	lb
15	The weight of iron in a portion of breakfast cereal.	mg	oz

Exercise 9E

1 (a) 2.2 m (b) 75 cm
(c) 85 cm (d) 3 cm/30 mm
(e) 15 cm (f) 50 cm
(g) 45 cm (h) 1.6 m
2 (a) canary 50 g, crow 0.5 kg, swan 5 kg
(b) Corgi 6 kg, Labrador 20 kg, St Bernard 60 kg
(c) wolf 30 kg, bear 100 kg, elephant 4000 kg
(d) carp 8 kg, shark 250 kg, whale 8000 kg
(e) sheep 20 kg, pig 80 kg, horse 200 kg
3 (a) 8 l (b) 2 l
(c) 275 l (d) 18 l
(e) 50 l (f) 10 000 l
(g) 500 ml (h) 250 ml

Exercise 9F

1. (a) 30 mm   (b) 80 mm
    (c) 29 mm   (d) 47 mm
    (e) 52.6 mm   (f) 62.1 mm
2. (a) 12.9 cm   (b) 63 cm
    (c) 200 cm,   (d) 347 cm
    (e) 2100 cm
3. (a) 3000 g   (b) 4100 g
    (c) 2970 g   (d) 132 g
    (e) 5.7 g   (f) 0.23 g
    (g) 8 g   (h) 7.55 g
4. (a) 15 kg   (b) 6.5 kg
    (c) 2000 kg   (d) 3720 kg
    (e) 13 kg   (f) 0.02 kg
    (g) 1 kg
5. (a) 5000 ml   (b) 22 600 ml
    (c) 3712 ml,   (d) 500 ml
    (e) 260 ml   (f) 2000 ml
6. (a) 23 l   (b) 3.7 l
    (c) 5 l   (d) 6.32 l
    (e) 105 l   (f) 0.5 l
    (g) 0.85 l

Exercise 9G

1. (a) 15.4 lb   (b) 48.4 lb   (c) 86.24 lb
    (d) 8.954 lb   (e) 1.32 lb
2. (a) 1.36 kg (2 d.p.)   (b) 68.18 kg (2 d.p.)
    (c) 43.86 kg (2 d.p.)   (d) 11 kg
    (e) 0.45 kg (2 d.p.)
3. 80.9 kg (1 d.p.)
4. 379.2 km
5. 13 miles
6. 44.8 km
7. 26 full bottles
8. 443p per gallon
9. 3267
10. 6 ft
11. 167.5 cm

Exercise 9H

1. (a) Minimum = 71.5 cm   (b) Minimum = 15.5 cm
      Maximum = 72.5 cm   Maximum = 16.5 cm
    (c) Minimum = 4.5 km   (d) Minimum = 99.5 m
      Maximum = 5.5 km   Maximum = 100.5 m
2. (a) Minimum = 49.5 kg   (b) Minimum = 124.5 g
      Maximum = 50.5 kg   Maximum = 125.5 g
    (c) Minimum = 2.5 tonnes   (d) Minimum = 81.5 mg
      Maximum = 3.5 tonnes   Maximum = 82.5 mg
3. (a) Minimum = 3.5 h   (b) Minimum = 22.5 min
      Maximum = 4.5 h   Maximum = 23.5 min
    (c) Minimum = 6.5 seconds   (d) Minimum = 64.5 years
      Maximum = 7.5 seconds   Maximum = 65.5 years
4. (a) Minimum = 25.5 °C   (b) Minimum = 54.5 °F
      Maximum = 26.5 °C   Maximum = 55.5 °F
    (c) Minimum = 749.5 ml   (d) Minimum = 7.5 litres
      Maximum = 750.5 ml   Maximum = 8.5 litres
5. (a) Minimum = 259.5 cm   (b) Minimum = 5.275 m
      Maximum = 260.5 cm   Maximum = 5.285 m
    (c) Minimum = 595 mm   (d) Minimum = 1995 mm
      Maximum = 605 mm   Maximum = 2005 mm
6. (a) $\frac{1}{2}$ hour   (b) 5 g   (c) 7.5 minutes
    (d) $\frac{1}{2}$ second   (e) 25 cm   (f) 0.1 seconds
    (g) 12.5 ml   (h) 2.5 °C

Exercise 9I

1.

	Distance	Time	Average speed
(a)	128 km	2 hours	64 km/h
(b)	58 miles	$7\frac{1}{4}$ h	8 mph
(c)	600 m	20 s	30 m/s
(d)	2.3 km	50 s	46 m/s
(e)	175 miles	$3\frac{1}{2}$ hours	50 mph
(f)	165 km	$2\frac{1}{2}$ hours	66 km/h
(g)	750 m	30 s	25 m/s
(h)	6 km	$2\frac{1}{2}$ min	40 m/s
(i)	100 km	50 min	120 km/h
(j)	254 miles	1 h 15 min	203.2 mph
(k)	76 km	5 h 4 min	15 km/h
(l)	27.15 km	16 min 10 s	101 km/h
(m)	127 miles	2 h 18 min 33 s	55 mph
(n)	99 miles	3 h 18 min	30 mph
(o)	2350 km	$1\frac{1}{2}$ days	65.3 km/h

2. 129 miles
3. 51.0 mph (3 s.f.)
4. 10.8 m/s (3 s.f.)
5. 3 h 27 min 16 s (nearest second)
6. 7200 m or 7.2 km
7. 6.07 km (3 s.f.)
8. 4 h 37 min 30 s
9. 9 h 3 min 15 s (nearest second)
10. 12.4 mph (3 s.f.)
11. 40 km per hour
12. 45 km
13. 164 km per hour (3 s.f.)
14. 108 km

Exercise 9J

1. 108 km/h
2. 20 m/s
3. 2 miles/min
4. 30 mph
5. 240 km/h
6. 1 350 000 mph
7. 53.3 m/s
8. 14.22 km/litre
9. 112.5 miles/gallon
10. 16 000 gallons/h
11. 4.2 litres/s
12. (a) 82.7 m/s (3 s.f.)
    (b) 298 km/h (3 s.f.)
13. 266.5 m apart (4 s.f.)

Exercise 9K

1. 804 cm³ (3 s.f.)
2. 91.44 g
3.

Substance	Mass	Volume	Density
Hydrogen	900 000 tonnes	1 km³	0.0009 g/cm³
Air	20 kg	15.38 m³	0.0013 g/cm³
Aluminium	15 kg	5556 cm³	2.70 g/cm³

4 Density of dish = 11.7 g/cm³, so it is unlikely that the dish is solid silver.
5 0.17 cm³ (2 d.p.)
6 2.5 g per cm³
7 (a) 8.96 g/cm3
(b) 35 650 kg

Exercise 9L

1 105 km/hour is faster.
2 3 for £1.19 is the better buy.
3 The 1 litre bottle is the best value.
4 small jar £2.70/100 g
medium jar £2.75/100 g
large jar £2.60/100 g
The large jar is the best buy.
5 London to Wycombe was the faster average speed.
6 £4.20 per gallon is equivalent to 93.3p per litre, which is cheaper.
7 The train is travelling faster.
In 10 minutes the distance between these is 1.25 miles or 2 km.

Mixed exercise 9

1 (a) quarter to eight
(b) ten minutes past three
(c) ten minutes to twelve
2 (a) quarter to five
(b) half past twelve
(c) five minutes past nine
(d) twenty-five minutes to two
3 (a) 7:15   (b) 8:50   (c) 10:45
4 (a) 03:50   (b) 13:20   (c) 22:15   (d) 00:05
5 5 h 10 min
6 16 h 20 min
7 3 h 10 min
8 (a) A 16, B 34
(b) C 0.9, D 0.2
9 (a) 203 cm
(b) 1.5 kg
(c) (i) 50 *l*   (ii) 50 000 m*l*
(d) (i) 40 m   (ii) 40 000 mm
10 272 km
11 112.5 litres
12 25.45 kg
13 greatest 400.5 m, least 399.5 m
14 (a) 126.5 g
(b) 127.5 g
15 3.2 h or 3 hours 12 minutes
16 8.3 m/s
17 12.1 mph
18 09 25
19 465 g
20 87.4 cm³
21 16 m/s
22 (a) Iron has the greater density.
(b) 1609 g
23 50 kg
24 The 1 kg box is the better buy.

Exercise 10A

1 12	**2** 14	**3** 14
4 16	**5** 12	**6** 16
7 30	**8** 22	**9** 32
10 28 cm	**11** 26 cm	**12** 128 slabs
13 £298.77		

Exercise 10B

1 5	**2** 8	**3** 9
4 11	**5** 5	**6** 10
7 14	**8** 11	**9** 16
10 (a) 14 cm		
(b) 6 cm²		

Exercise 10C

1 15 cm²	**2** 32 cm²
3 12.6 cm²	**4** 17.28 cm²
5 22.32 cm²	**6** 0.24 m²
7 0.81 m²	**8** 71.98 cm²
9 8 cm	**10** 10 cm
11 8 cm	**12** 12.2 cm
13 4.45 cm (3 s.f.)	**14** 0.05 m

Exercise 10D

1 10.5 cm²	**2** 12 cm²	**3** 12 cm²
4 20 cm²	**5** 24 cm²	**6** 30 cm²
7 24 cm²	**8** 35 cm²	**9** 22 cm²
10 19.5 cm²	**11** 27 cm²	**12** 35 m²
13 8 cm²	**14** 56 cm²	**15** 33 cm²
16 5.6 packs		

Exercise 10E

1

	Length	Width	Height	Surface area
(a)	4	7	2	100
(b)	16	8	3	400
(c)	21	4	5	418
(d)	16	3	2	172
(e)	10	5	3	190

2 388 cm²

3 168 cm²

4 £75.30

Exercise 10F

1 (a) 60   (b) 30   (c) 32
2 (a) 192 cm³   (b) 81 cm³   (c) 168 cm³
3 (a) 33.852 cm³   (b) 92.872 cm³   (c) 10.7 cm³
4 144 cm³
5 64 cm³
6 30 cm

7

	Length	Width	Height	Volume
(a)	2 m	3 m	5 m	30 m³
(b)	2 m	4 m	5 m	40 m³
(c)	4 m	6 m	3 m	72 m³
(d)	5 m	5 m	8 m	200 m³
(e)	1.5 m	4 m	5 m	30 m³
(f)	8 m	3 m	2.5 m	60 m³
(g)	50 cm	0.2 cm	4 cm	40 cm³
(h)	0.4 cm	6 cm	0.5 cm	1.2 cm³

8 (a) $135 \, \text{m}^2$ (b) $38 \, \text{cm}^2$ (c) $72 \, \text{cm}^2$
9 (a) $22\,500 \, \text{cm}^3$ (b) $22.5 \, \text{kg}$
10 36 drinks

Exercise 10G

1 (a) $45 \, \text{cm}^3$ (b) $12\,500 \, \text{cm}^3$
2 (a) $175 \, \text{cm}^3$ (b) $180 \, \text{cm}^3$
   (c) $540 \, \text{cm}^3$ (d) $432 \, \text{cm}^3$
3 $36.8 \, \text{m}^3$
4 $10 \, \text{cm}$

Exercise 10H

1 1000
2 250
3 60
4 (a) 40
   (b) 192
   (c) 960
5 500
6 9
7 100

Mixed exercise 10

1 (a) 34   (b) 36   (c) 48
2 (a) $66 \, \text{cm}^2$, $34 \, \text{cm}$
   (b) $53 \, \text{cm}^2$, $44 \, \text{cm}$
   (c) $45 \, \text{cm}^2$, $32 \, \text{cm}$
3 (a) 25   (b) 30   (c) 32   (d) 34   (e) 72
4 (a) $1000 \, \text{cm}^2$ (b) $222 \, \text{cm}^2$
5 $120 \, \text{cm}^3$
6 $6.5 \, \text{cm}$
7 (a) $240 \, \text{cm}^3$ (b) $280 \, \text{cm}^3$ (c) $120 \, \text{cm}^3$
8 20 tiles
9 £1408
10 $102 \, \text{cm}^2$
11 $105 \, \text{cm}^3$
12 36
13 For example, $18 \, \text{cm} \times 20 \, \text{cm} \times 28 \, \text{cm}$
14 90
15 360 bricks

Examination practice paper

Stage 1 (multiple choice)

1 B	2 C	3 D	4 B	5 E
6 A	7 D	8 D	9 A	10 A
11 E	12 C	13 B	14 A	15 E
16 B	17 C	18 E	19 D	20 C
21 E	22 A	23 C	24 E	25 B

Practice questions

Stage 1 (multiple choice)

1 D	2 B	3 E	4 B	5 C
6 B	7 D	8 B	9 E	10 C
11 E	12 B	13 D	14 A	15 C
16 A	17 E	18 C	19 B	20 C
21 E	22 C	23 A	24 B	25 C
26 D				